Outdoor Gas
Griddle **Cookbook**

1200 Days Affordable Griddle Recipes for Beginners and Advanced Users

Debbie Person

Table of Contents

Introduction

Cooking for all kinds of outdoor activities can be very challenging. This is because you usually don't have all of the kitchen appliances and utensils that you need when you are away from home and outdoors. Gas stoves with more than one burner, with the option of cooking a variety of foods are a bliss. An outdoor gas griddle meets all those requirements without compromising on quality. It is made up of high-quality stainless -steel material. For the storage and distribution of heat energy, there is thick, hot-rolled steel, which makes it easier for you to Prepare food, no matter your skill level. An outdoor gas griddle is one of those must-have devices if you are planning to host an outdoor barbecue for the whole family. This Outdoor Gas Griddle Cookbook is a useful, quick-start book for beginners, with a wonderful guide on healthy and easy recipes to make delicious and nutritious meals outdoors, with professional tips. Here you will discover the best recipes to cook outside. This is a book that contains the most delicious recipes for your griddle, perfect for beginners to start using this griddle without facing any trouble on the way. It includes illustrated instructions and pictures, as well as more than one hundred of the best recipes written for the outdoor gas griddle.

Outdoor Gas Griddle Basics

A Brief History of Outdoor Gas Griddle

Traditional versions of griddles involve the use of stones and brick slabs as flat surfaces placed above the fire to heat up to cooking temperature. The resulting heated flat surface is then removed, and food is placed on the surface to cook. As you can see, the historical griddle-cooking method was stressful and left room for several modifications and evolution. In the early 2000s, the company sought a cooking appliance that was capable of performing the functions of a regular indoor cooking appliance along with the ability to barbecue like a grill. By 2005, they were able to manufacture their cornerstone product, the 36" Griddle that kick-started the company's long chain of griddle-cooking products.

Components of Outdoor Gas Griddle

The griddle is designed to be easy to operate. The company manufactured many accessories to accompany the griddle, but here are a few basic components present when an outdoor gas griddle is purchased.

Griddle Top: This is the main component of the outdoor gas griddle; it is where the cooking takes place. It is made of steel and designed as a slope to prevent disturbances from juices while cooking. The griddle top is placed over multiple burners and heated up to the selected cooking temperature.

Side Shelf: This is fixed to the side of the griddle. It can hold seasonings and other ingredients of the food to be Prepared. However, do not put heavy materials on the shelf.

Portable Legs: The griddle comes with foldable legs and wheels to allow for easy movement. The caster wheels will have the grill positioned precisely where you want, and it has a lock mechanism to prevent any unwanted movement.

Griddle Drip Dish: This pan is responsible for collecting the juices produced while cooking. The griddle top is positioned at an angle that allows the liquid present on the surface to drip down to the drip pan through a mini steel channel.

Removable Drip Tray: It is present at the bottom of the grill and positioned between the four portable legs. It helps to collect juice when present in excessive amounts.

Control Valves: This controls the direction of all the cooking done on the griddle. The valves are used to set the cooking temperature of the burner.

Ignition Switch: This button makes igniting the outdoor gas griddle easy. It is battery powered and automatic. Once you press the button, the griddle comes alive and starts to heat up to the temperature selected with the control valve.

How Does the Outdoor Gas Griddle Work?

The mechanism of operation of the Outdoor Gas Griddle is similar to the process of traditional griddle-cooking. They both involve the heating of a flat surface, which eventually performs the cooking. But with the Outdoor Gas Griddle, there is no need to remove the cooking surface from direct heat because it has control valves that regulate the temperature. The Outdoor Gas Griddle uses propane or butane LPG bottle gas as a fuel source for creating controlled fire. When the griddle is set to a particular temperature with the control valves and switched on with the ignition switch, the inbuilt igniter needles create a fire in the burner tube. The burner tube is positioned below the griddle top and is responsible for heating it to the desired temperature level/mark.

Unlike the traditional griddle-cooking, food is Prepared directly on the heated Outdoor Gas Griddle Top. The heat generated allows the griddle to fry, grill, and sear. Here is a step-by-step direction for igniting the Outdoor Gas Griddle:

1. Check the battery of the ignition switch to ensure it is correctly installed.
2. Release the gas with the control valve on the gas bottle and at the cylinder.
3. Turn the control valves on the griddle until the indicator line points to HIGH
4. Press the ignition switch quickly. You should hear a click, then the spread of the flame.
5. Preheat the griddle for 3-5 minutes before cooking every meal.

Benefits of Outdoor Gas Griddle

An outdoor gas griddle is a great way to feed a crowd and have your breakfast or lunch spot serve the crowds at the same time. Featuring an innovative design that incorporates all the features of a standard grill, plus additional open space for pancakes, eggs, bacon and more! This flat top grill has 3 removable, stainless steel cooking surfaces. The bottom heated area is perfect for cooking traditional food such as burgers or sausages with just enough clearance to accommodate bread slices and buns. The center piece features two fully adjustable burners which can be set up in either a "V" formation or parallel for different size pans available on the market today. The third section is a gas powered griddle with a cast aluminum top. The heat retention and even cooking temperature of the outdoor gas griddle allows for perfect cooking results every time.

This commercial grade restaurant equipment is perfect for any food service operation or home owner looking to bring the taste of the restaurant into their own home!

The outdoor gas griddle is one of the best choices for your outdoor weekend parties. It comes with lots of benefits, as follows:

Strong Built Quality

The outdoor gas griddle is made from stainless steel material protected with a black powder coating layer. It helps to increase the lifespan of the griddle by protecting them from rust. The topmost 28-inch cooking surface plate is made from thick 7-gauge cold-rolled steel material. Overall Outdoor Gas griddle comes with strongly built quality materials.

Versatile Cooking

The outdoor gas griddle provides versatile cooking options while cooking different foods on the flat cooking surface area at the same time but different temperature settings. It allows you to make breakfast like tacos, pancakes, French toast, bacon eggs and cheese sandwich and more. For lunch you can make dishes like chicken, burger, pasta, steak, hotdogs and more. For a perfect dinner you can make special tuna, shrimp, salmon and more dishes. The outdoor gas griddle provides you with an endless cooking experience like a professional chef.

Large and Flat Cooking Surface Area

The outdoor gas griddle having the 28-inch large cooking surface area. It is large enough to hold 16 steaks, 28 hamburgers and 72 hotdogs into a single cooking cycle at a time. The flat griddle cooking surface area helps easily glide the spatula and scrapper over the cooking surface to flip your food. One of the main benefits of having a large cooking surface area is that food doesn't hold the moisture and you will get crispy results. The outdoor gas griddle is one of the best cooking tools for enjoying your weekend parties.

Perfect Heat Control

The gas griddle comes with a heat control system. It is equipped with two separate gas control valve which creates two different temperature zones on flat griddle surface to cook food at two different temperature settings in a single cooking batch. The gas controller switches having heat settings from high to low.

Easy to Clean

The greasy area of the top cooking surface of the griddle is clean easily with the help of scraper or spatula. You can also clean the top cooking surface of the griddle with the help of a paper towel. All the extra oil and juices drip from the food is collected into drip tray you just need to empty the drip tray and wash it with the help of soapy water.

Quick Start and Tips for Using Outdoor Gas Griddles

Use Basic Griddle Tools While Cooking Food

Basic griddle tools like spatula, scraper, and squeeze bottles are important while using your griddle. Scrappers and spatula help to flip and mix your food and squeeze bottles are used to spray water, oil, and sausage while cooking your food on a griddle.

Food Preparations Is Important

Before starting the actual cooking process, make sure all the necessary ingredients and raw foods are ready for the cook. When you start the actual cooking process, there is no time for chopping and cutting your ingredients. Due to this, there are chances of food burning. So, always be ready with Prepared ingredients before starting the cooking process.

Use Extra Tools While Cooking Your Food

The extra tools include a basting cover which helps to use steaming, roasting, and melting your food. Another tool is the grill press which allows you to press your food while cooking to remove the extra fat and oils from your food.

Use Water While Cooking Your Food

The water will help to cook your food faster. Just squeeze a little amount of water over a hot griddle surface to produce steam which helps to cook your food faster.
Water is helpful while using a griddle, but not everyone uses it to its full potential. Water should be utilized for removing stuck-on food, washing leftover debris, and boiling veggies.
If you're scraping food off with your scraper and part of it is very stuck, spray the region with water, and the steam will assist in loosening it up. When you scrape it off with your scraper, it will come off much easier now.
Even after scraping off all the food with your scraper, there may still be a dark-colored residue on the cooktop. Using water and paper towels to scrub the griddle will assist remove it from the cooktop and ensuring that it is perfectly clean before putting your post-cook oil coating on.
Finally, water is excellent for steaming food on a flat top grill. If you prefer steamed vegetables, for example, you can do it with a basting cover and a little water.
Place the meal you want to steam on the stovetop, then spritz it with water and cover it with the basting cover. The water will evaporate due to the heat, but the basting cover will catch it, steaming your meal.

Use Drip Pans (Disposable)

Excess grease and food must be disposed of when cooking on a griddle, which is why they all feature a grease trap. Leftover food and grease are a pain to dispose of, so why not make it as simple as possible?
Use a tinfoil drip pan or create one yourself out of normal aluminum foil instead of cleaning out the debris from the metal trap. Lifting out the drip pan and dumping it in the garbage makes cleanup a breeze.
Replace it with a new one, and you'll be back up and running in minutes. Drip trays are available from the outdoor gas griddle, but comparable trays are also available from other manufacturers.
Use a sheet of aluminum foil to line the drip tray to save a few dollars, but the trays aren't too costly, thankfully. Using a liner eliminates the need to clean the drip tray of all fat and food.

You Can Use Different Temperatures

This tip is more suitable for those who have grills with two or more burners. In fact, you should not think that all the burners of the grill must be at the same temperature when cooking; this allows us to be able to cook different types of food at the same time.

Always Preheat the Griddle Before Cooking a Large Meal

Before you start cooking, preheat the Griddle, especially if you're organizing a tailgate party or perhaps a bash for the entire neighborhood. It only takes 10 minutes, and we guarantee the flavor will increase. Oil infuses with the steel and maintains seasoning when poured on a Prepared griddle. This creates a nonstick surface that allows for more flavorful foods.

Cover the Griddle Cooktop with Parchment Paper or Wax Paper Between Cooks

Covering your griddle cooktop with parchment paper or wax paper is one way to give it more protection. This adds an extra layer of defense and keeps moisture (which can cause corrosion) as well as bugs and other creatures like mice away.

After you've finished cooking, clean the cooktop thoroughly and apply a small layer of oil to it. Allow the Griddle to cool completely before placing a sheet of parchment paper or wax paper immediately on top of it. Cover the Griddle with a hard and soft cover as usual.

Don't Worry About What Oil You Use

Initially, the choice of oil is not a major factor, and you can use vegetable oil or extra virgin olive oil; the important thing is to start cooking and make your own evaluations.

When it comes to griddle cooking, vegetable oils are our go-to oil. It's ideal for high-temperature cooking because of its high smoke point and rather a neutral flavor. Canola oil is considered of the best oils for griddle cooking. The following oils are recommended for seasoning other than vegetable oil and canola oil: coconut oil, olive oil, and sesame oil. The griddle surface can also be seasoned with lard.

On the web, you can find many discussions about which oil to use and which to avoid.

For example, grape seed oil has the highest burning point of all. Or avocado oil is the healthiest one.

What we can tell you is to start cooking, and, with the experience, you will find the right oil for your way of cooking. But a cooking oil with the highest smoke point, say 400–450°F is the best choice.

Use Spray Oil—It Is a Convenient Way to Apply Oil

When working on your Griddle, you'll frequently need cooking oil or fat to coat the surface. Squirt bottles are ideal for this, but an oil spray bottle is a faster and easier option. You can rapidly apply a small coating of oil to the Griddle with them, and you won't have to clean out a squirt bottle afterward. Replace the cap, and you're good to go. A spray oil bottle is a fast and easy way to cover the cooktop or any meals you're cooking. A squirt bottle is still wonderful for pouring water or condiments in, but a spray oil bottle is a simple and effective way to coat the cooktop or any foods you're cooking.

Pretty much every single type of oil is now available in a spray bottle, so whatever your preferred cooking oil is, you should be able to find one.

Prepare in Advance

This may sound silly, but it's not.

Before you start cooking any recipe, make sure you have everything you need on hand near your grill.

It's best to have stuff ready to go before starting to cook. When cooking on a griddle, you'll need a lot of equipment as you'll be Preparing a lot of different foods.

An Outdoor Gas Griddle has the advantage of cooking meals quickly, but this does not leave you time to run inside or chop items while the meals are cooking.

Make sure you have every tool you'll need on hand and within arm's reach before you put the first piece of food on your Griddle. It's also crucial that any food you'll be cooking is ready to go on the Griddle.

You should also have all of your meals Prepared and ready to go. Any food that has to be diced or weighed into the right portion should be done ahead of time so that all you have to focus on when you start cooking is that.

Not only will it render things easier, but it will also allow you to focus entirely on cooking, resulting in superior results. Allowing things to overcook because you're fetching something from the house or Preparing dinner is a bad idea.

This will help you to have the right ingredient at the right time and will prevent you from missing the cooking time of your food that is cooking on the grill.

It is highly recommended to Prepare everything inside containers found in every kitchen and to use medium/large trays to carry everything near your grill station.

Cooking Time

Cooking food in the wrong order is a mistake that most of us make initially.

Obviously, every basic recipe has its own cooking procedures, but when you are and feel quite "ready and loose" in front of your grill, you can experiment according to your ideas on the various types and orders of cooking.

So initially, it's recommended not to go too far outside the basics until you have some experience.

Another tip is to follow this order (meat, potatoes, vegetables, eggs), i.e., start cooking the meat, then the potatoes and finally the vegetables/eggs (eggs cook almost as fast as vegetables), obviously all this following the criteria of the recipe you are cooking.

Here is a table concerning the meat cooking time to get the required level of doneness:

Doneness	Internal Temperature	Time
Medium-rare	135°F	3–5 minutes
Medium	140°F	5–7 minutes
Medium-well	150°F	8–10 minutes
Well	160°F	10–12 minutes

Cooking Temperatures

Before getting onto the griddling, it is pertinent to crack up the heat.

Cooking temperatures may seem intuitive. What isn't evident is that cooking may be done in several methods and that one of the most common mistakes that people do is cooking meats and veggies at the same temperature. But first, let's go over the fundamentals—the temperature is classed as high, medium, or low, so:

High heat: Cook dishes quickly and efficiently. It's what you'll find in a frying pan, a steaming pot, or even a hot griddle.

Medium heat: Maintains a constant temperature that is just right. Takes about the same amount of time as eggs, pancakes, toast, and other breakfast foods. It's what you'll find on the majority of kitchen appliances, such as an oven or a skillet.

Low heat: Cook gradually and take longer. It's what you get on a charcoal barbecue, a pit BBQ, or a low-heat griddle.

And since you know how to adjust the heat to high, medium, or low, do you know that Outdoor Gas Griddles can do all 3? This suggests you can make a variety of foods just by turning a few dials—more on that later. It's also a time saver. In one shot, cook every type of food you'll need for a meal!

You can Prepare the sautéed mushrooms, seared meats, and sizzling vegetables by following these steps:

1. Increase the heat to a medium setting. To optimize the distribution of heat, keep the flames running for 3–5 minutes.
2. Turn the dial to the desired temperature. Pancakes, for example, should be cooked at a lower temperature.
3. Keep in mind that the griddle surface heats up quickly. However, it takes a long time to cool down. The Griddle will continue to cook even if the propane is turned off.
4. Allow the Griddle to cool slightly before cleaning it. You don't want to get burned.

It is recommended to look closely at the cooking temperatures, for example:
- Eggs from 325–350°F
- Meat, potatoes, or pancakes from 375–400°F
- Steaks and hamburgers from 420–450°F

Best Griddle Tools to Use

When cooking with the outdoor gas griddle there are some tools that can help you do it faster and easier. You can try any of the following tools:

Spatula

It is a kind of a spoon and it is used to stir the foods and scrape the food from the griddle. It is made from a plastic material that is heat-resistant chip-resistant and break-resistant.

Tongs

It is a tool that will help you protect your hands from the heat of the gas griddle. It is made from metal that is long and is one of the best tools to use on the outdoor gas griddle.

Chafing Dish

It is a tool that cannot be missed on this type of griddle. You can use it to Prepare any kind of dishes. You have to make sure that your dishes are hot enough so that they can be used. You have to have an ample amount of hot water for chafing.

Rotisserie

It is an accessory that is used to hold the food item and turn it easily. It is commonly made from metal and very much effective in cooking.

Stirring Tool

You can use it for any kind of food that has to be Prepared slowly and effectively on your griddle. It will be easier to use this over the tong.

Scrapper Tool

It is a device that is used for scraping the food from the outdoor gas griddle. It is also made out of metal and very effective in Preparing all types of food. The main use of the scraper tool is for digging and scrapping purposes. It is used to clean the top cooking surface for derbies and also use to lift cake, pie, pizza, and tarts.

Squeeze Bottles

It is commonly known as condiment bottles. It is used for the condiments used for eating all types of food. It is made from a squeezable and leak-proof material.

Tea Kettle

It is made for making hot water for tea. When it is hot it is very convenient to use it for tea. You can also use it for hot water when you are Preparing your food on the grill. It has a safety lock to prevent any accidents.

With all the tools that you can use, you can cook any food with more effectiveness and efficiency. If you are a beginner in using this kind of griddle, it is highly advised that you use the above tools in order to make it easier for you to get used to it.

As you can see, Outdoor Gas Griddles are very useful and helpful and, if you decide to have one, surely it will Prepare you all kinds of cooking, breakfast, lunch, dinner, and snacks that can all be cooked just through fire. There's no need for electricity as well. So, be spontaneous and have fun with the griddle.

Honey-Lime Glazed Fruit Salad

Servings: 4
Preparation Time: 10 minutes
Cooking Time: 4 minutes
Ingredients:
- ½ pound strawberries, washed, hulled and halved
- 1 (9 oz.) can pineapple chunks, drained, juice reserved
- 2 peaches, pitted and sliced
- 6 tbsps. honey, divided
- 1 tbsp. freshly squeezed lime juice

Directions:
1. Preheat your griddle to medium high.
2. While the unit is preheating, combine the strawberries, pineapple, and peaches in a large bowl with 3 tablespoons of honey. Toss to coat evenly.
3. Place the fruit on the grill top. Gently press the fruit down to maximize grill marks. Grill for 4 minutes without flipping.
4. Meanwhile, in a small bowl, combine the remaining 3 tablespoons of honey, lime juice, and 1 tablespoon of reserved pineapple juice.
5. When cooking is complete, place the fruit in a large bowl and toss with the honey mixture. Serve immediately.
Nutrition: Calories: 178kcal; fat: 1g; Carbs: 47g; Protein: 2g

Cheddar Mushroom Frittata

Servings: 4 slices
Preparation Time: 10 minutes
Cooking Time: 10 minutes
Ingredients:
- 4 large eggs
- ¼ cup whole milk
- Sea salt
- Freshly ground black pepper
- ½ bell pepper, seeded and diced
- ½ onion, chopped
- 4 cremini mushrooms, sliced
- ½ cup shredded Cheddar cheese

Directions:
1. Preheat the griddle to medium high.
2. In a medium bowl, whisk together the eggs and milk. Season with the salt and pepper. Add the bell pepper, onion, mushrooms, and cheese. Mix until well combined.
3. Pour the egg mixture into the Ninja Multi-Purpose Pan or baking pan, spreading evenly.
4. Place the pan directly to the grill and cook for 10 minutes, or until lightly golden.
Nutrition: Calories: 153kcal; Fat: 10g; Carbs: 5g; Protein: 11g

Tasty Buttermilk Pancakes

Servings: 4
Preparation Time: 5 minutes
Cooking Time: 10 minutes
Ingredients:
- 2 cup all-purpose flour
- 3 tbsps. sugar
- 1-½ tsps. baking powder
- 1-½ tsps. baking soda
- 1-¼ tsps. salt
- 2-½ cup buttermilk
- 2 eggs
- 3 tbsps. unsalted butter, melted
- 2 tbsps. vegetable oil

Directions:
1. In a large bowl, combine the flour, sugar, baking soda, baking powder, and salt.
2. Stir in the buttermilk, eggs, and butter, and mix until combined but not totally smooth.
3. Heat your griddle to medium heat and add a small amount of oil. Using a paper towel, spread the oil over the griddle in a very thin layer.
4. Use a ladle to pour the batter onto the griddle allowing a few inches between pancakes.
5. When the surface of the pancakes is bubbly, flip and cook a few additional minutes. Remove the pancakes from the griddle and serve immediately with butter and maple syrup.
Nutrition: Calories: 432kcal, Fat: 12.8.g, Carbs: 65.1g, Protein: 14.4g

Fabulous Blueberry Pancakes

Servings: 2
Preparation Time: 10 minutes
Cooking Time: 10 minutes
Ingredients:
- 1 cup flour
- ¾ cup milk
- 2 tbsps. white vinegar
- 2 tbsps. sugar
- 1 tsp. baking powder
- ½ tsp. baking soda
- ½ tsp. salt
- 1 egg
- 2 tbsps. butter, melted
- 1cup fresh blueberries
- butter for cooking

Directions:
1. In a bowl, combine the milk and vinegar. Set aside for two minutes.
2. In a large bowl, combine the flour, sugar, baking powder, baking soda, and salt. Stir in the milk, egg, blueberries, and melted butter. Mix until combined but not totally smooth.
3. Heat your griddle to medium heat and add a little butter. Pour the pancakes onto the griddle and cook until one side is golden brown.
4. Flip the pancakes and cook until the other side is golden.
5. Remove the pancakes from the griddle and serve with warm maple syrup.
Nutrition: Calories: 499kcal, Fat: 16.5.g, Carbs: 76.2g, Protein: 12.9g

Traditional French Toast

Servings: 4
Preparation Time: 5 minutes
Cooking Time: 10 minutes
Ingredients:
- 6 eggs, beaten
- ¼ cup "half and half" or heavy cream
- 8 slices thick cut white or sourdough bread
- 2 tablespoons sugar
- 1 tablespoon cinnamon
- 1 teaspoon salt - butter
- powdered sugar
- maple syrup

Directions:
1. Heat your griddle to medium heat.
2. In a large bowl, combine the eggs, cream, sugar, cinnamon, and salt. Mix well until smooth.
3. Lightly grease the griddle with butter or vegetable oil.
4. Dip each slice of bread in the mixture until well saturated with egg then place onto the griddle.
5. When the French toast has begun to brown, flip and cook until the other side has browned as well. About four minutes. Remove the French toast from the griddle, dust with powdered sugar, and serve with warm maple syrup.

Nutrition: Calories: 332, Sodium: 593 mg, Dietary Fiber: 2.4g, Fat: 10.5.g, Carbs: 44.2g Protein: 16g

Yummy Hash Browns

Servings: 4
Preparation Time: 10 minutes
Cooking Time: 15 minutes
Ingredients:
- 3 russet potatoes, peeled
- 1 tablespoon onion powder
- 1 tablespoon salt
- 1 teaspoon black pepper
- vegetable oil

Directions:
1. Using the largest holes on a box grater, grate the potatoes and place in a large bowl. When all of the potatoes have been grated, rinse with water.
2. Squeeze as much water out of the potatoes as possible and return to the bowl.
3. Add the onion powder, salt, and pepper to the bowl and stir to combine.
4. Preheat your griddle to medium heat and add a thik layer of oil. Spread the potato mixture onto the grill creating a layer about ½ inch thick. Cook for approximately 8 minutes.
5. Working in sections using a large spatula, turn the potatoes and cook an additional 5 to 8 minutes or until both sides are golden brown.
6. Remove the potatoes from the griddle in sections and add to plates. Sprinkle with a pinch of salt and serve immediately.

Nutrition: Calories: 118. Sodium: 1755 mg, Dietary Fiber: 4.1g, Fat: 0.2.g, Carbs: 26.8g Protein: 2.9g

Gruyere Bacon Omelet

Servings: 2
Preparation Time: 5 minutes
Cooking Time: 15 minutes
Ingredients:
- 6 eggs, beaten
- 6 strips bacon
- ¼ pound gruyere, shredded
- 1 tsp. black pepper
- 1 tsp. salt
- 1 tbsp. chives, finely chopped
- vegetable oil

Directions:
1. Add salt to the beaten eggs and set aside for 10 minutes.
2. Heat your griddle to medium heat and add the bacon strips. Cook until most of the fat has rendered, but bacon is still flexible. Remove the bacon from the griddle and place on paper towels.
3. Once the bacon has drained, chop into small pieces.
4. Add the eggs to the griddle in two even pools. Cook until the bottom of the eggs starts to firm up. Add the gruyere to the eggs and cook until the cheese has started to melt and the eggs are just starting to brown.
5. Add the bacon pieces and use a spatula to turn one half of the omelet onto the other half.
6. Remove from the griddle, season with pepper and chives and serve.

Nutrition: Calories: 734kcal, Fat: 55.3.g, Carbs: 2.8g, Protein: 54.8g

Homemade French Crepes

Servings: 4
Preparation Time: 1 hour
Cooking Time: 15 minutes
Ingredients:
- 1 ¼ cups flour
- ¾ cup whole milk
- ½ cup water
- 2 eggs
- 3 tablespoons unsalted butter, melted
- 1 teaspoon vanilla
- 2 tablespoon sugar

Directions:
1. In a large bowl, add all the ingredients and mix with a whisk. Make sure the batter is smooth. Rest for 1 hour.
2. Heat your Griddle to medium heat and add a thin layer of butter. Add about ¼ cup of the batter. Using a crepe spreading tool, form your crepe and cook for 1-2 minutes. Use your Crepe Spatula and flip. Cook for another minute.
3. Top with Nutella and strawberries for a sweet crepe, or top with scrambled eggs and black forest ham for a savory crepe

Nutrition: Calories: 303, Sodium: 112mg, Dietary Fiber: 1.1g, Fat: 12.7g, Carbs: 38.2g Protein: 8.4g

Grilled Berries Toast with Cinnamon

Servings: 4 slices
Preparation Time: 15 minutes
Cooking Time: 10 minutes
Ingredients:
* 1 (15-ounce) can full-fat coconut milk, refrigerated overnight
* ½ tablespoon powdered sugar
* 1-½ teaspoons vanilla extract, divided
* 1 cup halved strawberries
* 1 tablespoon maple syrup, plus more for garnish
* 1 tablespoon brown sugar, divided
* ¾ cup lite coconut milk
* 2 large eggs
* ½ teaspoon ground cinnamon
* 2 tablespoons unsalted butter, at room temperature
* 4 slices challah bread

Directions:
1. Turn the chilled can of full-fat coconut milk upside down (do not shake the can), open the bottom, and pour out the liquid coconut water. Scoop the remaining solid coconut cream into a medium bowl. Using an electric hand mixer, whip the cream for 3 to 5 minutes, until soft peaks form.
2. Add the powdered sugar and ½ teaspoon of the vanilla to the coconut cream, and whip it again until creamy. Place the bowl in the refrigerator.
3. Preheat the griddle to medium high. While the unit is preheating, combine the strawberries with the maple syrup and toss to coat evenly.
4. Sprinkle evenly with ½ tablespoon of the brown sugar.
5. In a large shallow bowl, whisk together the lite coconut milk, eggs, the remaining 1 teaspoon of vanilla, and cinnamon.
6. Place the strawberries on the grill top. Gently press the fruit down to maximize grill marks. Grill for 4 minutes without flipping.
7. Meanwhile, butter each slice of bread on both sides. Place one slice in the egg mixture and let it soak for 1 minute. Flip the slice over and soak it for another minute. Repeat with the remaining bread slices. Sprinkle each side of the toast with the remaining ½ tablespoon of brown sugar.
8. After 4 minutes, remove the strawberries from the grill and set aside. Decrease the temperature to medium low. Place the bread on the Grill and cook for 4 to 6 minutes, until golden and caramelized. Check often to ensure desired doneness.
9. Place the toast on a plate and top with the strawberries and whipped coconut cream.
10. Drizzle with maple syrup, if desired.
Nutrition: Calories: 386kcal; Fat: 19g; Carbs: 49g; Protein: 7g

Authentic Denver Omelet

Servings: 2
Preparation Time: 5 minutes
Cooking Time: 10 minutes
Ingredients:
* 6 large eggs
* ¼ cup country ham, diced
* ¼ cup yellow onion, finely chopped
* ¼ cup green bell pepper, chopped
* ⅔ cup cheddar cheese, shredded
* ¼ teaspoon cayenne pepper
* salt and black pepper
* 2 tablespoons butter

Directions:
1. Heat your griddle to medium heat and place the butter onto the griddle.
2. Add the ham, onion, and pepper to the butter and cook until the vegetables have just softened.
3. Beat the eggs in a large bowl and add a pinch of salt and the cayenne pepper.
4. Split the vegetables into to portions on the griddle and add half of the eggs to each portion. Cook until the eggs have begun to firm up, and then add the cheese to each omelet.
5. Fold the omelets over and remove from the griddle. Serve immediately.
Nutrition: Calories: 507, Sodium: 747 mg, Dietary Fiber: 0.8g, Fat: 40.5g, Carbs: 4.9g Protein: 31.5g

Flavorful Bacon Burrito

Servings: 2
Preparation Time: 5 minutes
Cooking Time: 20 minutes
Ingredients:
* 4 eggs
* 4 strips bacon
* 1 large russet potato, peeled and cut into small cubes
* 1 red bell pepper
* ½ yellow onion
* 1 ripe avocado, sliced
* 2 tablespoons hot sauce
* 2 large flour tortillas
* vegetable oil

Directions:
1. Preheat the griddle to medium-high heat on one side and medium heat on the other side. Brush with vegetable oil and add the bacon to the medium heat side and peppers and onions to the medium-high side. When the bacon finishes cooking, place on paper towels and chop into small pieces. Add the potatoes to the bacon fat on the griddle. Cook the potatoes until softened.
2. Add the eggs to the vegetable side and cook until firm. Place the ingredients onto the tortillas and top with slices of avocado and a tablespoon of hot sauce.
3. Fold the tortillas and enjoy.
Nutrition: Calories: 793, Sodium: 1800 mg, Dietary Fiber: 10.7g, Fat: 41.3.g, Carbs: 73.4g Protein: 35.8g

Fried Dill Pickles

Servings: 4
Preparation Time: 10 minutes
Cooking Time: 10 minutes
Ingredients:
* 20 dill pickle slices
* ¼ cup all-purpose flour
* ⅛ tsp. baking powder
* 3 tbsps. beer or seltzer water
* ⅛ tsp. sea salt
* 2 tbsps. water, plus more if needed
* 2 tbsps. cornstarch
* 1-½ cups panko bread crumbs
* 1 tsp. paprika
* 1 tsp. garlic powder
* ¼ tsp. cayenne pepper
* 2 tbsps. canola oil, divided

Directions:
1. Preheat the griddle to medium-high.
2. Pat the pickle slices dry, and place them on a dry plate in the freezer.
3. In a medium bowl, stir together the flour, baking powder, beer, salt, and water. The batter should be the consistency of cake batter. If it is too thick, add more water, 1 teaspoon at a time.
4. Place the cornstarch in a small shallow bowl.
5. In a separate large shallow bowl, combine the bread crumbs, paprika, garlic powder, and cayenne pepper.
6. Remove the pickles from the freezer. Dredge each one in cornstarch.
7. Tap off any excess, then coat in the batter. Lastly, coat evenly with the bread crumb mixture.
8. Set on the griddle top and gently brush the breaded pickles with 1 tablespoon of oil. Cook for 5 minutes.
9. After 5 minutes, turn and gently brush the pickles with the remaining 1 tablespoon of oil and resume cooking.
10. When cooking is complete, serve immediately.
Nutrition: Calories: 296kcal; Fat: 10g; Carbs: 44g; Protein: 7g

Scrambled Vegetables and Sausage

Servings: 4
Preparation Time: 10 minutes
Cooking Time: 20 minutes
Ingredients:
* 8 eggs, beaten
* ½ lb sausage, sliced into thin rounds or chopped
* 1 green bell pepper, sliced
* 1 yellow onion, sliced
* 1 cup white mushrooms, sliced
* 1 teaspoon salt
* ½ teaspoon black pepper
* vegetable oil

Directions:
1. Preheat the griddle to medium-high heat.
2. Brush the griddle with vegetable oil and add the peppers and mushrooms.
3. Cook until lightly browned and then add the onions. Season with salt and pepper and cook until the onions are soft.
4. Add the sausage to the griddle and mix with the vegetables. Cook until lightly browned.
5. Add the eggs and mix with the vegetables and cook until eggs reach desired doneness. Use a large spatula to remove the scramble from the griddle and serve immediately.
Nutrition: Calories: 342, Sodium: 1131 mg, Dietary Fiber: 1.2g, Fat: 24.9.g, Carbs: 6.3g, Protein: 23.2g

Fabulous Eggs and Sirloin

Servings: 4
Preparation Time: 10 minutes
Cooking Time: 10 minutes
Ingredients:
* 1 pound Sirloin, cut into 4 ½-inch thick pieces
* 8 large eggs
* 3 tablespoons vegetable oil
* salt and black pepper

Directions:
1. Preheat griddle to medium-high heat on one side and medium heat on the other.
2. Season the steaks with a generous amount of salt and pepper.
3. Place steaks on the medium high side and cook for 3 minutes and add the oil to the medium heat side.
4. Flip the steaks and crack the eggs onto the medium heat side of the griddle.
5. After 3 minutes remove the steaks from the griddle and allow to rest 5 minutes. Finish cooking the eggs and place two eggs and one piece of steak on each plate to serve. Season the eggs with a pinch of salt and pepper.
Nutrition: Calories: 444, Sodium: 215 mg, Dietary Fiber: 0g, Fat: 27.2g, Carbs: 0.8g, Protein: 47g

Classic English Toad in the Hole

Servings: 4
Preparation Time: 10 minutes
Cooking Time: 5 minutes
Ingredients:
* 4 slices white, wheat, or sourdough bread
* 4 eggs
* 2 tablespoons butter
* salt and black pepper

Directions:
1. Preheat griddle to medium heat add the butter, spreading it around.
2. Cut a hole in the center of each slice of bread.
3. Place the slices of bread on the griddle and crack an egg into the holes in each slice of bread.
4. Cook until the bread begins to brown, then flip and cook until the egg whites are firm.
5. Remove from the griddle and season with salt and black pepper before serving.
Nutrition: Calories: 206, Sodium: 311 mg, Dietary Fiber: 0.8g, Fat: 10.7g, Carbs: 18.4g, Protein: 9.4g

Mexican Scrambled Eggs and Black Beans

Servings: 4
Preparation Time: 5 minutes
Cooking Time: 10 minutes
Ingredients:
- 8 eggs, beaten
- 1 lb Chorizo
- ½ yellow onion
- 1 cup cooked black beans
- ½ cup green chilies
- ½ cup jack cheese
- ¼ cup green onion, chopped
- ½ teaspoon black pepper
- vegetable oil

Directions:
1. Preheat a griddle to medium heat. Brush the griddle with vegetable oil and add the chorizo to one side and the onions to the other side. When the onion has softened, combine it with the chorizo and add the beans and chilies. Add the eggs, cheese, and green onion and cook until eggs have reached desired firmness.
2. Remove the scramble from the griddle and season with black pepper before serving.
Nutrition: Calories: 843, Sodium: 1554 mg, Dietary Fiber: 9.2g, Fat: 54.1.g, Carbs: 38.2g Protein: 50.7g

Cheesy Hash Brown with Bacon

Servings: 4
Preparation Time: 10 minutes
Cooking Time: 10 minutes
Ingredients:
- 2 russet potatoes, shredded, rinsed, and drained
- 8 eggs, beaten
- 1 cup cheddar cheese
- 6 slices bacon, cut into small pieces
- ⅓ cup green onion, chopped
- vegetable oil

Directions:
4. Preheat griddle to medium heat and brush with vegetable oil.
5. On one side, place the potatoes on the griddle and spread in a ½-inch thick layer. Cook the potatoes until golden brown and then flip. Add the bacon to the other side of the griddle and cook until the fat has rendered.
6. Add the eggs and cheese to the top of the hash browns and stir in the bacon and green onion. Cook until the cheese has melted and divide equally among 4 plates.
Nutrition: Calories: 470, Sodium: 965 mg, Dietary Fiber: 2.8g, Fat: 30.2g, Carbs: 18.8g Protein: 30.6g

Garlicky Potato Bacon Hash

Servings: 6 – 8
Preparation Time: 30 minutes
Cooking Time: 3 hours
Ingredients:
- 6 slices thick cut bacon
- 2 russet potatoes, cut into ½ inch chunks

- 1 yellow onion, chopped
- 1 red bell pepper, chopped
- 1 clove garlic, finely chopped
- 1 teaspoon salt
- ½ teaspoon black pepper
- 1 tablespoon Tabasco sauce

Directions:
1. Set your griddle to medium heat and cook the bacon until just crispy.
2. Add the potato, onion, and bell pepper to the griddle and cook until the potato has softened. Use the large surface of the griddle to spread out the ingredients.
3. When the potato has softened, add the garlic, salt, and pepper.
4. Chop the bacon into small pieces and add it to the griddle. Stir the mixture well and add the hot sauce right before removing the hash from the griddle. Serve immediately.
Nutrition: Calories: 154, Sodium: 475 mg, Dietary Fiber: 1.8g, Fat: 10.2g, Carbs:11.3g Protein: 4.5g

Cheesy Bacon Egg Sandwich

Servings 4
Preparation Time: 5 minutes
Cooking Time: 10 minutes
Ingredients:
- 4 large eggs
- 8 strips of bacon
- 4 slices cheddar or American cheese
- 8 slices sourdough bread
- 2 tablespoons butter
- 2 tablespoons vegetable oil

Directions:
1. Heat your griddle to medium heat and place the strips of bacon on one side. Cook until just slightly crispy.
2. When the bacon is nearly finished, place the oil on the other side of the griddle and crack with eggs onto the griddle. Cook them either sunny side up or over medium.
3. Butter one side of each slice of bread and place them butter side down on the griddle. Place a slice of cheese on 4 of the slices of bread and when the cheese has just started to melt and the eggs are finished, stack the eggs on the bread.
4. Add the bacon to the sandwiches and place the other slice of bread on top. Serve immediately.
Nutrition: Calories: 699, Sodium: 1148 mg, Dietary Fiber: 1.5g, Fat: 47.7g, Carbs: 37.8g Protein: 29.3g

Cheesy Pizza with Greens

Servings: 2 slices
Preparation Time: 10 minutes
Cooking Time: 8 minutes

Ingredients:
- 2 tbsps. all-purpose flour, plus more as needed
- ½ store-bought pizza dough (about 8 ounces)
- 1 tbsp. canola oil, divided
- 1 cup fresh ricotta cheese
- 4 large eggs
- Sea salt
- Freshly ground black pepper
- 4 cups arugula, torn
- 1 tbsp. extra-virgin olive oil
- 1 tsp. freshly squeezed lemon juice
- 2 tbsps. grated Parmesan cheese

Directions:
1. Preheat the griddle to medium high.
2. Dust a clean work surface with flour. Place the dough on the floured surface, and roll it into a 9-inch round of even thickness. Dust your rolling pin and work surface with additional flour, as needed, to ensure the dough does not stick.
3. Brush the surface of the rolled-out dough evenly with ½ tablespoon of canola oil. Flip the dough over and brush with the remaining ½ tablespoon oil. Poke the dough with a fork 5 or 6 times across its surface to prevent air pockets from forming during cooking.
4. Place the dough to the grill and cook for 4 minutes.
5. After 4 minutes, flip the dough, then spoon teaspoons of ricotta cheese across the surface of the dough, leaving a 1-inch border around the edges.
6. Crack one egg into a ramekin or small bowl. This way you can easily remove any shell that may break into the egg and keep the yolk intact. Imagine the dough is split into four quadrants. Pour one egg into each. Repeat with the remaining 3 eggs. Season the pizza with salt and pepper.
7. Continue cooking for the remaining 3 to 4 minutes, until the egg whites are firm.
8. Meanwhile, in a medium bowl, toss together the arugula, oil, and lemon juice, and season with salt and pepper. Transfer the pizza to a cutting board and let it cool. Top it with the arugula mixture, drizzle with olive oil, if desired, and sprinkle with Parmesan cheese.
9. Cut into pieces and serve.

Nutrition: Calories: 788kcal; Fat: 46g; Carbs: 58g; Protein: 34g

Big Creamy Burger

Servings: 4
Preparation Time: 5 Minutes
Cooking Time: 9 Minutes
Ingredients:
- 1¼ pounds lean ground beef
- ½ teaspoon salt
- ½ teaspoon freshly ground black pepper
- Seasoning of your choice (such as a dash of Worcestershire or hot sauce, or 1 teaspoon Spicy Spanish Rub
- 4 slices cheese such as American, cheddar, or Swiss (about 4 ounces), or ¼ cup
- crumbled blue or goat cheese
- 4 toasted buns
- 4 beefsteak tomato slices
- 4 leaves romaine lettuce

Directions:
1. Bring the griddle to medium-high heat. Put the beef in a medium bowl and add the salt, pepper, and your preferred seasonings.
2. Using a fork, mix the seasonings into the meat and then, with your hands, form the mixture into 4 patties, each about 1 inch thick. When the griddle is hot, place the burgers on the Griddle and cook for 4 minutes without flipping.
3. Cooking is complete when the internal temperature of the beef reaches at least 145°F on a food thermometer. If needed, cook for up to 5 more minutes.
4. Lay the cheese over the burgers and lower the griddle. Griddle for 30 seconds, just until the cheese melts.
5. Set the burgers onto the bottom halves of the buns, add a slice of tomato and a leaf of lettuce to each burger, and cover with the tops of the buns. Serve immediately.
Nutrition: Calories: 510; Fat: 30g; Protein: 36g

BBQ Pineapple Turkey Burgers

Servings: 4
Preparation Time: 5 Minutes
Cooking Time: 9 Minutes
Ingredients:
- 1 tsp. BBQ rub
- 1 can sliced pineapple
- 4 slices Swiss cheese
- 1 cup fresh raw spinach, stems removed
- 4 sets of hamburger buns
- PATTY
- 1 lb. ground turkey
- ½ cup bread crumbs
- ¼ cup teriyaki sauce
- 1 small yellow onion, diced
- 2 Tbsp. finely chopped parsley
- 2 cloves garlic, minced
- 1 egg, beaten

Directions:
1. In a large mixing bowl, combine all patty ingredients and mix thoroughly by hand.
2. Divide mixture into four equal parts. Form the four portions into patties and lay on parchment paper. Sprinkle each patty evenly with BBQ rub. Place in refrigerator for 30 minutes.
3. Bring the griddle to high heat. When the griddle is hot, place the burgers and pineapple slices. Cook for 4 minutes without flipping. Remove the burgers and cover to keep warm.
4. After burgers are flipped over, add a slice of Swiss cheese to each patty and allow to melt as patty finishes cooking. Remove from griddle.
5. Layer burgers on buns with spinach and pineapple.
Nutrition: Calories: 554; Fat: 11g; Protein:26g; Fiber:2g

Dijon Salmon Burgers

Servings: 4
Preparation Time: 5 Minutes
Cooking Time: 11 Minutes
Ingredients:
- 1½ pounds salmon fillet, skin and any remaining pin bones removed, cut into chunks
- 2 teaspoons Dijon mustard
- 3 scallions, trimmed and chopped
- ¼cup bread crumbs (preferably fresh)
- Salt and pepper
- Good-quality olive oil for brushing
- sesame hamburger buns or 8–10 slider buns (like potato or dinner rolls)
- 1 large tomato, cut into 4 thick slices

Directions:
1. Put about one quarter of the salmon and the mustard in a food processor and purée into a paste. Add the rest of the salmon and pulse until chopped. Transfer to a bowl, add the scallions, bread crumbs, and a sprinkle of salt and pepper. Mix gently just enough to combine. Form into 4 burgers ¾ to 1 inch thick. Transfer to a plate, cover with plastic wrap, and chill until firm, at least 2 or up to 8hours.
2. Turn control knob to the high position, when the griddle is hot, brush the burgers with oil on both sides, then put them on the griddle. Cook for 11 minutes.
3. After 11 minutes, check the burgers for doneness. Cooking is complete when the internal temperature reaches at least 165°F on a food thermometer.
4. If necessary, close the hood and continue cooking for up to 2 minutes more.
5. Remove the burgers from the griddle. Put the buns on the griddle, cut side down, and toast for 1 to 2minutes. Serve the burgers on the buns, topped with the tomato if using.
 Nutrition: Calories: 123; Fat: 21g; Protein:16g; Fiber:12g

Griddle Pepperoni Cheese Pizza

Servings: 4
Preparation Time: Time: 10 minutes
Cooking Time: 20 minutes

Ingredients:
- 8 slices French bread
- 3 tablespoons butter, softened
- ½ cup pizza sauce
- ¼ cup mozzarella cheese
- ½ cup pepperoni diced
- Garlic powder, for dusting
- Oregano, for dusting

Directions:
1. Spread butter on one side of each French bread slice.
2. Place butter side down on a piece of aluminum foil and dust with garlic powder and oregano.
3. Spread pizza sauce on opposite side of all French bread slices.
4. Top 4 slices of bread with mozzarella cheese, a few slices of pepperoni, and additional mozzarella.
5. Place remaining French bread slices on top of pizza topped bread, butter side up, to create 4 sandwiches.
6. Preheat the griddle to medium heat and place one slice of bread, buttered side down into the griddle.
7. Cook, 3 minutes and flip to cook 3 minutes on the other side; cook until bread is golden and cheese is melted.
8. Serve warm and enjoy!

Nutrition: Calories:305, Sodium: 664 mg, Dietary Fiber: 2.3g, Fat: 12g, Carbs: 40.4g Protein: 9.4g

Mayo Poultry Burgers

Servings: 4
Preparation Time: 5 Minutes
Cooking Time: 15 Minutes

Ingredients:
- ¼cup mayonnaise
- 2 cloves garlic, 1 minced, 1 peeled and left whole
- 2 oil-packed anchovy fillets, drained and mashed
- 2 tablespoons freshly grated Parmesan cheese
- 1 tablespoon fresh lemon juice
- ½ teaspoon Worcestershire sauce
- 1½ pounds ground chicken or turkey
- Good-quality vegetable oil for oiling the grates
- ciabatta rolls, split, or 8–10 slider buns
- Good-quality olive oil for brushing the rolls
- leaves heart of romaine, trimmed

Directions:
1. Line a baking sheet with wax paper. Whisk the mayonnaise, minced garlic, anchovies, Parmesan, lemon juice, and Worcestershire together in a small bowl until smooth. Put the chicken in a medium bowl and add 2tablespoons of the dressing. Cover and refrigerate the remaining dressing. Work the dressing into the chicken with your hands gently but completely. Form the mixture into 4 burgers

¾ to 1 inch thick. Put them on the Prepared pan, cover, and refrigerate until firm, at least 1hour.
2. Turn control knob to the high position, when the griddle is hot, brush the cut sides of the rolls with olive oil. Brush the burgers with oil on both sides, put them on the griddle. Carefully turning once with two spatulas, until browned on the outside and no longer pink in the center, 5 to 7minutes per side.
3. 2 For the last couple of minutes, toast the rolls on the griddle, cut side down. To serve, rub the cut side of the top of each roll with the whole garlic clove.
4. Put a burger on the bottom half, add a dollop of the remaining dressing, a leaf of romaine, and the top of the roll.

Nutrition: Calories: 200; Fat: 11g; Protein: 12g; Fiber:2g

Garlic-Ginger Shrimp Burgers

Servings: 4
Preparation Time: 5 Minutes
Cooking Time: 10 Minutes

Ingredients:
- 1 large clove garlic, peeled
- 1 1-inch piece fresh ginger, peeled and sliced
- 1½ pounds shrimp, peeled (and deveined if you like)
- ½ cup lightly packed fresh basil leaves
- ¼ cup roughly chopped shallots, scallions, or red onion
- Salt and pepper
- Sesame oil for brushing the burgers
- sesame hamburger buns or 8–10 slider buns
- Lime wedges for serving
- Lettuce, sliced tomato, and other
- condiments for serving (optional)

Directions:
1. Put the garlic, ginger, and one-third of the shrimp in a food processor; purée until smooth, stopping the machine to scrape down the sides as necessary. Add the remaining shrimp, the basil, and shallots, season with salt and pepper, and pulse to chop. Form into 4 burgers about ¾ inch thick (or 8 to 10 sliders). Transfer to a plate, cover with plastic wrap, and chill until firm, at least 1 or up to 8hours.
2. Turn control knob to the high position, when the griddle is hot, brush the burgers on both sides with oil then put them on the griddle-and cook until the bottoms brown and they release easily, 5 to 7minutes. Carefully turn and cook until opaque all the way through, 3 to 5minutes.
3. Put the buns, cut side down, on the griddle to toast. Serve the burgers on the toasted buns with lime wedges, as is or dressed however you like.

Nutrition: Calories: 194; Fat: 21g; Protein:6g; Fiber:2g

Feta Lamb Burgers

Servings: 5
Preparation Time: 5 Minutes
Cooking Time:12 Minutes
Ingredients:
• 1½ pounds boneless lamb shoulder or leg or good-quality ground lamb
• 1 tablespoon chopped fresh oregano
• 1 teaspoon salt
• 1 teaspoon black pepper
• 1 tablespoon minced garlic
• ½ cup Greek yogurt
• 1 tablespoon olive oil, plus more for brushing
• 1 tablespoon red wine vinegar
• 2 tablespoons crumbled feta cheese
• 4 or 5 ciabatta rolls, split, or 8–10 slider buns (like potato or dinner rolls)
• Thinly sliced cucumbers for serving
Directions:
1. Put the lamb, oregano, salt, pepper, and garlic in a food processor and pulse until coarsely ground—finer than chopped, but not much. (If you're using preground meat, put it in a bowl with the seasonings and work them together gently with your hands.)
2. Take a bit of the mixture and fry it up to taste for seasoning; adjust if necessary.
3. Handling the meat as little as possible to avoid compressing it, shape the mixture lightly into 4 or 5 burgers or 8 to 10 sliders.
4. Refrigerate the burgers until you're ready to griddle; if you make them several hours in advance, cover with plastic wrap.
5. Whisk the yogurt, oil, and vinegar together in a small bowl until smooth. Stir in the feta. Taste and adjust the seasoning with salt and pepper.
6. Bring the griddle to high heat. When the griddle is hot, place the burgers and cook for 11 minutes.
7. Transfer the burgers to a plate. Brush the cut sides of the rolls lightly with oil and toast directly over the griddle, 1 to 2minutes. Top with a burger, then several slices of cucumber, a dollop of the sauce, and the other half of the roll. Serve with the remaining sauce on the side.
Nutrition: Calories: 134; Fat: 21g; Protein:36g; Fiber:2g

Authentic New Mexican Salsa Verde

Servings: 1 Cup
Preparation Time: 5 Minutes
Cooking Time: 15 Minutes
Ingredients:
• garlic (leave the skins on), as needed
• skewered on a wooden toothpick or small bamboo skewer
• 1 cup roasted New Mexican green chiles or Anaheim chiles cut into ¼-inch strips (8 to 10 chiles
• 2 tablespoons chopped fresh cilantro
• 2 teaspoons fresh lime juice, or more to taste
• ½ teaspoon ground cumin
• ½ teaspoon dried oregano
• Coarse salt (kosher or sea) and freshly ground black pepper
Directions:
1. Preheat the griddle to high. When ready to cook, lightly oil the griddle surface. Place the burgers on the hot griddle. The burgers will be done after cooking 4 to 6 minutes. Put the garlic cloves until they are lightly browned and tender, 2 to 3 minutes per side (4 to 6 minutes in all). Scrape any really burnt skin off the garlic. Place the garlic, chile strips, cilantro, lime juice, cumin, oregano, and 4 tablespoons of water in a blender and purée until smooth, scraping down the sides of the blender with a spatula.
2. Transfer the salsa to a saucepan and bring to a gentle simmer over medium heat. Let simmer until thick and flavorful, 5 to 8 minutes, stirring with a wooden spoon. The salsa should be thick (roughly the consistency of heavy cream) but pourable; add more water as needed. Taste for seasoning, adding more lime juice as necessary and salt and pepper to taste; the salsa should be highly seasoned.
Nutrition: Calories: 214; Fat: 16g; Protein:36g; Fiber:2g

Worcestershire Bruch Burgers

Servings: 4
Preparation Time: 5 Minutes
Cooking Time: 5 Minutes
Ingredients:
• ¼ cup light sour cream
• 5 tablespoons white horseradish
• ¼ teaspoon salt
• 1¼ pounds lean ground beef
• ¼ cup tomato sauce
• 2 tablespoons Worcestershire sauce
• A dash or 2 of hot sauce
• 1 teaspoon celery salt
• 4 beefsteak tomato slices
• 4 brioche buns or hamburger buns, toasted
• 2 celery stalks, with leafy greens, each cut into 4 pieces
Directions:
1. In a small bowl, combine the sour cream, 2 tablespoons of the horseradish, and the salt.
2. Put the beef in a medium bowl and add the remaining 3 tablespoons horseradish, the tomato sauce, the Worcestershire sauce, hot sauce, and celery salt.
3. Using a fork, mix the seasonings into the meat and then, with your hands, form the mixture into 4 patties, each about 1 inch thick.
4. Turn control knob to the high position, when the griddle is hot, place the burgers and cook for 4 minutes without flipping. Remove the burgers and cover to keep warm. Top with a tablespoon of the horseradish sour cream and a tomato slice before sandwiching between a toasted bun. Serve immediately with the celery sticks.
Nutrition: Calories: 447; Fat: 27g; Protein: 35g

Savory Beef Burgers

Servings: 6
Preparation Time: time: 15 minutes
Cooking Time: 35 minutes
Ingredients:
- 2 lbs. ground beef, at least 20% fat
- kosher salt
- black pepper
- 1 tomato, sliced
- 1 yellow or red onion, sliced
- 1 head iceberg lettuce, cut into flats
- thick pieces of American or medium cheddar cheese
- seeded buns or potato buns, toasted

Directions:
1. Divide the ground beef into 6 equal loosely formed balls. Press the balls on a flat surface to make patties. Do not over work them.
2. Generously season the patties with salt and black pepper.
3. Heat your griddle to medium-high heat.
4. Place the patties on the griddle and press down to ensure that the surface makes contact. Cook for three to four minutes.
5. Flip the patties and top with cheese. Cook an additional three to four minutes. The cheese should melt by then.
6. Remove the burgers from the griddle and place them on the buns. Top with lettuce, tomato, and onion, as well as your favorite condiments.

Nutrition: Calories: 410, Sodium: 305 mg, Dietary Fiber: 0.9g, Fat: 18.8g, Carbs: 4.1g Protein: 53.4g

Griddle Garlic Parmesan Sandwiches

Servings: 1
Preparation Time: time: 2 minutes
Cooking Time: 7 minutes
Ingredients:
- 2 slices Italian bread, sliced thin
- 2 slices provolone cheese
- 2 tablespoons butter, softened
- Garlic powder, for dusting
- Dried parsley, for dusting
- Parmesan Cheese, shredded, for dusting

Directions:
1. Spread the butter evenly across 2 slices of bread and sprinkle each buttered side with garlic and parsley.
2. Sprinkle a few tablespoons of Parmesan cheese over each buttered side of bread and gently press the cheese into the bread.
3. Preheat the griddle to medium heat and place one slice of bread, buttered side down, into the griddle.
4. Top with provolone slices and second slice of bread with the butter side up.
5. Cook 3 minutes, and flip to cook 3 minutes on the other side; cook until bread is golden and parmesan cheese is crispy.
6. Serve warm with your favorite sides!

Nutrition: Calories: 575, Sodium: 1065 mg, Dietary Fiber: 2.8g, Fat: 45.1g, Carbs: 18.1g Protein: 27.6g

Spiced Lamb Burger with Cucumber

Servings: 4
Preparation Time: 5 Minutes
Cooking Time: 5 Minutes
Ingredients:
- 1¼ pounds lean ground lamb
- ground cumin
- ¼ teaspoon ground cinnamon
- ½ teaspoon salt
- ½ teaspoon freshly ground black pepper
- whole wheat pitas
- ½ medium cucumber, peeled and sliced
- ½ cup Simple Garlic Yogurt Sauce

Directions:
1. Put the lamb in a medium bowl with the cumin, cinnamon, salt, and pepper. Using a fork, mix the seasonings into the meat and then, with your hands, form the mixture into 4 patties, each about 1 inch thick.
2. Turn control knob to the high position, when the griddle is hot place the burgers and cook for 5 minutes without flipping. Remove the burgers and cover to keep warm. Put a burger into each pita, stuff a few cucumber slices in there too, and spoon some of the yogurt sauce over the top. Serve immediately.

Nutrition: Calories: 354; Fat: 21g; Protein:36g; Fiber:2g

Pork Burgers with Garlic

Servings: 4
Preparation Time: 5 Minutes
Cooking Time: 10 Minutes
Ingredients:
- 1 teaspoon salt
- 1 teaspoon black pepper
- 4 cloves garlic, chopped
- 4 hard rolls, split, or 8–10 slider buns

Directions:
1. Put the meat, salt, pepper, and garlic in a food processor and pulse until coarsely ground—finer than chopped, but not much. (If using preground meat, put it in a bowl with the salt, pepper, and garlic and work them together gently with your hands.)
2. Handling the meat as little as possible to avoid compressing it, shape it lightly into 4 burgers, 1 to 1½ inches thick. (You can do this several hours in advance; cover with plastic wrap and refrigerate until you're ready to griddle.)
3. Turn control knob to the high position, when the griddle is hot, place the burgers on and cook for 10 minutes without flipping; the internal temperature should be 160°F (check with an instant-read thermometer, or nick with a small knife and peek inside).
4. Transfer to a platter.
5. Toast the rolls. Serve the burgers on the rolls.

Nutrition: Calories: 144; Fat: 22g; Protein:11g; Fiber:0g

Classic Tex-Mex Turkey Burgers

Servings: 4
Preparation Time: 10 Minutes
Cooking Time: 15 Minutes
Ingredients:
- ⅓ cup finely crushed corn tortilla chips
- 1 egg, beaten
- ¼ cup salsa
- ⅓ cup shredded pepper Jack cheese
- Pinch salt
- Freshly ground black pepper
- 1 pound ground turkey
- 1 tablespoon olive oil
- 1 teaspoon paprika

Directions:
1. In a medium bowl, combine the tortilla chips, egg, salsa, cheese, salt, and pepper, and mix well.
2. Add the turkey and mix gently but thoroughly with clean hands.
3. Form the meat mixture into patties about ½ inch thick. Make an indentation in the center of each patty with your thumb so the burgers don't puff up while cooking.
4. Brush the patties on both sides with the olive oil and sprinkle with paprika.
5. Griddle. Turn control knob to the high position. When the griddle is hot, griddle for 14 to 16 minutes or until the meat registers at least 165°F.
Nutrition: Calories: 354; Fat: 21g; Protein:36g; Fiber:2g

Teriyaki Beef Burgers

Servings: 4
Preparation Time: 5 Minutes
Cooking Time: 4 Minutes
Ingredients:
- 1¼ pounds lean ground beef
- 1 small onion, minced
- ¼ cup teriyaki sauce
- 3 tablespoons Italian-flavored bread
- crumbs
- 2 tablespoons grated Parmesan cheese
- 1 teaspoon salt
- 1 teaspoon freshly ground black pepper
- 3 tablespoons sweet pickle relish
- 4 Kaiser rolls, toasted

Directions:
1. Put the beef in a medium bowl and add the onion, teriyaki sauce, bread crumbs, Parmesan cheese, salt, and pepper. Using a fork, mix the seasonings into the meat and then form the mixture into 4 patties, each about 1 inch thick. Bring the griddle to high heat. When the griddle is hot place the burgers and cook for 4 minutes without flipping.
2. Remove the burgers and cover to keep warm. Top each burger with a spoonful of sweet pickle relish before sandwiching between a bun. Serve immediately.
Nutrition: Calories: 519; Fat: 23g; Protein: 33g

Cheddar Chipotle Burgers

Servings: 4
Preparation Time: 5 Minutes
Cooking Time: 5 Minutes
Ingredients:
- 1¼ pounds lean ground beef
- 2 tablespoons chipotle puree
- ½ teaspoon salt
- ¼ teaspoon freshly ground black pepper
- slices cheddar cheese (about 4 ounces)
- 1 avocado, halved, pitted, and sliced
- ¼ head iceberg lettuce, shredded
- 4 hamburger buns, toasted

Directions:
1. Put the beef in a medium bowl and add the chipotle puree, salt, and pepper. Using a fork, mix the seasonings into the meat and then, with your hands, form the mixture into 4 patties, each about 1 inch thick.
2. Turn control knob to the high position, when the griddle is hot, place the burgers and cook for 4 minutes without Flippin. Topping each burger with a slice of cheese and cook for 1 minute more, until the cheese melts. Remove the burgers and cover to keep warm.
3. Top each burger with a few slices of avocado and some shredded lettuce before sandwiching between a bun.
4. Chipotle Puree: Put canned chipotles and their liquid in a blender or food processor and process until smooth.
5. The puree can be covered with plastic wrap and refrigerated for up to 2 weeks. This stuff is hot-hot-hot, so a little goes a long way. I use it in meat marinades and dips. The puree is sold in some grocery stores, in ethnic mark.
Nutrition: Calories: 590; Fat: 38g; Protein: 37g

Garlicky Artichokes

Servings: 4 slices
Preparation Time: 10 minutes
Cooking Time: 15 minutes
Ingredients:
- Juice of ½ lemon
- ½ cup canola oil
- 3 garlic cloves, chopped - Sea salt
- Freshly ground black pepper
- 2 large artichokes, trimmed and halved

Directions:
1. Preheat the griddle to medium high.
2. While the unit is preheating, in a medium bowl, combine the lemon juice, oil, and garlic. Season with salt and pepper, then brush the artichoke halves with the lemon-garlic mixture.
3. Place the artichokes on the Grill, cut side down. Gently press them down to maximize grill marks. Grill for 8 to 10 minutes, occasionally basting generously with the lemon-garlic mixture throughout cooking, until blistered on all sides.
Nutrition: Calories: 285kcal; Fat: 28g; Carbs: 10g; Protein: 3g

Blistered Green Beans with Peppers

Servings: 4 slices
Preparation Time: 5 minutes
Cooking Time: 10 minutes
Ingredients:
- 1-pound haricots verts or green beans, trimmed
- 2 tablespoons vegetable oil
- Juice of 1 lemon
- Pinch red pepper flakes
- Flaky sea salt
- Freshly ground black pepper

Directions:
1. Preheat the griddle to medium high. While the unit is preheating, in a medium bowl, toss the green beans in oil until evenly coated.
2. Place the green beans on the Grill and grill for 8 to 10 minutes, tossing frequently until blistered on all sides. When cooking is complete, place the green beans on a large serving platter. Squeeze lemon juice over the green beans, top with red pepper flakes, and season with sea salt and black pepper.
Nutrition: Calories: 100kcal; Fat: 7g; Carbs: 10g; Protein: 2g

Stir Fried Mushrooms with Garlic

Servings: 2
Preparation Time: 10 minutes
Cooking Time: 10 minutes
Ingredients:
- 10 oz mushrooms, sliced
- ¼ cup olive oil
- 1 tbsp garlic, minced
- ¼ tsp dried thyme
- Pepper - Salt

Directions:
1. Preheat the griddle to high heat.
2. Add 2 tablespoons of oil to the hot griddle top.
3. Add mushrooms, garlic, thyme, pepper, and salt and sauté mushrooms until tender.
4. Drizzle remaining oil and serve.
Nutrition: Calories 253; Fat 25.6 g; Carbohydrates 6.2 g; Sugar 2.5 g; Protein 4.7 g; Cholesterol 0 mg

Balsamic Grilled Broccoli

Servings: 4 slices
Preparation Time: 10 minutes
Cooking Time: 10 minutes
Ingredients:
- 4 tablespoons soy sauce
- 4 tablespoons balsamic vinegar
- 2 tablespoons canola oil
- 2 teaspoons maple syrup
- 2 heads broccoli, trimmed into florets
- Red pepper flakes, for garnish
- Sesame seeds, for garnish

Directions:
1. Preheat the griddle to medium high.
2. While the unit is preheating, in a large bowl, whisk together the soy sauce, balsamic vinegar, oil, and maple syrup. Add the broccoli and toss to coat evenly.
3. Place the broccoli on the Grill and grill for 8 to 10 minutes, until charred on all sides.
4. When cooking is complete, place the broccoli on a large serving platter. Garnish with red pepper flakes and sesame seeds. Serve immediately.
Nutrition: Calories: 133kcal; Fat: 8g; Carbs: 13g; Protein: 5g

Veggie Stir Fry

Servings: 4
Preparation Time: 10 minutes
Cooking Time: 20 minutes
Ingredients:
- 2 medium potatoes, cut into small pieces
- 3 medium carrots, peeled and cut into small pieces
- ¼ cup olive oil
- 1 small rutabaga, peeled and cut into small pieces
- 2 medium parsnips, peeled and cut into small pieces
- Pepper
- Salt

Directions:
1. Preheat the griddle to high heat.
2. In a large bowl, toss vegetables with olive oil. Transfer vegetables onto the hot griddle top and stir fry until vegetables are tender.
3. Serve and enjoy.
Nutrition: Calories 218 Fat 12.8 g Carbohydrates 25.2 g Sugar 6.2 g Protein 2.8 g Cholesterol 0 mg

Simple Fried Rice with Eggs

Servings: 2
Preparation Time: 10 minutes
Cooking Time: 10 minutes
Ingredients:
- 4 cups rice, cooked
- 2 large eggs
- 2 tbsp green onion, sliced
- 2 tbsp olive oil
- 1 tsp salt

Directions:
1. In a bowl, whisk eggs and set aside.
2. Preheat the griddle to high heat.
3. Spray griddle top with cooking spray.
4. Add cooked rice on hot griddle top and fry until rice separate from each other.
5. Push rice to one side of the griddle top. Add oil to the griddle and pour beaten egg.
6. Add salt and mix egg quickly with rice and cook until rice grains are covered by egg.
7. Add green onion and stir fry for 2 minutes. Serve and enjoy.
Nutrition: Calories 557 Fat 19.8 g Carbohydrates 79.6 g Sugar 0.7 g Protein 14 g Cholesterol 186 mg

Teriyaki Zucchini Noodles

Servings: 4
Preparation Time: 10 minutes
Cooking Time: 10 minutes
Ingredients:
- 4 small zucchinis, spiralized
- 1 tbsp soy sauce
- 2 onions, spiralized
- 2 tbsp olive oil
- 1 tbsp sesame seeds
- 2 tbsp teriyaki sauce

Directions:
1. Preheat the griddle to high heat.
2. Add oil to the hot griddle top.
3. Add onion and sauté for 4-5 minutes.
4. Add zucchini noodles and cook for 2 minutes.
5. Add sesame seeds, teriyaki sauce, and soy sauce and cook for 4-5 minutes. Serve and enjoy.
Nutrition: Calories 124 Fat 8.4 g Carbohydrates 11.3 g Sugar 5.7 g Protein 3.2 g Cholesterol 0 mg

Seared Green Beans with Sesame

Servings: 6
Preparation Time: 10 minutes
Cooking Time: 10 minutes
Ingredients:
- 1 ½ lbs green beans, trimmed
- 1 ½ tbsp rice vinegar
- 3 tbsp soy sauce
- 1 ½ tbsp sesame oil
- 2 tbsp sesame seeds, toasted
- 1 ½ tbsp brown sugar
- ¼ tsp black pepper

Directions:
1. Cook green beans in boiling water for 3 minutes and drain well.

2. Transfer green beans to chilled ice water and drain again. Pat dry green beans.
3. Preheat the griddle to high heat.
4. Add oil to the hot griddle top.
5. Add green beans and stir fry for 2 minutes.
6. Add soy sauce, brown sugar, vinegar, and pepper and stir fry for 2 minutes more.
7. Add sesame seeds and toss well to coat. Serve and enjoy.
Nutrition: Calories 100 Fat 5 g Carbohydrates 11.7 g Sugar 3.9 g Protein 3.1 g Cholesterol 0 mg

Stir Fried Buttery Bok Choy

Servings: 4
Preparation Time: 10 minutes
Cooking Time: 5 minutes
Ingredients:
- 2 heads bok choy, trimmed and cut crosswise
- 1 tsp sesame oil
- 2 tsp soy sauce
- 2 tbsp water
- 1 tbsp butter
- 1 tbsp peanut oil
- 1 tbsp oyster sauce
- ½ tsp salt

Directions:
1. In a small bowl, mix together soy sauce, oyster sauce, sesame oil, and water and set aside.
2. Preheat the griddle to high heat.
3. Add oil to the hot griddle top.
4. Add bok choy and salt and stir fry for 2 minutes.
5. Add butter and soy sauce mixture and stir fry for 1-2 minutes.
6. Serve and enjoy.
Nutrition: Calories 122 Fat 8.2 g Carbohydrates 9.5 g Sugar 5 g Protein 6.5 g Cholesterol 8 mg

Yummy Kale Chips

Servings: 6
Preparation Time: 10 minutes
Cooking Time: 20 minutes
Ingredients:
- 2 bunches of kale, stems removed
- ½ teaspoon of sea salt
- 4 tablespoons olive oil

Directions:
1. Switch on the griddle, set the temperature to 250 degrees F and let it preheat for a minimum of 15 minutes.
2. Meanwhile, rinse the kale leaves, pat dry, spread the kale on a sheet tray, drizzle with oil, season with salt and toss until well coated.
3. When the griddle has preheated, open the lid, place sheet tray on the griddle grate, shut the griddle and smoke for 20 minutes until crisp.
4. Serve straight away.
Nutrition: Calories: 110 Cal Fat: 5 g Carbs: 15.8 g Protein: 5.3 g Fiber: 5.6 g

Sautéed Veggies with Honey

Servings: 4
Preparation Time: 10 minutes
Cooking Time: 5 minutes
Ingredients:
- 2 medium zucchinis, cut into matchsticks
- 2 tbsp coconut oil
- 2 tsp garlic, minced
- 1 tbsp honey
- 3 tbsp soy sauce
- 1 tsp sesame seeds
- 2 cups carrots, cut into matchsticks
- 2 cups snow peas

Directions:
1. In a small bowl, mix together soy sauce, garlic, and honey and set aside.
2. Preheat the griddle to high heat.
3. Add oil to the hot griddle top.
4. Add carrots, snow peas, and zucchini, and sauté for 1-2 minutes.
5. Add soy sauce mixture and stir fry for 1 minute.
6. Garnish with sesame seeds and serve.
Nutrition: Calories 160 Fat 7.5 g Carbohydrates 20.2 g Sugar 12.1 g Protein 5.3 g Cholesterol 0 mg

Stir Fried Cabbage with Chilies

Servings: 4
Preparation Time: 10 minutes
Cooking Time: 5 minutes
Ingredients:
- 1 cabbage head, tear cabbage leaves, washed and drained
- 2 green onion, sliced
- 1 tbsp ginger, minced
- 2 garlic cloves, minced
- 1 tbsp soy sauce
- ½ tbsp vinegar
- 4 dried chilies
- 2 tbsp olive oil
- ½ tsp salt

Directions:
1. Preheat the griddle to high heat.
2. Add oil to the hot griddle top.
3. Add ginger, garlic, and green onion and sauté for 2-3 minutes.
4. Add dried chilies and sauté for 30 seconds.
5. Add cabbage, vinegar, soy sauce, and salt and stir fry for 1-2 minutes over high heat until cabbage wilted.
6. Serve and enjoy.
Nutrition: Calories 115 Fat 7.3 g Carbohydrates 12.7 g Sugar 6 g Protein 2.9 g Cholesterol 0 mg

Fried Rice with Pineapple

Servings: 4
Preparation Time: 10 minutes
Cooking Time: 10 minutes
Ingredients:
- 3 cups cooked brown rice
- ½ cup frozen corn
- 2 carrots, peeled and grated
- 1 onion, diced
- 2 garlic cloves, minced
- 2 tbsp olive oil
- ½ tsp ginger powder
- 1 tbsp sesame oil
- 3 tbsp soy sauce
- ¼ cup green onion, sliced
- ½ cup ham, diced
- 2 cups pineapple, diced
- ½ cup frozen peas

Directions:
1. In a small bowl, whisk soy sauce, ginger powder, and sesame oil and set aside.
2. Preheat the griddle to high heat.
3. Add oil to the hot griddle top.
4. Add onion and garlic and sauté for 3-4 minutes.
5. Add corn, carrots, and peas and stir constantly for 3-4 minutes.
6. Stir in cooked rice, green onions, ham, pineapple, and soy sauce mixture and stir continuously for 2-3 minutes.
7. Serve and enjoy.
Nutrition: Calories 375 Fat 13.3 g Carbohydrates 57.6 g Sugar 12.7 g Protein 9.4 g Cholesterol 10 mg

Griddle Potato Salad with Jalapeno

Servings: 8
Preparation Time: 15 minutes
Cooking Time: 10 minutes
Ingredients:
- 1 ½ pound fingerling potatoes, halved lengthwise
- 1 small jalapeno, sliced
- 10 scallions
- 2 teaspoons salt
- 2 tablespoons rice vinegar
- 2 teaspoons lemon juice
- ⅔ cup olive oil, divided

Directions:
1. Switch on the griddle, set the temperature to 450 degrees F and let it preheat for a minimum of 5 minutes.
2. Meanwhile, Prepare scallions, and for this, brush them with some oil.
3. When the griddle has preheated, open the lid, place scallions on the griddle grate, shut the griddle and smoke for 3 minutes until lightly charred.
4. Then transfer scallions to a cutting board, let them cool for 5 minutes, then cut into slices and set aside until required.
5. Brush potatoes with some oil, season with some salt and black pepper, place potatoes on the griddle grate, shut the griddle and smoke for 5 minutes until thoroughly cooked.
6. Then take a large bowl, pour in remaining oil, add salt, lemon juice, and vinegar and stir until combined.
7. Add Griddle scallion and potatoes, toss until well mixed, taste to adjust seasoning and then serve.
Nutrition: Calories: 223.7 Cal Fat: 12 g Carbs: 27 g Protein: 1.9 g Fiber: 3.3 g

Lemony Zucchini Slices

Servings: 4
Preparation Time: 10 minutes
Cooking Time: 5 minutes
Ingredients:
- 2 zucchini, cut into ½-inch thick slices
- 1 tsp Italian seasoning
- 2 garlic cloves, minced
- ¼ cup butter, melted
- 1 ½ tbsp fresh parsley, chopped
- 1 tbsp fresh lemon juice
- Pepper
- Salt

Directions:
1. In a small bowl, mix melted butter, lemon juice, Italian seasoning, garlic, pepper, and salt.
2. Brush zucchini slices with melted butter mixture.
3. Preheat the griddle to high heat.
4. Place zucchini slices on the griddle top and cook for 2 minutes per side.
5. Transfer zucchini slices on serving plate and garnish with parsley. Serve and enjoy.
Nutrition: Calories 125 Fat 12 g Carbohydrates 4.1 g Sugar 1.9 g Protein 1.5 g Cholesterol 31 mg

Griddle Green Beans with Bacon

Servings: 6
Preparation Time: 10 minutes
Cooking Time: 20 minutes
Ingredients:
- 4 strips of bacon, chopped
- 1 ½ pound green beans, ends trimmed
- 1 teaspoon minced garlic
- 1 teaspoon salt
- 4 tablespoons olive oil

Directions:
1. Switch on the griddle, set the temperature to 450 degrees F and let it preheat for a minimum of 15 minutes.
2. Meanwhile, take a sheet tray, place all the ingredients in it and toss until mixed.
3. When the griddle has preheated, open the lid, place Prepared sheet tray on the griddle grate, shut the griddle and smoke for 20 minutes until lightly browned and cooked. When done, transfer green beans to a dish and then serve.
Nutrition: Calories: 93 Cal Fat: 4.6 g Carbs: 8.2 g Protein: 5.9 g Fiber: 2.9 g

Roasted Root Vegetables with Cinnamon

Servings: 6
Preparation Time: 15 minutes
Cooking Time: 45 minutes
Ingredients:
- 1 large red onion, peeled
- 1 bunch of red beets, trimmed, peeled
- 1 large yam, peeled
- 1 bunch of golden beets, trimmed, peeled
- 1 large parsnip, peeled
- 1 butternut squash, peeled
- 1 large carrot, peeled
- 6 garlic cloves, peeled
- 3 tablespoons thyme leaves
- Salt as needed
- 1 cinnamon stick
- Ground black pepper as needed
- 3 tablespoons olive oil
- 2 tablespoons honey

Directions:
1. Switch on the griddle, set the temperature to 450 degrees F and let it preheat for a minimum of 15 minutes.
2. Meanwhile, cut all the vegetables into ½-inch pieces, place them in a large bowl, add garlic, thyme, and cinnamon, drizzle with oil and toss until mixed.
3. Take a large cookie sheet, line it with foil, spread with vegetables, and then season with salt and black pepper.
4. When the griddle has preheated, open the lid, place Prepared cookie sheet on the griddle grate, shut the griddle and smoke for 45 minutes until tender.
5. When done, transfer vegetables to a dish, drizzle with honey, and then serve.
Nutrition: Calories: 164 Cal Fat: 4 g Carbs: 31.7 g Protein: 2.7 g Fiber: 6.4 g

Caramelized Worcestershire Onion

Servings: 10
Preparation Time: 30 minutes
Cooking Time: 1 hour
Ingredients:
- Onions (2.5-lb., 1.1-kg.)
- Salted butter – ½ cup
- Brown sugar – 3 tablespoons
- Molasses – 1 tablespoon
- Apple cider vinegar – 2 tablespoons
- Worcestershire sauce – 1 tablespoon
- Dry mustard – 2 teaspoons
- Smoked paprika – 1 teaspoon
- Onion powder – 1 teaspoon

Directions:
1. Peel the onions then cut into slices. Place in a disposable aluminum pan.
2. Mix brown sugar, molasses, apple cider vinegar, Worcestershire sauce, dry mustard, smoked paprika, and onion powder then sprinkle over the sliced onions. Shake to coat.
3. Drop butter on top of the sliced onion then set aside.
4. Set the griddle for indirect heat then adjust the temperature to 225°F (107°C).
5. Place the disposable aluminum pan in the griddle and smoke for an hour and a half, until the spice mixture is caramelized.
6. Once it is done, take the smoked onion out of the griddle and transfer to a serving dish. Stir a little.
7. Serve and enjoy.
Nutrition: Calories: 170 Carbs: 0g Fat: 9g Protein: 2g

Tahini Vegetable Sandwich

Servings: 4
Preparation Time: 30 minutes
Cooking Time: 45 minutes
Ingredients:
For the Smoked Hummus:
- 1 ½ cups cooked chickpeas
- 1 tablespoon minced garlic
- 1 teaspoon salt
- 4 tablespoons lemon juice
- 2 tablespoons olive oil
- ⅓ cup tahini

For the Vegetables:
- 2 large Portobello mushrooms
- 1 small eggplant, destemmed, sliced into strips
- 1 teaspoon salt
- 1 small zucchini, trimmed, sliced into strips
- ½ teaspoon ground black pepper
- 1 small yellow squash, peeled, sliced into strips
- ¼ cup olive oil

For the Cheese:
- 1 lemon, juiced
- ½ teaspoon minced garlic
- ¼ teaspoon ground black pepper
- ¼ teaspoon salt
- ½ cup ricotta cheese

To Assemble:
- 1 bunch basil, leaves chopped
- 2 heirloom tomatoes, sliced
- 4 ciabatta buns, halved

Directions:
1. Switch on the griddle, set the temperature to 180 degrees F and let it preheat for a minimum of 15 minutes.
2. Meanwhile, Prepare the hummus, and for this, take a sheet tray and spread chickpeas on it.
3. When the griddle has preheated, open the lid, place sheet tray on the griddle grate, shut the griddle and smoke for 20 minutes.
4. When done, transfer chickpeas to a food processor, add remaining ingredients for the hummus in it, and pulse for 2 minutes until smooth, set aside until required.
5. Change the smoking temperature to 500 degrees F, shut with lid, and let it preheat for 10 minutes.
6. Meanwhile, Prepare vegetables and for this, take a large bowl, place all the vegetables in it, add salt and black pepper, drizzle with oil and lemon juice and toss until coated.
7. Place vegetables on the griddle grate, shut with lid and then smoke for eggplant, zucchini, and squash for 15 minutes and mushrooms for 25 minutes.
8. Meanwhile, Prepare the cheese and for this, take a small bowl, place all of its ingredients in it and stir until well combined.
9. Assemble the sandwich for this, cut buns in half lengthwise, spread Prepared hummus on one side, spread cheese on the other side, then stuff with Griddle vegetables and top with tomatoes and basil.
10. Serve straight away.
Nutrition: Calories: 560 Cal Fat: 40 g Carbs: 45 g Protein: 8.3 g Fiber: 6.8 g

Baked Green Bean Casserole with Almond

Servings:10-12
Preparation Time:10 mins
Cooking Time:50 mins
Ingredients:
- 3 lbs. trimmed green beans
- Kosher salt
- 2 tbsp olive oil
- 2 tbsp unsalted butter
- ½ lb. shitake or king trumpet mushrooms, sliced
- ¼ cup minced shallot
- ¼ cup rice flour
- 2 cups chicken stock
- ½ cup sherry cooking wine
- 1 cup heavy cream
- 1 cup grated parmigiana Reggiano
- 1 cup slivered almonds, for topping
- 4 cups canola or vegetable oil
- 8 whole, peeled shallots
- ½ cup rice flour
- 1 tsp kosher salt

Directions:
1. When ready to cook, set the temperature to High and preheat, lid closed for 15 minutes.
2. Fill a large stockpot ⅔ full of water and bring to a boil over high heat. Prepare a large ice bath. When the water is boiling, add 1 tbsp. of salt.
3. After the water has returned to a rolling boil, add half of the green beans. Cook until al dente, about 2 minutes. Remove with a strainer and place the beans in the ice bath to cool.
4. Remove the green beans from the water and place on paper towels to dry. Repeat with the remaining green beans. Alternatively, place the green beans on a clean dish cloth and roll up to remove the water.
5. To make the Sauce: Melt the butter and olive oil in a small saucepan over medium heat. Add the shallots and mushrooms and a generous pinch of salt and cook, stirring, until the mushrooms are soft, about 5 minutes.
6. Sprinkle the rice flour over the top and stir to coat the mushrooms and cook off the raw flour taste, about 2 minutes. Add the sherry, stir and reduce, then slowly stir in the stock, allowing to thicken and ensuring there are no lumps, about 3 minutes.
7. Stir in the cream and Parmigiano-Reggiano. Taste, adding salt and pepper as needed.
8. Combine the green beans with the sauce.
9. While the green beans are on the griddle, fry the shallots. Place the oil in a deep saucepan or Dutch oven and heat oil to 350°F.
10. Combine the rice flour and salt in a shallow bowl and mix with a fork
11. When the casserole is ready, garnish with the fried shallots. Enjoy!
Nutrition: Calories: 130 Carbs: 14g Fat: 6g Protein: 2g

Griddled Zucchini with Thyme

Servings: 6
Preparation Time: 5 minutes
Cooking Time: 10 minutes

Ingredients:
- 4 medium zucchini
- 2 tablespoons olive oil
- 1 tablespoon sherry vinegar
- 2 sprigs of thyme, leaves chopped
- ½ teaspoon salt
- ⅓ teaspoon ground black pepper

Directions:
1. Switch on the griddle, set the temperature to 350 degrees F and let it preheat for a minimum of 5 minutes. Meanwhile, cut the ends of each zucchini, cut each in half and then into thirds and place in a plastic bag.
2. Add remaining ingredients, seal the bag, and shake well to coat zucchini pieces.
3. When the griddle has preheated, open the lid, place zucchini on the griddle grate, shut the griddle and smoke for 4 minutes per side.
4. When done, transfer zucchini to a dish, garnish with more thyme and then serve.

Nutrition: Calories: 74 Cal Fat: 5.4 g Carbs: 6.1 g Protein: 2.6 g Fiber: 2.3 g

Garlic Sugar Snap Peas

Servings: 4
Preparation Time: 15 minutes
Cooking Time: 10 minutes

Ingredients:
- 2-pound sugar snap peas, ends trimmed
- ½ teaspoon garlic powder
- 1 teaspoon salt
- ⅔ teaspoon ground black pepper
- 2 tablespoons olive oil

Directions:
1. Switch on the griddle, or set the temperature to 450 degrees F and let it preheat for a minimum of 15 minutes.
2. Meanwhile, take a medium bowl, place peas in it, add garlic powder and oil, season with salt and black pepper, toss until mixed and then spread on the sheet pan.
3. When the griddle has preheated, open the lid, place the Prepared sheet pan on the griddle grate, shut the griddle and smoke for 10 minutes until slightly charred.
4. Serve straight away.

Nutrition: Calories: 91 Cal Fat: 5 g Carbs: 9 g Protein: 4 g Fiber: 3 g

Griddle Cauliflower with Parmesan

Servings: 4
Preparation Time: 15 minutes
Cooking Time: 45 minutes

Ingredients:
- 1 medium head of cauliflower
- 1 teaspoon minced garlic
- 1 teaspoon salt
- ½ teaspoon ground black pepper
- ¼ cup olive oil
- ½ cup melted butter, unsalted
- ½ tablespoon chopped parsley
- ¼ cup shredded parmesan cheese

Directions:
1. Switch on the griddle, set the temperature to 450 degrees F and let it preheat for a minimum of 15 minutes.
2. Meanwhile, brush the cauliflower head with oil, season with salt and black pepper and then place in a griddle pan.
3. When the griddle has preheated, open the lid, place Prepared griddle pan on the griddle grate, shut the griddle and smoke for 45 minutes until golden brown and the center has turned tender.
4. Meanwhile, take a small bowl, place melted butter in it, and then stir in garlic, parsley, and cheese until combined.
5. Baste cheese mixture frequently in the last 20 minutes of cooking and, when done, remove the pan from heat and garnish cauliflower with parsley.
6. Cut it into slices and then serve.

Nutrition: Calories: 128 Cal Fat: 7.6 g Carbs: 10.8 g Protein: 7.4 g Fiber: 5 g

Herbed Corn & Cheese Chile Rellenos

Servings: 8-12
Preparation Time: 30 mins
Cooking Time: 65 mins

Ingredients:
- 2 lbs. Ripe tomatoes, chopped
- 4 cloves garlic, chopped
- ½ cup sweet onion, chopped
- 1 jalapeno, stemmed, seeded, and chopped
- 8 large green new Mexican or poblano chiles
- 3 ears sweet corn, husked
- ½ tsp. Dry oregano, Mexican, crumbled
- 1 tsp. Ground cumin
- 1 tsp. Mild chile powder
- ⅛ tsp. Ground cinnamon
- Salt and freshly ground pepper
- 3 cups grated Monterey jack
- ½ cup Mexican crema
- 1 cup queso fresco, crumbled
- Fresh cilantro leaves

Directions:
1. Put the tomatoes, garlic, onion, and jalapeno in a shallow baking dish and place on the griddle
2. Put the cooled tomato mixture in a blender and liquefy. Pour into a saucepan.
3. Stir in the cumin, oregano, chile powder, cinnamon, and salt and pepper to taste.
4. Carefully peel the blistered outer skin off the New Mexican chiles: Leave the stem ends intact and try not to tear the flesh.
5. Slice the corn off the cobs and put in a large mixing bowl.
6. Bake the rellenos for 25 to 30 minutes, or until the filling is bubbling and the cheese has melted.
7. Sprinkle with queso fresco and garnish with fresh cilantro leaves, if desired. Enjoy!

Nutrition: Calories: 206 Carbs: 5g Fat: 14g Protein: 9g

Maple Vegetable Kebobs

Servings: 4
Preparation Time: 10 minutes
Cooking Time: 20 minutes
Ingredients:
- 2 cups whole white mushrooms
- 2 large yellow squash, peeled, chopped
- 1 cup chopped pineapple
- 1 cup chopped red pepper
- 1 cup halved strawberries
- 2 large zucchinis, chopped

For the Dressing:
- 2 lemons, juiced
- ½ teaspoon ground black pepper
- ½ teaspoon sea salt
- 1 teaspoon red chili powder
- 1 tablespoon maple syrup
- 1 tablespoon orange zest
- 2 tablespoons apple cider vinegar
- ¼ cup olive oil

Directions:
1. Switch on the griddle, set the temperature to 450 degrees F and let it preheat for a minimum of 5 minutes.
2. Meanwhile, Prepared thread vegetables and fruits on skewers alternately and then brush skewers with oil.
3. When the griddle has preheated, open the lid, place vegetable skewers on the griddle grate, shut the griddle, and smoke for 20 minutes until tender and lightly charred.
4. Meanwhile, Prepare the dressing and for this, take a small bowl, place all of its ingredients in it and then whisk until combined.
5. When done, transfer skewers to a dish, top with Prepared dressing and then serve.
Nutrition: Calories: 130 Cal Fat: 2 g Carbs: 20 g Protein: 2 g Fiber: 0.3 g

Creamy Mashed Potatoes

Servings:8-12
Preparation Time:5 minutes
Cooking Time:40 minutes
Ingredients:
- 5 lbs. Yukon gold potatoes, large dice
- 1 ½ sticks butter, softened
- 1 ½ cup cream, room temperature
- kosher salt, to taste
- white pepper, to taste

Directions:
1. When ready to cook, set temperature to 300 degrees F and preheat, lid closed for 15 minutes
2. Peel and dice potatoes into ½" cubes.
3. Place the potatoes in a foil tin and cover. Roast on the griddle until tender (about 40 minutes).
4. In a medium saucepan, combine cream and butter. Cook over medium heat until butter is melted.
5. Mash potatoes using a potato masher. Gradually add in cream and butter mixture, and mix using the masher. Be careful not to overwork, or the potatoes will become gluey.
6. Season with salt and pepper to taste. Enjoy!
Nutrition: Calories: 122 Carbs: 12g Fat: 2g Protein: 2g

Honey Carrots and Asparagus

Servings: 6
Preparation Time: 10 minutes
Cooking Time: 30 minutes
Ingredients:
- 1-pound whole carrots, with tops
- 1 bunch of asparagus, ends trimmed
- Sea salt as needed
- 1 teaspoon lemon zest
- 2 tablespoons honey
- 2 tablespoons olive oil

Directions:
1. Switch on the griddle, or set the temperature to 450 degrees F and let it preheat for a minimum of 15 minutes.
2. Meanwhile, take a medium dish, place asparagus in it, season with sea salt, drizzle with oil and toss until mixed.
3. Take a medium bowl, place carrots in it, drizzle with honey, sprinkle with sea salt and toss until combined.
4. When the griddle has preheated, open the lid, place asparagus and carrots on the griddle grate, shut the griddle and smoke for 30 minutes.
5. When done, transfer vegetables to a dish, sprinkle with lemon zest, and then serve.
Nutrition: Calories: 79.8 Cal Fat: 4.8 g Carbs: 8.6 g Protein: 2.6 g Fiber: 3.5 g

Smoked Acorn Squash with Brown Sugar

Servings: 10
Preparation Time: 20 minutes
Cooking Time: 2 hours
Ingredients:
- Acorn squash (2-lbs., 0.9-kg.)
- Butter – 3 tablespoons
- Brown sugar – ¼ cup
- Salt – ¼ teaspoon
- Ground cinnamon – ¼ teaspoon
- Ground ginger – ¼ teaspoon
- Ground nutmeg – ¼ teaspoon

Directions:
1. Combine brown sugar, salt, ground cinnamon, ground ginger, and ground nutmeg in a bowl then mix well. Set aside.
2. Cut the acorn squash into halves then place in a disposable aluminum pan with the cut sides on top.
3. Brush butter onto the halved acorn squash then sprinkle the brown sugar mixture over the squash. Set aside.
4. Set the griddle for indirect heat then adjust the temperature to 225°F (107°C).
5. Place the acorn squash in the griddle and smoke for 2 hours or until tender.
6. Once it is done, remove the smoked acorn squash from the griddle and place on a serving dish.
7. Serve and enjoy.
Nutrition: Calories: 125 Carbs: 25g Fat: 4g Protein: 2g

Roasted Tomatoes with Garlic and Parsley

Servings:4-6
Preparation Time:20 minutes
Cooking Time:90 minutes
Ingredients:
- 2 lbs. roman fresh tomatoes
- 3 tbsp parsley, chopped
- 2 tbsp garlic, chopped
- Black pepper, to taste
- ½ cup olive oil
- Hot pepper, to taste
- 1 lb. spaghetti or other pasta

Directions:
1. When ready to cook, set the temperature to 400°F and preheat, lid closed for 15 minutes
2. Wash tomatoes and cut them in half, length width. Place them in a baking dish cut side up.
3. Sprinkle with chopped parsley, garlic, add salt and black pepper and pour ¼ cup of olive oil over them.
4. Place on pre-heated griddle and bake for 1 ½ hours. Tomatoes will shrink and the skins will be partly blackened.
5. Remove tomatoes from baking dish and place in a food processor leaving the cooked oil and puree them.
6. Drop pasta into boiling salted water and cook until tender. Drain and toss immediately with the pureed tomatoes.
7. Add the remaining ¼ cup of raw olive oil and crumbled hot red pepper to taste. Toss and serve. Enjoy!
Nutrition: Calories: 111 Carbs: 5g Fat: 11g Protein: 1g

Lemony Griddle Potato Salad

Servings:6-8
Preparation Time:15 mins
Cooking Time:15 mins
Ingredients:
- 1-½ lbs. Fingerling potatoes cut in half lengthwise
- 10 scallions
- ⅔ cup Evo (extra virgin olive oil), divided use
- 2 tbsp rice vinegar
- 2 tsp lemon juice
- 1 small jalapeno, sliced
- 2 tsp kosher salt

Directions:
1. When ready to cook, set temperature to High and preheat, lid closed for 15 minutes. Brush the scallions with the oil and place on the griddle. Cook until lightly charred, about 2-3 minutes. Remove and let cool. Once the scallions have cooled, slice and set aside.
2. Brush the Fingerlings with oil (reserving ⅓ cup for later use), then salt and pepper. Place cut side down on the griddle until cooked through, about 4-5 minutes.
3. In a bowl, whisk the remaining ⅓ cup olive oil, rice vinegar, salt, and lemon juice, then mix in the scallions, potatoes, and sliced jalapeno. Season with salt and pepper and serve. Enjoy!
Nutrition: Calories: 270 Carbs: 18g Fat: 18g Protein: 3g

Smoked Jalapeño Poppers with Bacon

Servings: 4-6
Preparation Time: 15 minutes
Cooking Time: 60 minutes
Ingredients:
- 12 medium jalapeños
- 6 slices bacon, cut in half
- 8 oz cream cheese, softened
- 1 cup cheese, grated
- 2 tbsp pork & poultry rub

Directions:
1. When ready to cook, set temperature to 180 degrees F and preheat, lid closed for 15 minutes.
2. Slice the jalapeños in half lengthwise. Scrape out any seeds and ribs with a small spoon or paring knife.
3. Mix softened cream cheese with Pork & Poultry rub and grated cheese.
4. Spoon mixture onto each jalapeño half. Wrap with bacon and secure with a toothpick.
5. Place the jalapeños on a rimmed baking sheet. Place on griddle and smoke for 30 minutes.
6. Increase the griddle temperature to 375 degrees F and cook an additional 30 minutes or until bacon is cooked to desired doneness. Serve warm, enjoy!
Nutrition: Calories: 280 Carbs: 24g Fat: 19g Protein: 4g

Griddle Zucchini Squash with Thyme

Servings: 4-6
Preparation Time: 5 minutes
Cooking Time: 10 minutes
Ingredients:
- 4 medium zucchinis
- 2 tbsp olive oil
- 1 tbsp cherry vinegar
- 2 springs thyme, leaves pulled
- Salt and pepper, to taste

Directions:
1. Clean the zucchini and cut each end off. Cut each in half, then each half into thirds.
2. When ready to cook, set the temperature to 350 degrees F and preheat, lid closed for 15 minutes.
3. Cooking Time for 3-4 minutes per side, until griddle marks appear, and zucchini is tender.
4. Remove from griddle and finish with more thyme leaves if desired. Enjoy!
Nutrition: Calories: 76 Carbs: 17g Fat: 1g Protein: 4g

Griddle Tahini Veggie Sandwich

Servings: 4-6
Preparation Time: 30 minutes
Cooking Time: 30 minutes
Ingredients:
- Smoked hummus
- 1-½ cups chickpeas
- ⅓ cup tahini
- 1 tbsp minced garlic
- 2 tbsp olive oil
- 1 tsp kosher salt
- 4 tbsp lemon juice
- Griddle veggie sandwich
- 1 small eggplant, sliced into strips
- 1 small zucchini, sliced into strips
- 1 small yellow squash, sliced into strips
- 2 large Portobello mushrooms
- Olive oil
- Salt and pepper to taste
- 2 heirloom tomatoes, sliced
- 1 bunch basil, leaves pulled
- 4 ciabatta buns
- ½ cup ricotta
- Juice of 1 lemon
- 1 garlic clove minced
- Salt and pepper to taste

Directions:
1. When ready to cook, set temperature to 180 degrees F and preheat, lid closed for 15 minutes.
2. In the bowl of a food processor, combine smoked chickpeas, tahini, garlic, olive oil, salt and lemon juice and process until mixed well but not completely smooth. Transfer to a bowl and reserve.
3. Increase griddle temp to high (400-500 degrees F).
4. While the veggies are cooking combine the ricotta, lemon juice, garlic, salt and pepper in a small bowl.
5. Cut the ciabatta buns in half and open them up. Spread hummus on one side and ricotta on the other. Stack the Griddle veggies and top with tomatoes and basil. Enjoy!
Nutrition: Calories: 376 Carbs: 57g Fat: 16g Protein: 10g

Smoked Buttery Cabbage

Servings: 5
Preparation Time: 10 minutes
Cooking Time: 2 hours
Ingredients:
- 1 head cabbage, cored
- 4 tablespoons butter
- 2 tablespoons rendered bacon fat
- 1 chicken bouillon cube
- 1 teaspoon fresh ground black pepper
- 1 garlic clove, minced

Directions:
1. Pre-heat your griddle to 240 degrees Fahrenheit.
2. Fill the hole of your cored cabbage with butter, bouillon cube, bacon fat, pepper and garlic
3. Wrap the cabbage in foil about two-thirds of the way up
4. Make sure to leave the top open

5. Transfer to your griddle rack and smoke for 2 hours
6. Unwrap and enjoy!
Nutrition: Calories: 231 Fats: 10g Carbs: 26g Fiber: 1g

Garlicky Potato Wedges with Rosemary

Servings:4
Preparation Time: 15 minutes
Cooking Time: 1 hour 30 minutes
Ingredients:
- 4-6 large russet potatoes, cut into wedges
- ¼ cup olive oil
- 2 garlic cloves, minced
- 2 tablespoons rosemary leaves, chopped
- 2 teaspoon salt
- 1 teaspoon fresh ground black pepper
- 1 teaspoon sugar
- 1 teaspoon onion powder

Directions:
1. Pre-heat your griddle to 250 degrees Fahrenheit
2. Take a large bowl and add potatoes and olive oil
3. Toss well
4. Take another small bowl and stir garlic, salt, rosemary, pepper, sugar, onion powder
5. Sprinkle the mix on all sides of the potato wedge
6. Transfer the seasoned wedge to your griddle rack and smoke for 1 and a ½ hours
7. Serve and enjoy!
Nutrition: Calories: 291 Fats: 10g Carbs: 46g Fiber: 2g

Sesame Smoked Asparagus

Servings: 10
Preparation Time: 20 minutes
Cooking Time: 1 hour
Ingredients:
- Asparagus (2-lbs., 0.9-kg.)
- Sesame oil – 2 tablespoons
- Lemon juice – 2 tablespoons
- Grated lemon zest – ¼ teaspoon
- Garlic powder – 1 teaspoon
- Salt – ½ teaspoon
- Pepper – ¼ teaspoon

Directions:
1. Combine grated lemon zest, garlic powder, salt, and pepper in a bowl then drizzle lemon juice and sesame oil over the spices. Mix well.
2. Cut and trim the asparagus then rub with the spice mixture.
3. Next, wrap the seasoned asparagus with aluminum foil then set aside.
4. Set the griddle for indirect heat then adjust the temperature to 225°F (107°C).
5. Place the wrapped asparagus in the griddle and smoke for an hour, until tender.
6. Once it is done, remove the smoked asparagus from the griddle then transfer to a serving dish.
7. Serve and enjoy.
Nutrition: Calories: 250 Carbs: 26g Fat: 9g Protein: 19g

Smoked Tomato and Cheeses Dip

Servings:4
Preparation Time: 5 minutes
Cooking Time: 1 hour
Ingredients:
- 8 ounces smoked mozzarella cheese, shredded
- 8 ounces Colby cheese, shredded
- ½ cup parmesan cheese, grated
- 1 cup sour cream
- 1 cup sun-dried tomatoes
- 1 and ½ teaspoon salt
- 1 teaspoon fresh ground pepper
- 1 teaspoon dried basil
- 1 teaspoon dried oregano
- 1 teaspoon red pepper flakes
- 1 garlic clove, minced
- ½ teaspoon onion powder
- French toast, serving

Directions:
1. Pre-heat your griddle to 275 degrees Fahrenheit
2. Take a large bowl and stir in the cheeses, tomatoes, pepper, salt, basil, oregano, red pepper flakes, garlic, onion powder and mix well
3. Transfer the mix to a small metal pan and transfer to a griddle
4. Smoke for 1 hour
5. Serve with toasted French bread
6. Enjoy!
Nutrition: Calories: 174 Fats: 11g Carbs: 15g Fiber: 2g

Roasted Cauliflower with Parmesan

Servings:4
Preparation Time: 15 minutes
Cooking Time:10 minutes
Ingredients:
- 1 cauliflower head, cut into florets
- 1 tablespoon oil
- 1 cup parmesan, grated
- 2 garlic cloves, crushed
- ½ teaspoon pepper
- ½ teaspoon salt
- ¼ teaspoon paprika

Directions:
1. Pre-heat your Griddle to 180 degrees F
2. Transfer florets to griddle and smoke for 1 hour
3. Take a bowl and add all ingredients except cheese
4. Once smoking is done, remove florets
5. Increase temperature to 450 degrees F, brush florets with the brush and transfer to griddle
6. Smoke for 10 minutes more
7. Sprinkle cheese on top and let them sit (Lid closed) until cheese melts
8. Serve and enjoy!
Nutrition: Calories: 45 Fats: 2g Carbs: 7g Fiber: 1g

Spicy Pickled Green Beans

Servings:4-6
Preparation Time:15 minutes
Cooking Time:45 minutes
Ingredients:
- 1 lb. green beans, blanched
- ½ cup salt
- ½ cup sugar
- 1 tbsp red pepper flake
- 2 cups white wine vinegar
- 2 cups ice water

Directions:
1. When ready to cook, set temperature to 180°F and preheat, lid closed for 15 minutes.
2. Place the blanched green beans on a mesh griddle mat and place mat directly on the griddle grate. Smoke the green beans for 30-45 minutes until they've picked up the desired amount of smoke. Remove from griddle and set aside until the brine is ready.
3. In a medium sized saucepan, bring all remaining ingredients, except ice water, to a boil over medium high heat on the stove. Simmer for 5-10 minutes then remove from heat and steep 20 minutes more. Pour brine over ice water to cool.
4. Once brine has cooled, pour over the green beans and weigh them down with a few plates to ensure they are entirely submerged. Let sit 24 hours before use.
5. Enjoy!
Nutrition: Calories: 20 Carbs: 3g Fat: 0g Protein: 1g

Peppered Maple Brussels Sprouts

Servings: 10
Preparation Time: 10 minutes
Cooking Time: 40 minutes
Ingredients:
- Brussels sprouts (2-lbs., 0.9-kg.)
- Maple syrup – 3 tablespoons
- Olive oil – 2 tablespoons
- Salt – ¼ teaspoon
- Pepper – ¼ teaspoon
- Smoked paprika – ¼ teaspoon

Directions:
1. Combine maple syrup with olive oil, salt, pepper, and smoked paprika then stir until incorporated.
2. Drizzle the mixture over the Brussels sprouts then shake to coat. Spread the seasoned Brussels sprouts over a disposable aluminum pan.
3. Set the griddle for indirect heat then adjust the temperature to 400°F (204°C).
4. Place the glazed Brussels sprouts on the griddle and smoke for 30 minutes, until brown and tender.
5. Once the smoked Brussels sprouts are done, remove from the griddle and transfer to a serving dish.
6. Serve and enjoy.
Nutrition: Calories: 380 Carbs: 30g Fat: 26g Protein: 8g

Griddle Beer Cabbage with Cinnamon

Servings: 10
Preparation Time: 40 minutes
Cooking Time: 3 hours

Ingredients:
- Whole cabbages (3-lb., 1.4-kg.)
- Olive oil – 3 tablespoons
- Garlic powder – 2 teaspoons
- Salt – ¼ teaspoon
- Chili powder – ¼ teaspoon
- Ground cinnamon – ½ teaspoon
- Beer – 1 can

Directions:
1. Combine garlic powder, salt, chili powder, and ground cinnamon in a bowl.
2. Drizzle olive oil over the spices then mix well.
3. Rub the spice mixture over the cabbage and in between the cabbage leaves.
4. Set the griddle for indirect heat then adjust the temperature to 275°F (135°C).
5. Place the seasoned cabbage on a sheet of aluminum foil then wrap the cabbage. Let the top of the cabbage open.
6. Pour beer over the cabbage then place it on the griddle. Smoke the cabbage for 3 hours, until tender.
7. Once it is done, remove the smoked cabbage from the griddle and unwrap it.
8. Cut the smoked cabbage into wedges then serve.
9. Enjoy!

Nutrition: Calories: 300 Carbs: 70g Fat: 2g Protein: 18g

Chapter 4 Poultry Recipes

Sesame Smoked Teriyaki Chicken Wings

Servings: 1
Preparation Time: 30 minutes
Cooking Time: 4 Hours
Ingredients:
• Chicken wings
For the homemade Teriyaki Glaze:
• ⅔ cup mirin
• 2 tablespoons of minced ginger
• 3 tablespoons of cornstarch
• 2 tablespoon of rice vinegar
• 1 cup of soy sauce
• ⅓ cup of brown sugar
• 8 minced garlic cloves
• 2 teaspoon of sesame oil
• 3 tablespoons of water
For creamy sesame dressing:
• 1 green onion, chopped
• ½ cup of mayonnaise
• ¼ cup rice wine vinegar
• 1 teaspoon of ground garlic
• 1 tablespoon of soy sauce
• 2 tablespoon of sesame oil
• ½ teaspoon of ground ginger
• 1 teaspoon siracha
• 2 tablespoon of maple syrup
• Salt and pepper to taste
Directions:
1. Set the griddle to smoke mode by keeping the temperature to 225 degrees F
2. Now trim the wings and make them into drumettes and season with sea salt and black pepper
3. Smoke them for nearly 45 minutes
4. For the teriyaki glaze
5. Mince both garlic and ginger by using a teaspoon of sesame oil
6. Then mix all the ingredients except for cornstarch and water
7. Take a pan and boil cornstarch and water on low heat
8. Simmer for 15 minutes and then when done, mix it with an immersion blender
9. Now add cornstarch and water and stir it until it has mixed well
10. Add this mix to the teriyaki glaze and mix it well until it thickens. Set it aside
11. For the creamy dressing
12. Take a blender and blend all the ingredients thoroughly until you get a smooth mixture
13. Now set the griddle for direct flame griddling and put the temperature to medium
14. Griddle the wings for approx. 10 minutes
15. The internal temperature should reach 165 degrees F when you remove the wings from the griddle
16. Toss them in the glaze when done
17. Sprinkle some sesame seeds along with green onion
18. Serve hot and spicy
Nutrition: Carbohydrates: 39 g Protein: 29 g Sodium: 15 mg Cholesterol: 19 mg

Herbed Chicken Beasts

Servings: 4
Preparation Time: 5 Minutes
Cooking Time: 8 Minutes
Ingredients:
• 2 whole boneless chicken breasts (each 12 to 16 ounces), or 4 half chicken breasts (each half 6 to 8 ounces)
• Coarse salt (kosher or sea) and freshly ground black pepper
• ¼ cup white wine vinegar or red wine vinegar
• ½ sweet onion, finely diced (about ½ cup)
• 3 cloves garlic, coarsely chopped
• dried oregano
• ½ teaspoon ground cumin
• ¾ cup extra-virgin olive oil
• ⅓ cup chopped fresh flat-leaf parsley
Directions:
1. If using whole breasts, cut each breast in half. Remove the tenders from the chicken breasts, place a breast half between 2 pieces of plastic wrap and gently pound it to a thickness of ½ inch using a meat pounder, the side of a heavy cleaver, a rolling pin, or the bottom of a heavy saucepan. Repeat with the remaining breast halves. Place the chicken breasts in a large baking dish and season them on both sides with salt and pepper.
2. Place the vinegar, onion, garlic, oregano, and cumin in a nonreactive mixing bowl. Add ½ teaspoon of salt and ¼ teaspoon of pepper and whisk until the salt dissolves. Whisk in the olive oil. Correct the seasoning, adding salt and pepper to taste. The mixture should be highly seasoned. Pour half of this mixture into another nonreactive serving bowl and set aside for use as a sauce. Whisk 2 tablespoons of the parsley into the mixture in the mixing bowl then pour it over the chicken, turning the breasts to coat on both sides. Let the chicken breasts marinate in the refrigerator, covered, for at least 2 hours or as long as overnight, turning them a few times so that they marinate evenly.
3. Drain the chicken breasts well and discard the marinade.
4. Turn control knob to the high position, when the griddle is hot, place the chicken breasts and cook for 5 minutes. Use the poke test to check for doneness; the chicken should feel firm when pressed. Or insert an instant-read meat thermometer into the breast through one end: The internal temperature should be about 160°F. You may need to cook the chicken breasts in more than one batch; cover the Griddle chicken with aluminum foil to keep warm until ready to serve.
Whisk the remaining parsley into the reserved bowl of vinegar mixture. Spoon half of it over the chicken breasts and serve the remainder on the side.
Nutrition: Calories: 211; Fat: 5g; Protein:32g; Fiber:23g

Korean-Style Grilled Chicken Wings

Servings: 6
Preparation Time: time: 30 minutes
Cooking Time: 30 minutes to 1 hour
Ingredients:
• 2 pounds chicken wings (flats and drumettes attached or separated)
• For the marinade:
• olive oil
• sea salt, plus more
• ½ teaspoon black pepper
• ½ cup gochujang, Korean hot pepper paste
• 1 scallion, thinly sliced, for garnish
Directions:
1. Rinse and pat wings dry with paper towels.
2. Whisk marinade ingredients together in a large mixing bowl until well-combined.
3. Add wings to bowl and toss to coat.
4. Cover bowl with plastic wrap and chill in the refrigerator for 30 minutes.
5. Preparation time are one side of the griddle for medium heat and the other side on medium-high.
6. Working in batches, cook wings over medium heat, turning occasionally, until skin starts to brown; about 12 minutes.
7. Move wings to medium-high area of griddle for 5 minutes on each side to sear until cooked through; meat thermometer should register 165°F when touching the bone. Transfer wings to a platter, garnish with scallions, and serve warm with your favorite dipping sauces.
Nutrition: Calories: 312, Sodium:476 mg, Dietary Fiber: 0.4 g, Fat: 13.5g, Carbs:1.1g, Protein: 43.9g.

Maple Smoked Chicken

Servings: 1
Preparation Time: 30 minutes
Cooking Time: 6 Hours
Ingredients:
• Boneless chicken breast (5-lbs., 2.3-kgs)
• The Spice
• Chipotle powder – 1 tablespoon
• Salt – 1 ½ teaspoons
• Garlic powder – 2 teaspoons
• Onion powder – 2 teaspoons
• Pepper – 1 teaspoon
• The Glaze
• Maple syrup – ½ cup
Directions:
1. Preheat a griddle to 225°F.
2. Place chipotle, salt, garlic powder, onion powder, and pepper in a bowl then mix to combine.
3. Rub the chicken with the spice mixture then place on the griddle's rack.
4. Smoke the chicken for 4 hours and brush with maple syrup once every hour.
5. When the internal temperature has reached 160°F (71°C), remove the smoked chicken breast from the griddle and transfer to a serving dish.
6. Serve and enjoy right away.

Nutrition: Carbohydrates: 27 g Protein: 19 g Sodium: 65 mg Cholesterol: 49 mg

Savory Boneless Chicken

Servings: 4
Preparation Time: 5 Minutes
Cooking Time: 15 Minutes
Ingredients:
• 1½ pounds boneless, skinless, chicken breasts
• 2 tablespoons good-quality olive oil
• Salt and pepper
Directions:
1. Pat the chicken dry with paper towels, then pound to an even thickness if necessary. Brush with the oil and sprinkle with salt and pepper on both sides.
2. Turn control knob to the high position, when the griddle is hot, place the chicken breasts and cook for 10 to 14 minutes.
3. Transfer the chicken to a platter, let rest for 5minutes, slice across the grain if you like, and serve.
Nutrition: Calories: 111; Fat: 19g; Protein: 22g; Fiber:2g

BBQ Turkey Sandwiches

Servings: 1
Preparation Time: 30 minutes
Cooking Time: 4 Hours
Ingredients:
• 6 skin-on turkey thighs
• 6 split and buttered buns
• 1 ½ cups of chicken broth
• 1 cup of BBQ sauce
• Poultry rub
Directions:
1. Season the turkey thighs on both the sides with poultry rub
2. Set the griddle to preheat by pushing the temperature to 180 degrees F
3. Arrange the turkey thighs on the grate of the griddle and smoke it for 30 minutes
4. Now transfer the thighs to an aluminum foil which is disposable and then pour the brine right around the thighs
5. Cover it with a lid
6. Now increase the griddle, temperature to 325 degrees F and roast the thigh till the internal temperature reaches 180 degrees F
7. Remove the foil from the griddle but do not turn off the griddle
8. Let the turkey thighs cool down a little
9. Now pour the dripping and serve
10. Remove the skin and discard it
11. Pull the meat into shreds and return it to the foil
12. Add 1 more cup of BBQ sauce and some more dripping
13. Now cover the foil with lid and re-heat the turkey on the griddle for half an hour Serve and enjoy
Nutrition: Carbohydrates: 39 g Protein: 29 g Sodium: 15 mg Cholesterol: 19 mg

Hellfire Grilled Chicken Wings

Servings: 1
Preparation Time: 30 minutes
Cooking Time: 6 Hours
Ingredients:
- For Hellfire chicken wings
- 3 lbs. of chicken wings
- 2 tablespoon of vegetable oil
- For the rub
- 1 teaspoon of onion powder
- 1 tablespoon of paprika
- 1 teaspoon of celery seed
- 1 teaspoon of salt
- 1 teaspoon of cayenne pepper
- 1 teaspoon of freshly ground black pepper
- 1 teaspoon of granulated garlic
- 2 teaspoons of brown sugar
- For the sauce
- 2 -4 thinly sliced crosswise jalapeno poppers
- 2 tablespoons of butter; unsalted
- ½ cup of hot sauce
- ½ cup of cilantro leaves

Directions:
1. Take the chicken wings and cut off the tips and discard them
2. Now cut each of the wings into two separate pieces through the joint
3. Move this in a large mixing bowl and pour oil right over it
4. For the rub: Take a small-sized bowl and add sugar, black pepper, paprika, onion powder, salt, celery seed, cayenne, and granulated garlic in it
5. Now sprinkle this mixture over the chicken and toss it gently to coat the wings thoroughly
6. Put the griddle to preheat by putting the temperature to 350 degrees F
7. Griddle the wings for approximately 40 minutes or till the time the skin turns golden brown and you feel that it has cooked through. Make sure to turn it once when you are halfway.
8. For the sauce: Take a small saucepan and melt the butter by keeping the flame on medium-low heat. Now add jalapenos to it and cook for 3 minutes, stir cilantro along with a hot sauce
9. Now, pour this freshly made sauce over the wings and toss it to coat well Serve and enjoy
Nutrition: Carbohydrates: 27 g Protein: 19 g Sodium: 65 mg Cholesterol: 49 mg

Garlicky Chicken Drumsticks

Servings: 1
Preparation Time: 30 minutes
Cooking Time: 2 Hours
Ingredients:
- 8 pieces of chicken drumsticks
- 2 tablespoon of rice wine vinegar
- 3 tablespoon brown sugar
- 1 cup of ketchup
- ¼ cup of soy sauce
- Minced garlic
- 2 tablespoons of honey
- 1 tablespoon of sweet heat rub
- Minced ginger
- ½ lemon juice
- ½ juiced lime

Directions:
1. Take a mixing bowl and add soy sauce along with brown sugar, ketchup, lemon, rice wine vinegar, sweet heat rub, honey, ginger, and garlic.
2. Now keep half of the mixture for dipping sauce and therefore set it aside
3. Take the leftover half and pour it in a plastic bag that can be re-sealed
4. Now add drumsticks to it and then seal the bag again
5. Refrigerate it for 4 to 12 hours
6. Take out the chicken from the bag and discard the marinade
7. Fire the griddle and set the temperature to 225 degrees F
8. Now smoke the chicken over indirect heat for 2 to 3 hours a make sure to turn it once or twice
9. Add more glaze if needed
10. Remove it from the griddle and let it stand aside for 10 minutes
11. Add more sauce or keep it as a dipping sauce
12. Serve and enjoy
Nutrition: Carbohydrates: 29 g Protein: 19 g Sodium: 25 mg Cholesterol: 19 mg

Honey-Glazed Smoked Whole Chicken

Servings: 1
Preparation Time: 30 minutes
Cooking Time: 3 Hours
Ingredients:
- 1 4 pounds of chicken with the giblets thoroughly removed and patted dry
- 1 ½ lemon
- 1 tablespoon of honey
- 4 tablespoons of unsalted butter
- 4 tablespoon of chicken seasoning

Directions:
1. Fire up your griddle and set the temperature to 225 degrees F.
2. Take a small saucepan and melt the butter along with honey over a low flame
3. Now squeeze ½ lemon in this mixture and then move it from the heat source
4. Take the chicken and smoke by keeping the skin side down. Do so until the chicken turns light brown and the skin starts to release from the grate.
5. Turn the chicken over and apply the honey butter mixture to it
6. Continue to smoke it making sure to taste it every 45 minutes until the thickest core reaches a temperature of 160 degrees F
7. Now remove the chicken from the griddle and let it rest for 5 minutes.
8. Serve with the leftover sliced lemon and enjoy
Nutrition: Carbohydrates: 29 g Protein: 19 g Sodium: 25 mg Cholesterol: 19 mg

Beer-Braised Adobo Chicken Tacos

Servings: 1
Preparation Time: 30 minutes
Cooking Time: 3 Hours
Ingredients:
- For the braised chicken
- 2 lbs. of chicken thighs; boneless, skinless
- ½ small-sized diced onion
- 1 de-seeded and chopped jalapeno
- 1 (12 oz) can of Modelo beer
- 1 tablespoon of olive oil
- 1 EA chipotle Chile in adobo
- 1 clove of minced garlic
- 4 tablespoon of adobo sauce
- 1 teaspoon of chili powder
- 1 teaspoon of garlic powder
- 1 teaspoon of salt
- 1 teaspoon of black pepper
- Juice of 2 limes
- For the tacos
- 8-12 tortillas; small flour
- Hot sauce
- Cilantro
- Cotija cheese
- For the jalapeno relish
- ¼ cup of finely diced red onion
- 3 seeded and diced jalapenos
- 1 clove of minced garlic
- ⅓cup of water
- 1 tablespoon of sugar
- ⅔ cup of white wine vinegar
- 1 tablespoon of salt
- For pickled cabbage
- 2 cups of red cabbage; shredded
- ½ cup of white wine vinegar
- 1 tablespoon of sugar
- 1 tablespoon of salt

Directions:
1. For the jalapeño relish: take all the ingredients and mix then in a non-reactive dish and then keep it aside to be used.
2. For the pickled cabbage: take another non-reactive dish and mix all its respective ingredients and keep it aside
3. Now, transfer both the relish along with the pickled cabbage to your refrigerator and allow it to see for a couple of hours or even overnight if you so desire
4. Take the chicken thighs and season it with an adequate amount of salt and pepper
5. Take a Dutch oven and keep the flame over medium-high heat. Heat 1 tablespoon of olive oil in it
6. Now place the chicken thighs skin side down and brown
7. Remove them from the heat and then set it aside
8. Now, add 1 tablespoon of butter and keep the flame to medium-high
9. When the butter has melted, add jalapeno along with onion and sauté it for 3 to 5 minutes until they turn translucent
10. Add minced garlic to it and sauté it for 30 more seconds
11. Now add adobo sauce along with lime juice, chili powder, and chipotle chile.

12. Add the chicken thighs in the oven and pour in the beer
13. Now set the griddle to pre-heat by keeping the temperature to 350 degrees F
14. Place the oven on the griddle and let it braise for 30 minutes
15. Remove the chicken from the braising liquid and slowly shred it
16. For the tacos: place the shredded part of chicken on the tortillas. Top it with jalapeno relish along with cotija, cabbage, and cilantro and pour the hot sauce
17. Serve and enjoy
Nutrition: Carbohydrates: 29 g Protein: 19 g Sodium: 25 mg Cholesterol: 19 mg

Flavorful Roasted Shawarma

Servings: 1
Preparation Time: 30 minutes
Cooking Time: 4 Hours
Ingredients:
- 5 ½ lbs. of chicken thighs; boneless, skinless
- 4 ½ lbs. of lamb fat
- Pita bread
- 5 ½ lbs. of top sirloin
- 2 yellow onions; large
- 4 tablespoons of rub
- Desired toppings like pickles, tomatoes, fries, salad and more

Directions:
1. Slice the meat and fat into ½" slices and place then in 3 separate bowls
2. Season each of the bowls with the rub and massage the rub into the meat to make sure it seeps well
3. Now place half of the onion at the base of each half skewer. This will make for a firm base
4. Add 2 layers from each of the bowls at a time
5. Make the track as symmetrical as you can
6. Now, put the other 2 half onions at the top of this
7. Wrap it in a plastic wrap and let it refrigerate overnight
8. Set the griddle to preheat keeping the temperature to 275 degrees F
9. Lay the shawarma on the griddle grate and let it cook for approx. 4 hours. Make sure to turn it at least once
10. Remove from the griddle and shoot the temperature to 445 degrees F
11. Now place a cast iron griddle on the griddle grate and pour it with olive oil
12. When the griddle has turned hot, place the whole shawarma on the cast iron and smoke it for 5 to 10 minutes per side
13. Remove from the griddle and slice off the edges
14. Repeat the same with the leftover shawarma
15. Serve in pita bread and add the chosen toppings Enjoy
Nutrition: Carbohydrates: 39 g Protein: 29 g Sodium: 15 mg Cholesterol: 19 mg

Ranch Buffalo Chicken Thighs

Servings: 1
Preparation Time: 30 minutes
Cooking Time: 6 Hours
Ingredients:
- 4-6 skinless, boneless chicken thighs
- Pork and poultry rub
- 4 tablespoons of butter
- 1 cup of sauce; buffalo wing
- Bleu cheese crumbles
- Ranch dressing

Directions:
1. Set the griddle to preheat by keeping the temperature to 450 degrees F and keeping the lid closed
2. Now season the chicken thighs with the poultry rub and then place it on the griddle grate
3. Cook it for 8 to 10 minutes while making sure to flip it once midway
4. Now take a small saucepan and cook the wing sauce along with butter by keeping the flame on medium heat. Make sure to stir in between to avoid lumps
5. Now take the cooked chicken and dip it into the wing sauce and the butter mix. Make sure to coat both the sides in an even manner
6. Take the chicken thighs that have been sauced to the griddle and then cook for further 15 minutes. Do so until the internal temperature reads 175 degrees
7. Sprinkle bleu cheese and drizzle the ranch dressing
8. Serve and enjoy
Nutrition: Carbohydrates: 29 g Protein: 19 g Sodium: 25 mg Cholesterol: 19 mg

Simple Duck Breasts

Servings: 6
Preparation Time: 5 Minutes
Cooking Time: 15 Minutes
Ingredients:
- skin-on duck breasts (about 8 ounces each)
- Salt and pepper

Directions:
1. Trim the excess fat and skin from the duck without exposing the meat; reserve the scraps. With a sharp knife, cut slashes into the skin without slicing all the way down to the flesh; this will help render the fat as the duck cooks. Pat the duck dry with paper towels, then sprinkle both sides with salt and pepper.
2. Put the breasts in a cold large, heavy griddle, skin side down, along with the trimmings, and turn the heat to low. Let the breasts cook, rendering their fat, until the skin is golden brown and dry, 13 to 15minutes; the flesh side of the breast should still be cool or room temperature to the touch. Remove the breasts from the griddle. (At this point, you can let the breasts cool, cover them, and refrigerate for up to a day.)
3. Bring the griddle to high heat. When the griddle is hot, put the duck skin side up and cook until the breasts are one stage less done than you eventually want them, 3 to 10minutes; nick the thickest places with a small knife and peek inside.
4. Turn the breasts over to let the skin crisp, just 1 to 2minutes. Transfer the duck breasts to a platter, let rest for 5minutes, slice, and serve with any accumulated juices.
Nutrition: Calories: 127; Fat: 7g; Protein: 23g; Fiber: 5g

Balsamic Chicken Breasts with Rosemary

Servings: 4
Preparation Time: 5 Minutes
Cooking Time: 6 Minutes
Ingredients:
- ½ cup balsamic vinegar
- 2 tablespoons olive oil
- 2 rosemary sprigs, coarsely chopped
- 2 pounds boneless, skinless chicken breasts, pounded to ½-inch thickness

Directions:
1. Combine the balsamic vinegar, olive oil, and rosemary in a shallow baking dish.
2. Add the chicken breasts and turn to coat. Cover with plastic wrap and refrigerate for at least 30 minutes or overnight.
3. Bring the griddle to high heat. When the griddle is hot, place the s chicken breasts on the Griddle and cook for 6 minutes until they have taken on griddle marks and are cooked through.
Nutrition: Calories: 299; Fat: G; Protein:52g;

Sriracha Duck Poppers

Servings: 1
Preparation Time: 30 minutes
Cooking Time: 4 Hours
Ingredients:
- 8 – 10 pieces of bacon, cut event into same-sized pieces measuring 4 inches each
- 3 duck breasts; boneless and with skin removed and sliced into strips measuring ½ inches
- Sriracha sauce
- 6 de-seeded jalapenos, with the top cut off and sliced into strips

Directions:
1. Wrap the bacon around one trip of pepper and one slice of duck
2. Secure it firmly with the help of a toothpick
3. Fire the griddle on low flame and keep this wrap and griddle it for half an hour until the bacon turns crisp
4. Rotate often to ensure even cooking
5. Serve with sriracha sauce
Nutrition: Carbohydrates: 39 g Protein: 29 g Sodium: 15 mg Cholesterol: 19 mg

Black Tea Smoked Chicken

Servings: 1
Preparation Time: 30 minutes
Cooking Time: 10 Hours
Ingredients:
• Chicken breast (6-lbs., 2.7-kgs)
• The Rub
• Salt – ¼ cup
• Chili powder – 2 tablespoons
• Chinese five-spice – 2 tablespoons
• Brown sugar – 1 ½ cups
• The Smoke
• Preheat the griddle an hour prior to smoking.
• Black tea – 2 cups
Directions:
1. Place salt, chili powder, Chinese five-spice, and brown sugar in a bowl then stir to combine.
2. Rub the chicken breast with the spice mixture then marinate overnight. Store in the refrigerator to keep it fresh.
3. In the morning, preheat a griddle to 225°F (107°C)
4. Pour black tea into a disposable aluminum pan then place in the griddle.
5. Remove the chicken from the refrigerator then thaw while waiting for the griddle.
6. Once the griddle has reached the desired temperature, place the chicken on the griddle's rack.
7. Smoke the chicken breast for 2 hours then check whether the internal temperature has reached 160°F (71°C).
8. Take the smoked chicken breast out from the griddle and transfer to a serving dish.
9. Serve and enjoy immediately.
Nutrition: Carbohydrates: 27 g Protein: 19 g Sodium: 65 mg Cholesterol: 49 mg

Herbed Chicken Salad with Mango

Servings: 4
Preparation Time: 10 Minutes
Cooking Time: 8 Minutes
Ingredients:
• 1½ pounds boneless, skinless chicken breasts
• ¼ cup olive oil, plus more for brushing
• Salt and pepper
• Grated zest of 1 lime
• 2 tablespoons fresh lime juice
• 1 head Boston lettuce, torn into pieces
• ½ cup whole fresh mint leaves
• 1 ripe mango, peeled, pitted, and cut into 1-inch pieces
Directions:
1. Brush with oil and sprinkle with salt and pepper on both sides.
2. Turn control knob to the high position, when the griddle is hot, place the chicken on the griddle and cook for 8 minutes. Transfer the chicken to a plate and let rest while you put the rest of the salad together.
3. Make the dressing: Put the ¼ cup oil in a small bowl with the lime zest and juice and a pinch of salt.
4. Whisk until the dressing thickens; taste and adjust the seasoning. Put the lettuce and mint in a salad bowl and toss to mix. Cut the chicken across the grain into ½-inch slices and put over the greens. Top with the mango pieces, then drizzle with the dressing and serve (or toss before serving if you like).
Nutrition: Calories: 115; Fat: 8g; Protein: 28g; Fiber: 9g

Smoked BBQ Turkey Legs

Servings: 1
Preparation Time: 30 minutes
Cooking Time: 6 Hours
Ingredients:
• 4 turkey legs
• 2 bay leaves
• 1 cup of BBQ rubs
• 1 tablespoon of crushed allspice berries
• 2 teaspoons of liquid smoke
• ½ gal of cold water
• 4 cups of ice
• 1 gal of warm water
• ½ cup of brown sugar
• ½ cup of curing salt
• 1 tablespoon of peppercorns; whole black
Directions:
1. Take a large stockpot and mix a gallon of warm water to curing salt, rub, peppercorns, brown sugar, liquid smoke, allspice and bay leaves
2. Bring this mix to boil by keeping the flame on high heat and let all salt granules dissolve thoroughly
3. Now let it cool to room temperature
4. Now add ice and cold water and let the whole thing chill in the refrigerator
5. Add turkey legs and make sure they are submerged in the brine
6. Let it stay for a day
7. Now drain the turkey legs and get rid of the brine
8. Wash off the brine from the legs with the help of cold water and then pat it dry
9. Set the griddle to preheat by keeping the temperature to 250 degrees F
10. Lay the legs directly on the grate of the griddle
11. Smoke it for 4 to 5 hours till the internal temperature reaches 165 degrees F
12. Serve and enjoy
Nutrition: Carbohydrates: 39 g Protein: 29 g Sodium: 15 mg Cholesterol: 19 mg

Spiced Chicken Burgers

If you're looking for a great alternative to traditional beef burgers, these chicken burgers are lighter and packed with flavor.

Servings: 3
Preparation Time: time: 10 minutes
Cooking Time: 20 minutes

Ingredients:
- 1 lb. ground chicken
- ½ red onion, finely chopped
- 1 teaspoon garlic powder
- ½ teaspoon onion powder
- ¼ teaspoon black pepper
- ½ teaspoon salt
- 3 tablespoons vegetable oil
- 3 potato buns, toasted

Directions:
1. In a large bowl, combine the ground chicken, onion, garlic powder, onion powder, pepper, and salt. Mix well to combine. Form the chicken mixture into three equal patties. Don't work the mixture too much or the burgers will be too dense.
2. Heat your griddle to medium-high heat. Add the vegetable oil.
3. When the oil is shimmering, add the chicken patties and cook 5 minutes per side, or until the patties reach 165°F.
4. Remove the patties from the griddle and allow to rest for five minutes before serving on the toasted buns.

Nutrition: Calories: 420, Sodium: 519 mg, Dietary Fiber: 0.6 g, Fat: 24.8g, Carbs: 2.8g, Protein: 44.2g.

Sweet Smoked Lemony Chicken

Servings: 1
Preparation Time: 30 minutes
Cooking Time: 6 Hours

Ingredients:
- Whole chicken 2 (4-lbs., 1.8-kgs)
- Olive oil – ¼ cup
- The Rub
- Salt – ¼ cup
- Pepper – 2 tablespoons
- Garlic powder – ¼ cup
- The Filling
- Fresh Ginger – 8, 1-inch each
- Cinnamon sticks – 8
- Sliced lemon – ½ cup
- Cloves - 6
- The Smoke
- Preheat the griddle an hour prior to smoking.

Directions:
1. Preheat a griddle to 225°F (107°C).
2. Rub the chicken with salt, pepper, and garlic powder then set aside.
3. Fill the chicken cavities with ginger, cinnamon sticks, cloves, and sliced lemon then brush olive oil all over the chicken.
4. When the griddle is ready, place the whole chicken on the griddle's rack.
5. Smoke the whole chicken for 4 hours then check whether the internal temperature has reached 160°F (71°C).

6. When the chicken is done, remove the smoked chicken from the griddle then let it warm for a few minutes.
7. Serve and enjoy right away or cut into slices.

Nutrition: Carbohydrates: 27 g Protein: 19 g Sodium: 65 mg Cholesterol: 49 mg

Smoked Cayenne Chicken Wings

Servings: 1
Preparation Time: 30 minutes
Cooking Time: 3 Hours

Ingredients:
- Chicken wings (6-lbs., 2.7-kgs)
- The Rub
- Olive oil – 3 tablespoons
- Chili powder – 2 ½ tablespoons
- Smoked paprika – 3 tablespoons
- Cumin – ½ teaspoon
- Garlic powder – 2 teaspoons
- Salt – 1 ¾ teaspoons
- Pepper – 1 tablespoon
- Cayenne – 2 teaspoons

Directions:
1. Preheat the griddle an hour prior to smoking.
2. Divide each chicken wing into two then place in a bowl. Set aside.
3. Combine olive oil with chili powder, smoked paprika, cumin, garlic powder, salt, pepper, and cayenne then mix well.
4. Rub the chicken wings with the spice mixture then let them sit for about an hour.
5. Meanwhile, preheat a griddle to 225°F
6. When the griddle is ready, arrange the spiced chicken wings on the griddle's rack.
7. Smoke the chicken wings for 2 hours or until the internal temperature of the chicken wings has reached 160°F (71°C).
8. Take the smoked chicken wings from the griddle and transfer to a serving dish.
9. Serve and enjoy immediately.

Nutrition: Carbohydrates: 17 g Protein: 29 g Sodium: 55 mg Cholesterol: 48 mg

Herbed Lemon Chicken

Servings: 1
Preparation Time: 30 minutes
Cooking Time: 5 Hours
Ingredients:
*   1 whole chicken
*   4 cloves of minced garlic
*   Zest of 2 fresh lemons
*   1 tablespoon of olive oil
*   1 tablespoon of smoked paprika
*   1 ½ teaspoon of salt
*   ½ teaspoon of black pepper
*   ½ teaspoon of dried oregano
*   1 tablespoon of ground cumin

Directions:
1. Preheat the griddle by pushing the temperature to 375 degrees F
2. Now take the chicken and spatchcock it by cutting it on both the sides right from the backbone to the tail via the neck
3. Lay it flat and push it down on the breastbone. This would break the ribs
4. Take all the leftover ingredients in a bowl except ½ teaspoon of salt and crush them to make a smooth rub
5. Spread this rub evenly over the chicken making sure that it seeps right under the skin
6. Now place the chicken on the griddle grates and let it cook for an hour until the internal temperature reads 165 degrees F
7. Let it rest for 10 minutes
8. Serve and enjoy
Nutrition: Carbohydrates: 39 g Protein: 29 g Sodium: 15 mg Cholesterol: 19 mg

Garlicky Bone-In Chicken Thighs

Servings: 4
Preparation Time: 10 Minutes
Cooking Time: 55 Minutes
Ingredients:
*   3 pounds bone-in, skin-on chicken thighs
*   Salt and pepper
*   ¼ cup fish sauce
*   2 tablespoons turbinado sugar
*   minced garlic
*   dried red chiles

Directions:
1. Trim excess fat and skin from the chicken without exposing the meat. Sprinkle with salt and pepper on both sides.

2. Turn control knob to the high position, when the griddle is hot, put the thighs on the griddle, skin side up, and cook for about 20minutes, then turn the pieces and rotate them 180 degrees for even browning. Cook until the meat is no longer pink at the bone, 40 to 55minutes total, depending on the size of the pieces.
3. While the thighs cook, put the fish sauce, sugar, garlic, and chiles in a small saucepan over low heat. Stir until the sugar dissolves completely. Let cool a few minutes before pouring into a large heatproof bowl; remove the chiles. When the thighs are done, transfer them to the bowl and toss to coat evenly with the glaze, using tongs. Turn the heat to medium. Remove the thighs from the glaze, let any excess glaze drip off, then arrange the thighs skin side up on the griddle. Cook, turning once, until crisp and brown, 1 to 3minutes per side; move the thighs away from the flames if the glaze starts to burn. Transfer to a platter and serve.
Nutrition: Calories: 400; Fat: 10g; Protein:34g; Fiber:17 g

Chicken and Tomato Kebabs

Servings: 4
Preparation Time: 5 Minutes
Cooking Time: 15 Minutes
Ingredients:
*   1½ to 2pounds boneless, skinless chicken breasts or thighs
*   2 cups cherry or grape tomatoes
*   3 tablespoons good-quality olive oil
*   Salt and pepper

Directions:
1. If you're using bamboo or wooden skewers, soak them in water for 30minutes. Cut the chicken into 1-to 1½-inch pieces, depending on the size of the tomatoes. Toss the chicken and tomatoes with the oil in a medium bowl and sprinkle with some salt and pepper. Alternate the chicken and tomatoes on the skewers.
2. Put the skewers on the griddle and cook until the chicken is no longer pink in the center, 10 to 15minutes total. Transfer to a platter and serve hot or at room temperature.
Nutrition: Calories: 467; Fat: 19g; Protein:19g; Fiber:12g

Chapter 5 Turkey Recipes

Peppered Roasted Turkey

Servings: 12
Preparation Time: 15 Minutes
Cooking Time: 3 Hours 30 Minutes
Ingredients:
- 14 pounds turkey, cleaned
- 2 tablespoons chopped mixed herbs
- Pork and poultry rub as needed
- ¼ teaspoon ground black pepper
- 3 tablespoons butter, unsalted, melted
- 8 tablespoons butter, unsalted, softened
- 2 cups chicken broth

Directions:
1. Clean the turkey by removing the giblets, wash it inside out, pat dry with paper towels, then place it on a roasting pan and tuck the turkey wings by tiring with butcher's string.
2. Switch on the griddle, set the temperature to 325 degrees F and let it preheat for a minimum of 15 minutes.
3. Meanwhile, Prepared herb butter and for this, take a small bowl, place the softened butter in it, add black pepper and mixed herbs and beat until fluffy.
4. Place some of the Prepared herb butter underneath the skin of turkey by using a handle of a wooden spoon, and massage the skin to distribute butter evenly.
5. Then rub the exterior of the turkey with melted butter, season with pork and poultry rub, and pour the broth in the roasting pan. When the griddle has preheated, open the lid, place roasting pan containing turkey on the griddle grate, shut the griddle and smoke for 3 hours and 30 minutes until the internal temperature reaches 165 degrees F and the top has turned golden brown.
6. When done, transfer turkey to a cutting board, let it rest for 30 minutes, then carve it into slices and serve.
Nutrition: Calories: 154.6 Fat: 3.1 g Carbs: 8.4 g Protein: 28.8 g

BBQ Turkey Legs

Servings: 4
Preparation Time: 10 Minutes
Cooking Time: 5 Hours
Ingredients:
- 4 turkey legs -
For the Brine:
- ½ cup curing salt
- 1 tablespoon whole black peppercorns -
- 1 cup BBQ rub
- ½ cup brown sugar
- 2 bay leaves
- 2 teaspoons liquid smoke
- 16 cups of warm water
- 4 cups ice -
- 8 cups of cold water

Directions:
1. Prepare the brine and for this, take a large stockpot, place it over high heat, pour warm water in it, add peppercorn, bay leaves, and liquid smoke

2. Stir in salt, sugar, and BBQ rub and bring it to a boil.
3. Remove pot from heat, bring it to room temperature, then pour in cold water, add ice cubes and let the brine chill in the refrigerator. Then add turkey legs in it, submerge them completely, and let soak for 24 hours in the refrigerator.
4. After 24 hours, remove turkey legs from the brine, rinse well and pat dry with paper towels.
5. When ready to cook, switch on the griddle, set the temperature to 250 degrees F and let it preheat for a minimum of 15 minutes.
6. When the griddle has preheated, open the lid, place turkey legs on the griddle grate, shut the griddle, and smoke for 5 hours until nicely browned and the internal temperature reaches 165 degrees F. Serve immediately.
Nutrition: Calories: 416 Fat: 13.3 g Carbs: 0 g Protein: 69.8 g

Savory Turkey Legs with Mandarin

Servings: 4
Preparation Time: 10 minutes
Cooking Time: 5 hours
Ingredients:
- 1-gallon hot water
- 1 cup curing salt (such as Morton Tender Quick)
- ¼ cup packed light brown sugar
- 1 teaspoon freshly ground black pepper
- 1 teaspoon ground cloves
- 1 bay leaf
- 2 teaspoons liquid smoke
- 4 turkey legs
- Mandarin Glaze, for serving

Directions:
1. In a huge container with a lid, stir together the water, curing salt, brown sugar, pepper, cloves, bay leaf, and liquid smoke until the salt and sugar are dissolved; let come to room temperature.
2. Submerge the turkey legs in the seasoned brine, cover, and refrigerate overnight.
3. When ready to smoke, remove the turkey legs from the brine and rinse them; discard the brine. Supply your griddle Preheat, with the lid closed, to 225°F.
4. Arrange the turkey legs on the griddle, close the lid, and smoke for 4 to 5 hours, or until dark brown and a meat thermometer inserted in the thickest part of the meat reads 165°F.
5. Serve with Mandarin Glaze on the side or drizzled over the turkey legs.
Nutrition: Calories: 190 Carbs: 1g Fat: 9g Protein: 24g

Sesame Hoisin Turkey Wings with Honey

Servings: 8
Preparation Time: 15 minutes
Cooking Time: 1 hour
Ingredients:
- 2 pounds turkey wings
- ½ cup hoisin sauce
- 1 tablespoon honey
- 2 teaspoons soy sauce
- 2 garlic cloves (minced)
- 1 teaspoon freshly grated ginger
- 2 teaspoons sesame oil
- 1 teaspoons pepper or to taste
- 1 teaspoons salt or to taste
- ¼ cup pineapple juice
- 1 tablespoon chopped green onions
- 1 tablespoon sesame seeds
- 1 lemon (cut into wedges)

Directions:
1. In a huge container, combine the honey, garlic, ginger, soy, hoisin sauce, sesame oil, pepper and salt. Put all the mixture into a zip lock bag and add the wings. Refrigerate for 2 hours.
2. Remove turkey from the marinade and reserve the marinade. Let the turkey rest for a few minutes, until it is at room temperature. Preheat your griddle to 300°F with the lid closed for 15 minutes.
3. Arrange the wings into a griddleing basket and place the basket on the griddle.
4. Griddle for 1 hour or until the internal temperature of the wings reaches 165°F.
5. Meanwhile, pour the reserved marinade into a saucepan over medium-high heat. Stir in the pineapple juice. Wait to boil then reduce heat and simmer for until the sauce thickens. Brush the wings with sauce and cook for 6 minutes more. Remove the wings from heat. Serve and garnish it with green onions, sesame seeds and lemon wedges.
Nutrition: Calories: 115 Fat: 4.8g Carbs: 11.9g Protein 6.8g

Garlicky Turkey Jerky with Sriracha

Servings: 6
Preparation Time: 15 minutes
Cooking Time: 4 hours
Ingredients:
- Marinade:
- 1 cup pineapple juice
- ½ cup brown sugar
- 2 tablespoons sriracha
- 2 teaspoons onion powder
- 2 tablespoons minced garlic
- 2 tablespoons rice wine vinegar
- 2 tablespoons hoisin
- 1 tablespoon red pepper flakes
- 1 tablespoon coarsely ground black pepper flakes
- 2 cups coconut amino
- 2 jalapenos (thinly sliced)
Meat:

- 3 pounds turkey boneless skinless breasts (sliced to ¼ inch thick)

Directions:
1. Pour the marinade mixture ingredients in a container and mix until the ingredients are well combined. Put the turkey slices in a gallon sized zip lock bag and pour the marinade into the bag. Massage the marinade into the turkey. Seal the bag and refrigerate for 8 hours.
2. Remove the turkey slices from the marinade.
3. Activate the griddle for smoking for 5 minutes until fire starts.
4. Close the lid and preheat your griddle to 180°F,.
5. Remove the turkey slices from the marinade and pat them dry with a paper towel.
6. Arrange the turkey slices on the griddle in a single layer. Smoke the turkey for about 3 to 4 hours, turning often after the first 2 hours of smoking. The jerky should be dark and dry when it is done.
7. Remove the jerky from the griddle and let it sit for about 1 hour to cool. Serve immediately or store in refrigerator.
Nutrition: Calories: 109 Carbs: 12g Fat: 1g Protein: 14g

Garlicky Turkey Drumstick

Servings: 3
Preparation Time: 20 minutes
Cooking Time: 2.5 hours to 3 hours
Ingredients:
- 3 fresh or thawed frozen turkey drumsticks
- 3 tablespoons extra virgin olive oil
- Brine component
- 4 cups of filtered water
- ¼Cup kosher salt
- ¼ cup brown sugar
- 1 teaspoon garlic powder
- Poultry seasoning 1 teaspoon
- ½ teaspoon red pepper flakes
- 1 teaspoon pink hardened salt

Directions:
1. Put the salt water ingredients in a 1 gallon sealable bag. Add the turkey drumstick to the salt water and refrigerate for 12 hours. After 12 hours, remove the drumstick from the saline, rinse with cold water, and pat dry with a paper towel.
2. Air dry the drumstick in the refrigerator without a cover for 2 hours. Remove the drumsticks from the refrigerator and rub a tablespoon of extra virgin olive oil under and over each drumstick.
3. Set the griddle for indirect cooking and preheat to 250 degrees
4. Place the drumstick on the griddle and smoke at 250 ° F for 2 hours. After 2 hours, increase griddle temperature to 325 ° F.
5. Cook the turkey drumstick at 325 ° F until the internal temperature of the thickest part of each drumstick is 180 ° F with an instant reading digital thermometer.
6. Place a smoked turkey drumstick under a loose foil tent for 15 minutes before eating.
Nutrition: Calories: 278 Carbs: 0gFat: 13g Protein: 37g

BBQ Turkey Breast

Servings: 6
Preparation Time: 12 Hours
Cooking Time: 8 Hours
Ingredients:
For the Brine:
- 2 pounds turkey breast, deboned
- 2 tablespoons ground black pepper
- ¼ cup salt
- 1 cup brown sugar
- 4 cups cold water
For the BBQ Rub:
- 2 tablespoons dried onions
- 2 tablespoons garlic powder
- ¼ cup paprika
- 2 tablespoons ground black pepper -
- 1 tablespoon salt
- 2 tablespoons brown sugar
- 2 tablespoons red chili powder
- 1 tablespoon cayenne pepper
- 2 tablespoons sugar
- 2 tablespoons ground cumin
Directions:
1. Prepare the brine and for this, take a large bowl, add salt, black pepper, and sugar in it, pour in water, and stir until sugar has dissolved. Place turkey breast in it, submerge it completely and let it soak for a minimum of 12 hours in the refrigerator.
2. Meanwhile, Prepare the BBQ rub and for this, take a small bowl, place all of its ingredients in it and then stir until combined, set aside until required. Then remove turkey breast from the brine and season well with the Prepared BBQ rub. When ready to cook, switch on the griddle, set the temperature to 180 degrees F and let it preheat for a minimum of 15 minutes. When the griddle has preheated, open the lid, place turkey breast on the griddle grate, shut the griddle, change the smoking temperature to 225 degrees F, and smoke for 8 hours until the internal temperature reaches 160 degrees F.
3. When done, transfer turkey to a cutting board, let it rest for 10 minutes, then cut it into slices and serve.
Nutrition: Calories: 250 Fat: 5 g Carbs: 31 g Protein: 18 g

Herbed Smoked Whole Turkey

Servings: 6
Preparation Time: 10 minutes
Cooking Time: 5 hours
Ingredients:
- 1 (10- to 12-pound) turkey, giblets removed
- Extra-virgin olive oil, for rubbing
- ¼ cup poultry seasoning
- 8 tablespoons (1 stick) unsalted butter, melted
- ½ cup apple juice
- 2 teaspoons dried sage
- 2 teaspoons dried thyme
Directions:
1. Supply your griddle follow the manufacturer's specific start-up procedure. Preheat, with the lid closed, to 250°F.

2. Rub the turkey with oil and season with the poultry seasoning inside and out, getting under the skin.
3. In a bowl, combine the melted butter, apple juice, sage, and thyme to use for basting.
4. Put the turkey in a roasting pan, place on the griddle, close the lid, and griddle for 5 to 6 hours, basting every hour, until the skin is brown and crispy, or until a meat thermometer inserted in the thickest part of the thigh reads 165°F.
5. Let the turkey meat rest for about 15 to 20 minutes before carving.
Nutrition: Calories: 180 Carbs: 3g Fat: 2g Protein: 39g

Marinated Turkey Breast with Honey

Servings: 6
Preparation Time: 15 minutes
Cooking Time: 4 hours
Ingredients:
- 1 (5 pounds) boneless chicken breast
- 4 cups water
- 2 tablespoons kosher salt
- 1 teaspoon Italian seasoning
- 2 tablespoons honey
- 1 tablespoon cider vinegar
Rub:
- ½ teaspoon onion powder
- 1 teaspoon paprika
- 1 teaspoon salt
- 1 teaspoon ground black pepper
- 1 tablespoons brown sugar
- ½ teaspoon garlic powder
- 1 teaspoon oregano
Directions:
1. In a huge container, combine the water, honey, cider vinegar, Italian seasoning and salt.
2. Add the chicken breast and toss to combine. Cover the bowl and place it in the refrigerator and chill for 4 hours.
3. Rinse the chicken breast with water and pat dry with paper towels.
4. In another mixing bowl, combine the brown sugar, salt, paprika, onion powder, pepper, oregano and garlic.
5. Generously season the chicken breasts with the rub mix.
6. Preheat the griddle to 225°F with lid closed for 15 minutes.
7. Arrange the turkey breast into a griddle rack. Place the griddle rack on the griddle.
8. Smoke for about 3 to 4 hours or until the internal temperature of the turkey breast reaches 165°F.
9. Remove the chicken breast from heat and let them rest for a few minutes. Serve.
Nutrition: Calories 903 Fat: 34g Carbs: 9.9g Protein 131.5g

Rosemary Maple Bourbon Turkey

Servings: 8
Preparation Time: 15 minutes
Cooking Time: 3 hours
Ingredients:
- 1 (12 pounds) turkey
- 8 cup chicken broth
- 1 stick butter (softened)
- 1 teaspoon thyme
- 2 garlic clove (minced)
- 1 teaspoon dried basil
- 1 teaspoon pepper
- 1 teaspoon salt
- 1 tablespoon minced rosemary
- 1 teaspoon paprika
- 1 lemon (wedged)
- 1 onion
- 1 orange (wedged)
- 1 apple (wedged)
- Maple Bourbon Glaze:
- ¾ cup bourbon
- ½ cup maple syrup
- 1 stick butter (melted)
- 1 tablespoon lime

Directions:
1. Wash the turkey meat inside and out under cold running water.
2. Insert the onion, lemon, orange and apple into the turkey cavity.
3. In a mixing bowl, combine the butter, paprika, thyme, garlic, basil, pepper, salt, basil and rosemary.
4. Brush the turkey generously with the herb butter mixture.
5. Set a rack into a roasting pan and place the turkey on the rack. Put a 5 cups of chicken broth into the bottom of the roasting pan.
6. Preheat the griddle to 350°F with lid closed for 15 minutes.
7. Place the roasting pan in the griddle and cook for 1 hour.
8. Meanwhile, combine all the maple bourbon glaze ingredients in a mixing bowl. Mix until well combined.
9. Baste the turkey with glaze mixture. Continue cooking, basting turkey every 30 minutes and adding more broth as needed for 2 hours, or until the internal temperature of the turkey reaches 165°F.
10. Take off the turkey from the griddle and let it rest for a few minutes. Cut into slices and serve.
Nutrition: Calories 1536 Fat 58.6g Carbs: 24g Protein 20.1g

Flavorful Herbed Turkey

Servings: 6
Preparation Time: 15 minutes
Cooking Time: 4 hours
Ingredients:
- 2 cups butter (softened)
- 1 tablespoon cracked black pepper
- 2 teaspoons kosher salt
- 2 tablespoons freshly chopped rosemary
- 2 tablespoons freshly chopped parsley
- 2 tablespoons freshly chopped sage –
- 2 teaspoons dried thyme
- 6 garlic cloves (minced)
- 1 (18 pound) turkey

Directions:
1. In a mixing bowl, combine the butter, sage, rosemary, 1 teaspoon black pepper, 1 teaspoon salt, thyme, parsley and garlic.
2. Use your fingers to loosen the skin from the turkey.
3. Generously, Rub butter mixture under the turkey skin and all over the turkey as well. 4. Season turkey generously with herb mix. 5. Preheat the griddle to 300°F with lid closed for 15 minutes.
4. Place the turkey on the griddle and roast for about 4 hours, or until the turkey thigh temperature reaches 160°F.
5. Take out the turkey meat from the griddle and let it rest for a few minutes. Cut into sizes and serve.
Nutrition: Calories 278 Fat 30.8g Carbs: 1.6g Protein 0.6g

Spiced Smoked Turkey

Servings: 6
Preparation Time: 15 minutes
Cooking Time: 4 hours 3 minutes
Ingredients:
- 1 (18 pounds) turkey
- 2 tablespoons finely chopped fresh parsley
- 1 tablespoon finely chopped fresh rosemary
- 2 tablespoons finely chopped fresh thyme
- ½ cup melted butter
- 1 teaspoon garlic powder
- 1 teaspoon onion powder
- 1 teaspoon ground black pepper
- 2 teaspoons salt or to taste
- 2 tablespoons finely chopped scallions

Directions:
1. Remove the turkey giblets and rinse turkey, in and out, under cold running water.
2. Place the turkey on a working surface, breast side down. Use a poultry shear to cut the turkey along both sides of the backbone to remove the turkey back bone.
3. Flip the turkey over, back side down. Now, press the turkey down to flatten it.
4. In a mixing bowl, combine the parsley, rosemary, scallions, thyme, butter, pepper, salt, garlic and onion powder.
5. Rub butter mixture over all sides of the turkey.
6. Preheat your griddle to HIGH (450°F) with lid closed for 15 minutes.
7. Place the turkey directly on the griddle grate and cook for 30 minutes. Reduce the heat to 300°F and cook for an additional 4 hours, or until the internal temperature of the thickest part of the thigh reaches 165°F. Take out the turkey meat from the griddle and let it rest for a few minutes. Cut into sizes and serve.
Nutrition: Calories: 780 Fat: 19g Carbs: 29.7g Protein 116.4g

Maple Smoked Turkey Breast

Servings: 6
Preparation Time: 10 Minutes
Cooking Time: 1 Hour 30 minutes
Ingredients:
For The Brine
- 1 Cup of kosher salt
- 1 Cup of maple syrup
- ¼ Cup of brown sugar
- ¼ Cup of whole black peppercorns
- 4 Cups of cold bourbon
- 1 and ½ gallons of cold water
- 1 Turkey breast of about 7 pounds
For The Turkey
- 3 Tablespoons of brown sugar
- 1 and ½ tablespoons of smoked paprika
- 1 ½ teaspoons of chipotle chili powder
- 1 ½ teaspoons of garlic powder
- 1 ½ teaspoons of salt
- 1 and ½ teaspoons of black pepper
- 1 Teaspoon of onion powder
- ½ teaspoon of ground cumin
- 6 Tablespoons of melted unsalted butter

Directions:
1. Before beginning; make sure that the bourbon; the water and the chicken stock are all cold
2. Now to make the brine, combine altogether the salt, the syrup, the sugar, the peppercorns, the bourbon, and the water in a large bucket.
3. Remove any pieces that are left on the turkey, like the neck or the giblets
4. Refrigerate the turkey meat in the brine for about 8 to 12 hours in a reseal able bag
5. Remove the turkey breast from the brine and pat dry with clean paper towels; then place it over a baking sheet and refrigerate for about 1 hour
6. Preheat your griddle to about 300°F;
7. In a bowl, mix the paprika with the sugar, the chili powder, the garlic powder, the salt, the pepper, the onion powder and the cumin, mixing very well to combine.
8. Carefully lift the skin of the turkey; then rub the melted butter over the meat
9. Rub the spice over the meat very well and over the skin
10. Smoke the turkey breast for about 1 ½ hours at a temperature of about 375°
Nutrition: Calories: 94 Fat: 2g Carbs: 1g Protein: 18g

Roasted Jalapeno Injection Turkey

Servings: 4
Preparation Time: 15 Minutes
Cooking Time: 4 Hours And 10 Minutes
Ingredients:
- 15 pounds whole turkey, giblet removed
- ½ of medium red onion, peeled and minced
- 8 jalapeño peppers
- 2 tablespoons minced garlic
- 4 tablespoons garlic powder
- 6 tablespoons Italian seasoning
- 1 cup butter, softened, unsalted

- ¼ cup olive oil
- 1 cup chicken broth
Directions:
1. Open hopper of the griddle, add dry pallets, make sure ash-can is in place, then open the ash damper, power on the griddle and close the ash damper.
2. Make the temperature of the griddle up to 200 degrees F, let preheat for 30 minutes or until the green light on the dial blinks that indicate griddle has reached to set temperature.
3. Meanwhile, place a large saucepan over medium-high heat, add oil and butter and when the butter melts, add onion, garlic, and peppers and cook for 3 to 5 minutes or until nicely golden brown.
4. Pour in broth, stir well, let the mixture boil for 5 minutes, then remove pan from the heat and strain the mixture to get just liquid.
5. Inject turkey generously with Prepared liquid, then spray the outside of turkey with butter spray and season well with garlic and Italian seasoning.
6. Place turkey on the griddle, shut with lid, and smoke for 30 minutes, then increase the temperature to 325 degrees F and continue smoking the turkey for 3 hours or until the internal temperature of turkey reach to 165 degrees F.
7. When done, transfer turkey to a cutting board, let rest for 5 minutes, then carve into slices and serve.
Nutrition: Calories: 131 Fat: 7 g Protein: 13 g Carbs: 3 g

Tasty Griddle Young Turkey

Servings: 6
Preparation Time: 20 Minutes
Cooking Time: 4 To 4 Hours 30 Minutes
Ingredients:
- 1 fresh or thawed frozen young turkey
- 6 glasses of extra virgin olive oil with roasted garlic flavor
- 6 original Yang dry lab or poultry seasonings
Directions:
1. Remove excess fat and skin from turkey breasts and cavities.
2. Slowly separate the skin of the turkey to its breast and a quarter of the leg, leaving the skin intact.
3. Apply olive oil to the chest, under the skin and on the skin.
4. Gently rub or season to the chest cavity, under the skin and on the skin.
5. Set up tailgate griddle for indirect cooking and smoking. Preheat to 225 ° F.
6. Put the turkey meat on the griddle with the chest up.
7. Suck the turkey for 4-4 hours at 225 ° F until the thickest part of the turkey's chest reaches an internal temperature of 170 ° F and the juice is clear.
8. Before engraving, place the turkey under a loose foil tent for 20 minutes
Nutrition: Calories: 240 Carbs: 27g Fat: 9g Protein: 15g

Savory Turkey Breast with Herbed Butter

Servings: 12
Preparation Time: 8 Hours and 10 Minutes
Cooking Time: 3 Hours
Ingredients:
- 7 pounds turkey breast, bone-in, skin-on, fat trimmed
- ¾ cup salt
- ⅓ cup brown sugar
- 4 quarts water, cold
- For Herbed Butter:
- 1 tablespoon chopped parsley
- ½ teaspoon ground black pepper
- 8 tablespoons butter, unsalted, softened
- 1 tablespoon chopped sage
- ½ tablespoon minced garlic
- 1 tablespoon chopped rosemary
- 1 teaspoon lemon zest
- 1 tablespoon chopped oregano
- 1 tablespoon lemon juice

Directions:
1. Prepare the brine and for this, pour water in a large container, add salt and sugar and stir well until salt and sugar has completely dissolved.
2. Add turkey breast in the brine, cover with the lid and let soak in the refrigerator for a minimum of 8 hours.
3. Then remove turkey breast from the brine, rinse well and pat dry with paper towels.
4. Open hopper of the griddle, add dry pallets, make sure ash-can is in place, then open the ash damper, power on the griddle and close the ash damper.
5. Set the temperature of the griddle to 350 degrees F, let preheat for 30 minutes or until the green light on the dial blinks that indicate griddle has reached to set temperature.
6. Meanwhile, take a roasting pan, pour in 1 cup water, then place a wire rack in it and place turkey breast on it. Prepare the herb butter and for this, place butter in a heatproof bowl, add remaining ingredients for the butter and stir until just mix.
7. Loosen the skin of the turkey from its breast by using your fingers, then insert 2 tablespoons of Prepared herb butter on each side of the skin of the breastbone and spread it evenly, pushing out all the air pockets.
8. Place the remaining herb butter in the bowl into the microwave wave and heat for 1 minute or more at high heat setting or until melted. Then brush melted herb butter on the outside of the turkey breast and place roasting pan containing turkey on the griddle.
9. Shut the griddle with lid and smoke for 2 hours and 30 minutes or until the turkey breast is nicely golden brown and the internal temperature of turkey reach to 165 degrees F, flipping the turkey and basting with melted herb butter after 1 hour and 30 minutes smoking.
10. When done, transfer the turkey breast to a cutting board, let it rest for 15 minutes, then carve it into pieces and serve.

Nutrition: Calories: 97 Fat: 4 g Protein: 13 g Carbs: 1 g

Roast Orange Turkey with Celery

Servings:6 to 8
Preparation Time: 30 Minutes
Cooking Time: 2 hours 30 minutes
Ingredients:
- 1 Frozen Long Island turkey
- 3 tablespoons west
- 1 large orange, cut into wedges
- Three celery stems chopped into large chunks
- Half a small red onion, a quarter
- Orange sauce:
- 2 orange cups
- 2 tablespoons soy sauce
- 2 tablespoons orange marmalade
- 2 tablespoons honey
- 3 teaspoons grated raw

Directions:
1. Remove the jibble from the turkey's cavity and neck and retain or discard for another use. Wash the duck and pat some dry paper towel.
2. Remove excess fat from tail, neck and cavity. Use a sharp scalpel knife tip to pierce the turkey's skin entirely, so that it does not penetrate the duck's meat, to help dissolve the fat layer beneath the skin.
3. Add the seasoning inside the cavity with one cup of rub or seasoning.
4. Season the outside of the turkey with the remaining friction or seasoning.
5. Fill the cavity with orange wedges, celery and onion. Duck legs are tied with butcher twine to make filling easier. Place the turkey's breast up on a small rack of shallow roast bread.
6. To make the sauce, mix the ingredients in the saucepan over low heat and cook until the sauce is thick and syrupy. Set aside and let cool.
7. Set the griddle for indirect cooking and preheat to 350 ° F.
8. Roast the turkey at 350 ° F for 2 hours.
9. After 2 hours, brush the turkey freely with orange sauce.
10. Roast the orange glass turkey for another 30 minutes, making sure that the inside temperature of the thickest part of the leg reaches 165 ° F.
11. Place turkey under loose foil tent for 20 minutes before serving.
12. Discard the orange wedge, celery and onion. Serve with a quarter of turkey with poultry scissors.

Nutrition: Calories: 216 Carbs: 2g Fat: 11g Protein: 34g

Mayo Smoked Turkey

Servings: 10
Preparation Time: 20 minutes
Cooking Time: 4 hours 10 minutes
Ingredients:
- Whole turkey (4-lbs., 1.8-kg.)
- The Rub
- Mayonnaise – ½ cup
- Salt – ¾ teaspoon
- Brown sugar – ¼ cup
- Ground mustard – 2 tablespoons
- Black pepper – 1 teaspoon
- Onion powder – 1 ½ tablespoons
- Ground cumin – 1 ½ tablespoons
- Chili powder – 2 tablespoons
- Cayenne pepper – ½ tablespoon
- Old Bay Seasoning – ½ teaspoon
- The Filling
- Sliced green apples – 3 cups

Directions:
1. Place salt, brown sugar, brown mustard, black pepper, onion powder, ground cumin, chili powder, cayenne pepper, and old bay seasoning in a bowl then mix well. Set aside.
2. Next, fill the turkey cavity with sliced green apples then baste mayonnaise over the turkey skin. Sprinkle the dry spice mixture over the turkey then wrap with aluminum foil.
3. Marinate the turkey for at least 4 hours or overnight and store in the fridge to keep it fresh.
4. On the next day, remove the turkey from the fridge and thaw at room temperature.
5. Set the griddle for indirect heat then adjust the temperature to 275°F (135°C). Unwrap the turkey and place in the griddle. Smoke the turkey for 4 hours or until the internal temperature has reached 170°F (77°C). Remove the smoked turkey from the griddle and serve.
Nutrition: Calories: 340 Carbs: 40g Fat: 10g Protein: 21g

Beer-Braised Smoked Turkey

Servings: 6
Preparation Time: 15 minutes
Cooking Time: 4 hours
Ingredients:
- Whole turkey (4-lbs., 1.8-kg.)
- The Brine
- Beer – 2 cans
- Salt – 1 tablespoon
- White sugar – 2 tablespoons
- Soy sauce – ¼ cup
- Cold water – 1 quart
- The Rub
- Unsalted butter – 3 tablespoons
- Smoked paprika – 1 teaspoon
- Garlic powder – 1 ½ teaspoons
- Pepper – 1 teaspoon
- Cayenne pepper – ¼ teaspoon

Directions:
1. Pour beer into a container then add salt, white sugar, and soy sauce then stir well. Put the turkey into the brine mixture cold water over the turkey. Make sure that the turkey is completely soaked. Soak the turkey in the brine for at least 6 hours or overnight and store in the fridge to keep it fresh. On the next day, remove the turkey from the fridge and take it out of the brine mixture.
2. Wash and rinse the turkey then pat it dry. Set the griddle for indirect heat then adjust the temperature to 275°F (135°C). Open the beer can then push it in the turkey cavity. Place the seasoned turkey in the griddle and make a tripod using the beer can and the two turkey-legs. Smoke the turkey for 4 hours or until the internal temperature has reached 170°F (77°C). Once it is done, remove the smoked turkey from the griddle and transfer it to a serving dish.
Nutrition: Calories: 229 Carbs: 34g Fat: 8g Protein: 3g

Barbecue Glazed Turkey Breast

Servings: 8
Preparation Time: 15 minutes
Cooking Time: 4 hours 20 minutes
Ingredients:
- Turkey breast (3-lb., 1.4-kg.)
- The Rub
- Salt – ¾ teaspoon
- Pepper – ½ teaspoon
- The Glaze
- Olive oil – 1 tablespoon
- Ketchup – ¾ cup
- White vinegar – 3 tablespoons
- Brown sugar – 3 tablespoons
- Smoked paprika – 1 tablespoons
- Chili powder – ¾ teaspoon
- Cayenne powder – ¼ teaspoon

Directions:
1. Score the turkey breast at several places then sprinkle salt and pepper over it.
2. Let the seasoned turkey breast rest for approximately 10 minutes. Set the griddle for indirect heat then adjust the temperature to 275°F (135°C).
3. Place the seasoned turkey breast in the griddle and smoke for 2 hours.
4. In the meantime, combine olive oil, ketchup, white vinegar, brown sugar, smoked paprika; chili powder, garlic powder, and cayenne pepper in a saucepan then stir until incorporated. Wait to simmer then remove from heat.
5. After 2 hours of smoking, baste the sauce over the turkey breast and continue smoking for another 2 hours.
6. Once the internal temperature of the smoked turkey breast has reached 170°F (77°C) remove from the griddle and wrap with aluminum foil.
7. Let the smoked turkey breast rest for approximately 15 minutes to 30 minutes then unwrap it. Cut the smoked turkey breast into thick slices then serve.
Nutrition: Calories: 290 Carbs: 2g Fat: 3g Protein: 63g

Cajun Smoked Turkey Tabasco

Servings: 8
Preparation Time: 20 minutes
Cooking Time: 4 hours 15 minutes
Ingredients:
• Whole turkey (4-lbs., 1.8-kg.)
• The Rub
• Brown sugar – ¼ cup
• Smoked paprika – 2 teaspoons
• Salt – 1 teaspoon
• Onion powder – 1 ½ teaspoons
• Oregano – 2 teaspoons
• Garlic powder – 2 teaspoons
• Dried thyme – ½ teaspoon
• White pepper – ½ teaspoon
• Cayenne pepper – ½ teaspoon
• The Glaze
• Ketchup – ½ cup
• Hot sauce – ½ cup
• Cider vinegar – 1 tablespoon
• Tabasco – 2 teaspoons
• Cajun spices – ½ teaspoon
• Unsalted butter – 3 tablespoons
Directions:
1. Rub the turkey with 2 tablespoons of brown sugar, smoked paprika, salt, onion powder, garlic powder, dried thyme, white pepper, and cayenne pepper. Let the turkey rest for an hour.
2. Set the griddle for indirect heat then adjust the temperature to 275°F (135°C).
3. Place the seasoned turkey in the griddle and smoke for 4 hours.
4. In the meantime, place ketchup, hot sauce, cider vinegar, Tabasco, and Cajun spices in a saucepan then bring to a simmer.
5. Remove the sauce from heat and quickly add unsalted butter to the saucepan. Stir until melted.
6. After 4 hours of smoking, baste the Tabasco sauce over the turkey then continue smoking for 15 minutes.
7. Once the internal temperature of the smoked turkey has reached 170°F (77°C), remove from the griddle and place it on a serving dish.
Nutrition: Calories: 160 Carbs: 2g Fat: 14g Protein: 7g

Griddle Rosemary Whole Turkey

Servings: 10

Preparation Time: 10 Minutes
Cooking Time: 7 Hours And 30 Minutes
Ingredients:
• 1 frozen whole turkey, giblets removed, thawed
• 2 tablespoons orange zest
• 2 tablespoons chopped fresh parsley
• 1 teaspoon salt
• 2 tablespoons chopped fresh rosemary
• 1 teaspoon ground black pepper
• 2 tablespoons chopped fresh sage
• 1 cup butter, unsalted, softened, divided
• 2 tablespoons chopped fresh thyme
• ½ cup water
• 14.5-ounce chicken broth
Directions:
1. Open hopper of the griddle, add dry pallets, make sure ash-can is in place, then open the ash damper, power on the griddle and close the ash damper.
2. Set the temperature of the griddle to 180 degrees F, let preheat for 30 minutes or until the green light on the dial blinks that indicate griddle has reached to set temperature.
3. Meanwhile, Prepare the turkey and for this, tuck its wings under it by using kitchen twine.
4. Place ½ cup butter in a bowl, add thyme, parsley, and sage, orange zest, and rosemary, stir well until combined and then brush this mixture generously on the inside and outside of the turkey and season the external of turkey with salt and black pepper.
5. Place turkey on a roasting pan, breast side up, pour in broth and water, add the remaining butter in the pan, then place the pan on the griddle and shut with lid.
6. Smoke the turkey for 3 hours, then increase the temperature to 350 degrees F and continue smoking the turkey for 4 hours or until thoroughly cooked and the internal temperature of the turkey reaches to 165 degrees F, basting turkey with the dripping every 30 minutes, but not in the last hour.
7. When you are done, take off the roasting pan from the griddle and let the turkey rest for 20 minutes.
8. Carve turkey into pieces and serve.
Nutrition: Calories: 146 Fat: 8 g Protein: 18 g Carbs: 1 g
Turkey Recipes

Chapter 6 Pork Recipes

Herb-Crusted Parmesan Pork Tenderloin

Herb-Crusted Tenderloin with Mediterranean style spices is one great way to griddle up juicy tenderloin. My favorite way to serve this dish is alongside lemon chili pasta and salad with a glass of Pinot Grigio.
Servings: 4
Preparation Time: 2 hours
Cooking Time: 30 minutes
Ingredients:
- 1 pound pork tenderloin
- 1 tablespoon olive oil
- 2 teaspoons dried oregano
- ¾ teaspoon lemon pepper
- 1 teaspoon garlic powder
- ¼ cup parmesan cheese, grated
- 3 tablespoons olive tapenade

Directions:
1. Place pork on a large piece of plastic wrap.
2. Rub tenderloin with oil, and sprinkle oregano, garlic powder, and lemon pepper evenly over entire tenderloin.
3. Wrap tightly in the plastic wrap and refrigerate for 2 hours.
4. Preheat griddle to medium-high heat.
5. Transfer pork to cutting board, remove plastic wrap, and make a lengthwise cut through center of tenderloin, opening meat so it lies flat, but do not cut all the way through.
6. Combine tapenade and parmesan in a small mixing bowl; rub into the center of the tenderloin and fold meat back together.
7. Tie together with twine in 2-inch intervals.
8. Sear tenderloin for 20 minutes, turning tenderloin once during griddleing, or until internal temperature reaches 145°F.
9. Transfer tenderloin to cutting board.
10. Tent with foil; let rest for 10 minutes.
11. Remove string and cut into ¼-inch-thick slices and serve.
Nutrition: Calories: 413, Sodium: 1279mg, Dietary Fiber: 0.5g, Fat: 30.5g, Carbs: 2.4g, Protein: 31.4g.

Dijon Pork Tenderloin with Paprika

This tender pork loin is paired perfectly with the earthy flavor of mustard for a dish that is sure to please guests or you family. The addition of a little smoked paprika compliments the robust mustard and delicate pork tenderloin.
Servings: 6
Preparation Time: 10 minutes
Cooking Time: 4 hours
Ingredients:
- 2 1 lb pork tenderloins
- 2 tablespoons Dijon mustard
- 1-½ teaspoons smoked paprika
- 1 teaspoon salt
- 2 tablespoons olive oil
Directions:

1. In a small bowl, combine the mustard and paprika.
2. Set your griddle to medium heat.
3. Rub the tenderloins with the mustard mixture, making sure they are evenly coated.
4. Place the tenderloins on the griddle and cook until all sides are well browned, and the internal temperature is 135°F.
5. Remove the tenderloins from the griddle and rest 5 minutes before slicing and serving.
Nutrition: Calories: 484, Sodium: 755mg, Dietary Fiber: 4.2g, Fat: 24.7g, Carbs: 13.8g, Protein: 50.9g.

Savory Bacon Pork Chops with Pineapple

Sweet and juicy pineapple compliments savory pork for one incredible dish! You'll love the sweet and spicy kick in this recipe - serve it with your favorite Griddle side dishes and vegetables and a cold glass of beer or iced tea.
Servings: 6
Preparation Time: 30 minutes
Cooking Time: 1 hour
Ingredients:
- 1 large whole pineapple
- 6 pork chops
- 12 slices thick-cut bacon
- Toothpicks, soaked in water
- For the glaze:
- ¼ cup honey
- ⅛ teaspoon cayenne pepper
Directions:
1. Turn both burners to medium-high heat; after about 15 minutes, turn off one of the middle burners and turn the remaining burners down to medium.
2. Slice off the top and bottom of the pineapple, and peel the pineapple, cutting the skin off in strips.
3. Cut pineapple flesh into six quarters.
4. Wrap each pineapple section with a bacon slice; secure each end with a toothpick.
5. Brush quarters with honey and sprinkle with cayenne pepper.
6. Put the quarters on the griddle, flipping when bacon is cooked so that both sides are evenly Griddle.
7. While pineapple quarters are cooking, coat pork chops with honey and cayenne pepper. Set on griddle.
8. Tent with foil and cook for 20 minutes. Flip, and continue cooking an additional 10 to 20 minutes or until chops are fully cooked.
9. Serve each chop with a pineapple quarter on the side.
Nutrition: Calories: 380, Sodium: 852mg, Dietary Fiber: 0.5g, Fat: 23.5g, Carbs: 18.2g, Protein: 25.8g.

Spiced Harissa Pork Tenderloin

Moroccan spice and creamy harissa make for one delicious way to serve up tender pork any night of the week. Enjoy this yummy dish with collard greens and potato salad for a taste twist on your next cookout.

Servings: 6
Preparation Time: 40 minutes
Cooking Time: 20 minutes

Ingredients:
- 2 (1 lb.) pork tenderloins
- 1 teaspoon ground cinnamon
- 1 teaspoon ground cilantro
- 1 teaspoon ground cumin
- 1 teaspoon paprika
- 1 teaspoon sea salt
- 2 tablespoons olive oil
- For Creamy Harissa Sauce:
- 1 cup Greek yogurt (8 ounces)
- 1 tablespoon fresh lemon juice
- 1 tablespoon extra-virgin olive oil
- 1 teaspoon harissa sauce
- 1 clove garlic, minced
- Kosher salt and cracked black pepper

Directions:
1. Combine harissa ingredients in a small mixing bowl and set aside.
2. Combine the cinnamon, coriander, cumin, paprika, salt and olive oil.
3. Rub the seasonings evenly over the pork tenderloins; cover and refrigerate for 30 minutes.
4. Preheat griddle to high heat and cook tenderloins until browned; about 8 to 10 minutes.
5. Turn and cook an additional 8 to 10 minutes. Transfer the tenderloins to a cutting board, tent with foil and rest for 10 minutes.
6. Slice and serve with creamy harissa sauce.

Nutrition: Calories: 376, Sodium: 458mg, Dietary Fiber: 0.4g, Fat: 17.9g, Carbs: 2.6g, Protein: 48.7g.

Marinated Pork Shoulder

Sweet and sticky sauce is the perfect complement to savory Griddle pork. Serve this delicious dish with your favorite sides or as a delicious stuffing for steamed buns or Griddle bread.

Servings: 6 – 8
Preparation Time: 8 hours
Cooking Time: 8 minutes

Ingredients:
- 1 (5 lbs.) Boston Butt pork shoulder
- For the marinade:
- 2 tablespoons garlic, minced
- 1 large piece ginger, peeled and chopped
- 1 cup hoisin sauce
- ¾ cup fish sauce
- ⅔ cup honey
- ⅔ cup Shaoxing
- ½ cup chili oil
- ⅓ cup oyster sauce
- ⅓ cup sesame oil
- For the glaze:
- ¾ cup dark brown sugar
- 1 tablespoon light molasses

Directions:

1. Place pork shoulder, fat side down, on a cutting board with a short end facing you. Holding a long sharp knife about 1"–1½" above cutting board, make a shallow cut along the entire length of a long side of shoulder.
2. Continue cutting deeper into meat, lifting and unfurling with your free hand, until it lies flat.
3. Purée marinade in a blender and reserve 1 ½ cups for glaze, cover and refrigerate.
4. Pour remaining marinade in a large sealable plastic bag.
5. Add pork shoulder to bag and marinate in the refrigerator for 8 hours.
6. Preheat griddle to medium heat (with cover closed, thermometer should register 350°). Remove pork from marinade, letting excess drip off.
7. Add glaze ingredients to reserved marinade until sugar is dissolved.
8. Griddle pork, for 8 minutes, basting and turning with tongs every minute or so, until thick coated with glaze, lightly charred in spots, and warmed through; an instant-read thermometer inserted into the thickest part should register 145°F.
9. Transfer to a cutting board and slice against the grain, ¼" thick, to serve.

Nutrition: Calories: 1286, Sodium: 2875mg, Dietary Fiber: 1g, Fat: 84.8g, Carbs: 58.3g, Protein: 68.7g.

Grilled Sausage Mix with Radicchio

Servings: 4 slices
Preparation Time: 5 minutes
Cooking Time: 22 minutes

Ingredients:
- 8 mini bell peppers
- 2 heads radicchio, each cut into 6 wedges
- Canola oil, for brushing
- Sea salt
- Freshly ground black pepper
- 6 breakfast sausage links
- 6 hot or sweet Italian sausage links

Directions:
1. Preheat the griddle to medium high.
2. Brush the bell peppers and radicchio with the oil. Season with salt and black pepper.
3. Place the bell peppers and radicchio on the Grill and cook for 10 minutes, without flipping.
4. Meanwhile, poke the sausages with a fork or knife and brush them with some of the oil.
5. After 10 minutes, remove the vegetables and set aside. Decrease the heat to medium. Place the sausages on the Grill and cook for 6 minutes.
6. Flip the sausages and cook for 6 minutes more. Remove the sausages from the Grill.
7. Serve the sausages and vegetables on a large cutting board or serving tray.

Nutrition: Calories: 473kcal; Fat: 34g; Carbs: 14g; Protein: 28g

Herbed Pork Chops with Apple Compote

Apples are one of my absolute favorite ingredients to pair with pork chops, and I hope you love this recipe too! Sweet meets juicy pork for a griddling flavor that is out of this world.
Servings: 4
Preparation Time: 5 minutes
Cooking Time: 20 minutes
Ingredients:
- 4 bone-in pork chops
- 2 honey crisp apples, peeled, cored and chopped
- ⅓ cup orange juice
- 1 teaspoon chopped fresh rosemary
- 1 teaspoon chopped fresh sage
- Sea salt
- Black pepper

Directions:
1. Add the apples, herbs and orange juice to a saucepan and simmer over medium heat until the apples are tender and the juices are thickened to a thin syrup, about 10 to 12 minutes.
2. Season pork chops with salt and pepper.
3. Place on the griddle and cook until the pork chop releases from the griddle, about 4 minutes.
4. Flip and cook on the other side for 3 minutes.
5. Transfer to a cutting board and tent with foil.
6. Top with apple compote and serve!
Nutrition: Calories: 284, Sodium: 173mg, Dietary Fiber: 1g, Fat: 20g, Carbs: 7.2g, Protein: 18.2g.

Yucatan-Style Marinated Pork

Elevate simple Griddle pork with Yucatan citrus combinations to make something different on your outdoor griddle Serve this with a side of Griddle plantains, veggies, and sparkling water.
Servings: 4
Preparation Time: 15 minutes
Cooking Time: 8 minutes
Ingredients:
- 2 pork tenderloins, trimmed
- 1 teaspoon annatto powder
- Olive oil
- For the marinade:
- 2 oranges, juiced
- 2 lemons, juiced, or more to taste
- 2 limes, juiced, or more to taste
- 6 cloves garlic, minced
- 1 teaspoon ground cumin
- ½ teaspoon cayenne pepper
- ½ teaspoon dried oregano
- ½ teaspoon black pepper

Directions:
1. Combine marinade ingredients in a mixing bowl and whisk until well-blended.
2. Cut the tenderloins in half crosswise; cut each piece in half lengthwise.
3. Place pieces in marinade and thoroughly coat with the mixture.
4. Cover with plastic wrap and refrigerate 4 to 6 hours.
5. Transfer pieces of pork from marinade to a paper-towel-lined bowl to absorb most of the moisture.
6. Discard paper towels. Drizzle olive oil and a bit more annatto powder on the pork.
7. Preheat griddle for medium-high heat and lightly oil.
8. Place pieces evenly spaced on griddle; cook 4 to 5 minutes.
9. Turn and cook on the other side another 4 or 5 minutes.
10. Transfer onto a serving platter and allow meat to rest about 5 minutes before serving.
Nutrition: Calories: 439, Sodium: 1382mg, Dietary Fiber: 1.5g, Fat: 33.1g, Carbs: 11.4g, Protein: 23.9g.

Cuban Pork Roast

Servings: 18
Preparation Time: 12 Hours
Cooking Time: 2.5 Hours
Ingredients:
- 1 - 8 lbs. pork shoulder
- 8 slices bacon
- ½ lb. ham
- 1 bottle Malta
- 1 cup guava shells
- 1 cup Mojo (pg. 125)
- 1 cup prunes
- 4 Tbsp. Adobo Spices
- 2 cups brown sugar
- 2 Tbsp. sea salt

Directions:
1. Debone and flatten meat so that it may be rolled.
2. If the pork shoulder is very fatty, a small amount may be removed.
3. Score fat well and marinate for a minimum of 12 hours in the Mojo, and Adobo.
4. Sear both sides of roast on a very hot grate until dark brown and charred in spots.
5. Remove roast to cutting board, and line unrolled roast with ham slices, bacon slices, prunes and guava shells. Roll meat carefully to keep the filling inside. Tie firmly with a butcher cord.
6. Cover with brown sugar and ½ bottle of Malta.
7. Cook for one hour in the griddle at 325. At this point, turn the meat, cover with the remaining Malta and cook for an extra hour, or until you reach a meat temperature of 180.
8. Allow to cool at least 30 minutes and cut into fine slices. Pour the drippings over the meat after slicing the meat.
9. These ingredients can be found at most Hispanic grocery stores.
Nutrition: Calories: 83 Carbs: 19g Fat: 0g Protein: 3g

Cheddar Baked Egg and Stuffed Peppers

Servings: 4 slices
Preparation Time: 10 minutes
Cooking Time: 15 minutes
Ingredients:
- 1 cup shredded Cheddar cheese
- 4 slices bacon, cooked and chopped
- 4 bell peppers, seeded and tops removed
- 4 large eggs
- Sea salt
- Freshly ground black pepper
- Chopped fresh parsley, for garnish

Directions:
1. Preheat the griddle to medium high.
2. Divide the cheese and bacon between the bell peppers. Crack one of the eggs into each bell pepper, and season with salt and pepper.
3. Place each bell pepper to the grill and cook for 10 to 15 minutes, until the egg whites are cooked and the yolks are slightly runny.
4. Remove the peppers, garnish with parsley, and serve.
Nutrition: Calories: 326kcal; Fat: 23g; Carbs: 10g; Protein: 22g

Marinated Pork Chops with Habanero

Kick things up a notch on your outdoor griddle with this spicy recipe. These yummy pork chops pair perfectly with yellow rice, black beans, and your favorite salad.
Servings: 4
Preparation Time: 30 minutes
Cooking Time: 13 minutes
Ingredients:
- 4-½-inch-thick bone-in pork chops
- 3 tablespoons olive oil, plus more for griddle
- Kosher salt and freshly ground black pepper
- For the marinade:
- 1 habanero chili, seeded, chopped fine
- 2 garlic cloves, minced
- ½ cup fresh orange juice
- 2 tablespoons brown sugar
- 1 tablespoon apple cider vinegar

Directions:
1. Combine marinade ingredients in a large sealable plastic bag.
2. Pierce pork chops all over with a fork and add to bag, seal, and turn to coat.
3. Marinate at room temperature, turning occasionally, for 30 minutes.
4. Prepare griddle for medium-high heat.
5. Brush the griddle with oil.
6. Remove pork chops from marinade and pat dry.
7. Sear for 8 minutes, turning occasionally, until charred and cooked through.
8. Transfer to a plate and let rest 5 minutes.
9. Serve with your favorite sides.
Nutrition: Calories: 490, Sodium: 171mg, Dietary Fiber: 1.1g, Fat: 39.2g, Carbs: 10.9g, Protein: 23.3g.

Flavorful Honey Soy Pork Chops Griddle

Sweet and tangy Griddle pork is absolutely delicious when Griddle to perfection on your outdoor griddle. Simply serve this dish with rice and Griddle vegetables for one delicious meal.
Servings: 6
Preparation Time: 1 hour
Cooking Time: 25 minutes
Ingredients:
- 6 (4 ounce) boneless pork chops
- ¼ cup organic honey
- 1 to 2 tablespoons low sodium soy sauce
- 2 tablespoons olive oil
- 1 tablespoon rice mirin

Directions:
1. Combine honey, soy sauce, oil, and white vinegar and whisk until well-combined. Add sauce and pork chops to a large sealable plastic bag and marinate for 1 hour.
2. Preheat the griddle to medium-high heat and cook for 4 to 5 minutes, or until the pork chop easily releases from the griddle.
3. Flip and continue to cook for 5 additional minutes, or until internal temperature reaches 145°F.
4. Serve and enjoy!
Nutrition: Calories: 251, Sodium: 187mg, Dietary Fiber: 0.1g, Fat: 8.7g, Carbs: 13.1g, Protein: 29.9g.

Salted Pork Chops

These authentic Cuban pork chops are easy to make are a packed with exotic flavors. Thanks to your outdoor griddle they are sure to cook to perfection.
Servings: 4
Preparation Time: 30 minutes
Cooking Time: 1 hour 30 minutes
Ingredients:
- 4 pork chops
- 4 cloves garlic, smashed
- 2 tablespoons olive oil
- ⅓ cup lime juice
- ¼ cup water
- 1 teaspoon ground cumin
- Salt and black pepper

Directions:
1. Set your griddle to medium. Salt the pork chops on both side and cook the chops until lightly browned.
2. Combine the water, garlic, and lime juice in a bowl and whisk until even.
3. Continue cooking the pork chops while basting them with the lime juice mixture.
4. When the pork chops have finished cooking, remove from the griddle and top with additional sauce and black pepper before serving.
Nutrition: Calories: 323, Sodium: 58mg, Dietary Fiber: 0.1g, Fat: 27g, Carbs: 1.5g, Protein: 18.3g.

Garlic Peppered Soy Pork Chops

Sweet and spicy ribs are a great way to griddle out with the whole family on the weekends. Serve these sticky ribs with mashed potatoes and Griddle vegetables for some decadent weekend backyard fun.
Servings: 4 – 6
Preparation Time: 8 hours
Cooking Time: 1 hour
Ingredients:
- 4 to 6 pork chops
- 4 cloves garlic, finely chopped
- ½ cup olive oil
- ½ cup soy sauce
- ½ teaspoon garlic powder
- ½ teaspoon salt –
- ½ black pepper
- ¼ cup butter

Directions:
1. In a large zipper lock bag, combine the garlic, olive oil, soy sauce, and garlic powder. Add the pork chops and make sure the marinade coats the chops. Set aside for 30 minutes.
2. Heat your griddle to medium-high heat. Add 2 tablespoons of olive oil and 2 tablespoons of butter to the griddle.
3. Add the chops to the griddle one at a time, making sure they are not crowded. Add another 2 tablespoons of butter to the griddle and cook the chops for 4 minutes. Cook an additional 4 minutes.
4. Remove the chops from the griddle and spread the remaining butter over them. Serve after resting for 5 minutes.
Nutrition: Calories: 398, Sodium: 1484mg, Dietary Fiber: 0.2g, Fat: 37.7g, Carbs: 2.5g, Protein: 13.6g.

Cajun Pork Chops with Paprika

Packed with flavor and a nice amount of heat, these Cajun pork chops are perfect for outdoor cooking any time of year. For best results, serve with a nice, rich coleslaw.
Servings: 4
Preparation Time: 10 minutes
Cooking Time: 15 minutes
Ingredients:
- 4 pork chops
- 1 tablespoon paprika
- ½ teaspoon ground cumin
- ½ teaspoon dried sage
- ½ teaspoon salt
- ½ teaspoon black pepper
- ½ teaspoon garlic powder
- ¼ teaspoon cayenne pepper
- 1 tablespoon butter
- 1 tablespoon vegetable oil

Directions:
1. In a medium bowl, combine the paprika, cumin, sage, salt, pepper, garlic, and cayenne pepper.
2. Heat your griddle to medium-high heat and add the butter and oil.

3. Rub the pork chops with a generous amount of the seasoning rub.
4. Place the chops on the griddle and cook for 4 to 5 minutes. Turn the pork chops and continue cooking an additional 4 minutes.
5. Remove the pork chops from the griddle and allow to rest 5 minutes before serving.
Nutrition: Calories: 320, Sodium: 368mg, Dietary Fiber: 0.8g, Fat: 26.5g, Carbs: 1.6g, Protein: 18.4g.

Teriyaki Pork Sirloin Tip Roast

Servings: 4
Preparation Time: 45 minutes
Cooking Time: 2 hours 30 minutes
Ingredients:
- 1 (1½ to 2 pounds) pork sirloin tip roast
- Teriyaki marinade, for example, Mr. Yoshida's Original Gourmet Marinade

Directions:
1. Dry the roast with a piece of paper
2. Utilizing a 1-gallon cooler stockpiling sack or a sealable compartment, spread the roast with the teriyaki marinade.
3. Refrigerate medium-term, turning at regular intervals whenever the situation allows.
4. Smoke the meat for 1 hour at 180°F.
5. After 60 minutes, increase your pit temperature to 325°F.
6. Cook the roast until the internal temperature, at the thickest part of the roast, arrives at 145°F, around 1 to 1½ hours.
7. Rest the roast under a free foil tent for 15 minutes.
8. Remove the cooking groups or twine and cut the roast contrary to what would be expected.
Nutrition: Calories: 214 Protein: 17 g Fat: 19 g

Flavorful Double-Smoked Ham

Servings: 8 to 12
Preparation Time: 15 minutes
Cooking Time: 2½ to 3 hours
Ingredients:
- 1 (10-pound) smoked, boneless, wholly cooked, ready-to-eat ham or bone-in smoked ham

Directions:
1. Remove the ham from its bundling and let sit at room temperature for 30 minutes.
2. Arrange the griddle for a non-direct cooking and preheat to 180°F.
3. Place the ham directly on the griddle grates and smoke the ham for 1 hour at 180°F.
4. After 60 minutes, increase pit temperature to 350°F.
5. Cooking Time the ham until the internal temperature arrives at 140°F, about 1½ to 2 additional hours.
6. Remove the ham and wrap in foil for 15 minutes before cutting contrary to what would be expected.
Nutrition: Calories: 215 kCal Protein: 21 g Fat: 19 g

Garlic Pork Sirloin Tip Roast

Servings: 3
Preparation Time: 30 minutes
Cooking Time: 3 hours
Ingredients:
- 1 (1½ to 2 pounds) pork sirloin tip roast
- 2 tablespoons roasted garlic–seasoned extra-virgin olive oil
- 5 tablespoons Jan's Original Dry Rub, Pork Dry Rub, or your preferred pork rub

Directions:
1. Pat the roast dry with a paper towel.
2. Rub the whole roast with the olive oil. Coat the roast with the rub.
3. Support the roast utilizing 2 to 3 silicone nourishment grade cooking groups or butcher's twine to ensure the roast keeps up its shape during cooking.
4. Wrap the tip roast in plastic wrap and refrigerate medium-term.
5. Place the roast directly on the griddle grates and smoke the roast until the internal temperature, at the thickest part of the roast, arrives at 145°F, around 3 hours.
6. Rest the roast under a free foil tent for 15 minutes.
7. Remove the cooking groups or twine and cut the roast contrary to what would be expected.
Nutrition: Calories: 276 kCal Protein: 28 g Fat: 12 g

Enticing Rib of Pork

Servings: 6
Preparation Time: 30 minutes
Cooking Time: 3 hours
Ingredients:
- 1 (5-pound) rack of pork, around 6 ribs
- ¼ cup roasted garlic–enhanced extra-virgin olive oil
- 6 tablespoons Jan's Original Dry Rub, Pork Dry Rub, or your preferred pork roast rub

Directions:
1. Trim of the fat cap and silver skin from the rack of pork. Much the same as a chunk of ribs a rack of pork has a membrane on the bones. Remove the membrane from the bones by working a spoon handle under the bone membrane until you can get the membrane with a paper towel to pull it off. Rub the olive oil generously on all sides of the meat. Season with the rub, covering all sides of the meat. Double wrap the seasoned rack of pork in plastic wrap and refrigerate for 2 to 4 hours or medium-term.
2. Remove the seasoned rack of pork from the refrigerator and let sit at room temperature for 30 minutes before cooking. Arrange the griddle for a non-direct cooking and preheat to 225°F. Add your griddle meat probe or a remote meat probe into the thickest part of the rack of pork. On the off chance that your griddle doesn't have meat probe capabilities or you don't claim a remote meat probe at that point, utilize a moment read computerized thermometer during the cook for internal temperature readings.

3. Place the rack rib-side down directly on the griddle grates.
4. Smoke the rack of pork for 3 to 3½ hours, until the internal temperature arrives at 140°F.
5. Remove from the meat from the griddle, and let it rest under a free foil tent for 15 minutes before cutting.
Nutrition: Calories: 189 kCal Protein: 17 g Fat: 12 g

Tender Grilled Loin Chops

Servings: 6
Preparation Time: 10 minutes
Cooking Time: 12 to 15 minutes
Ingredients:
- 6 boneless focus cut midsection pork cleaves, 1 to 1½ inches thick 2 quarts Pork Brine
- 2 tablespoons roasted garlic–seasoned extra-virgin olive oil
- 2 teaspoons black pepper

Directions:
1. Trim abundance fat and silver skin from the pork slashes.
2. Place the pork slashes and brine in a 1-gallon sealable pack and refrigerate for in any event 12 hours or medium-term.
3. Remove the pork slashes from the brine and pat them dry with paper towels.
4. Brined pork hacks cook quicker than unbrined cleaves, so be mindful so as to screen internal temperatures.
5. Rest the pork slashes under a foil tent for 5 minutes before serving.
Nutrition: Calories: 211 kCal Protein: 17 g Fat: 21 g

Naked Rib Racks

Servings: 6 to 8
Preparation Time: 30 minutes
Cooking Time: 5 to 6 hours
Ingredients:
- 3 St. Louis–style pork rib racks
- 1 cup in addition to 1 tablespoon Jan's Original Dry Rub or your preferred pork rub

Directions:
1. Remove the membrane on the underside of the rib racks by embedding a spoon handle between the membrane and rib bones. Get the membrane with a paper towel and gradually dismantle it down the rack to remove.
2. Rub the two sides of the ribs with a liberal measure of the rub.
3. Arrange the griddle for a non-direct cooking and preheat to 225°F. In the event of utilizing a rib rack, place the ribs in the rack on the griddle grates. Else you can utilize Teflon-covered fiberglass tangles or place the ribs directly on the griddle grates.
4. Smoke the ribs at 225°F for 5 to 6 hours until the internal temperature, at the thickest part of the ribs, arrives at 185°F to190°F.
5. Rest the ribs under a free foil tent for 10 minutes before cutting and serving.
Nutrition: Calories: 241kCal Protein: 23.6 g Fat: 13 g

Mozzarella Ribeye Pork Loin with Bacon

Servings: 6 to 8
Preparation Time: 30 minutes
Cooking Time: 60 to 75 minutes
Ingredients:
- 1 (3-pound) boneless ribeye pork loin roast
- 4 tablespoons extra-virgin olive oil, divided
- 2 tablespoons Pork Dry Rub or your favorite pork seasoning
- 4 bacon slices
- 6 cups fresh spinach
- 1 small red onion, diced
- 6 cloves garlic, cut into thin slivers
- ¾ cup shredded mozzarella cheese

Directions:
1. Trim away any abundance fat and silver skin.
2. Butterfly the pork loin or approach your butcher to butterfly it for you. There are numerous phenomenal recordings online with nitty gritty directions on the various systems for butterflying a loin roast.
3. Rub 2 tablespoons of the olive oil on each side of the butterflied roast and season the two sides with the rub.
4. Cook the bacon in a large griddle over medium heat. Disintegrate and set aside. Reserve the bacon fat.
5. Griddle the pork loin for 60 to 75 minutes, or until the internal temperature at the thickest part arrives at 140°F.
6. Rest the pork loin under a free foil tent for 15 minutes before cutting contrary to what would be expected.
Nutrition: Calories: 365 kCal Protein: 32.1 g Fat: 22 g

Worcestershire Glazed Pork Ribs

Country ribs are full of delicious flavor and make for one great main dish on weeknights or weekends with friends. Serve these ribs with your favorite sides and cold, crisp beer on summer holidays for traditional griddling fun.
Servings: 6
Preparation Time: 10 minutes
Cooking Time: 4 hours
Ingredients:
- 3 pounds country-style pork ribs
- 1 cup low-sugar ketchup
- ½ cup water
- ¼ cup onion, finely chopped
- ¼ cup cider vinegar or wine vinegar
- ¼ cup light molasses
- 2 tablespoons Worcestershire sauce
- 2 teaspoons chili powder
- 2 cloves garlic, minced

Directions:
1. Combine ketchup, water, onion, vinegar, molasses, Worcestershire sauce, chili powder, and garlic in a saucepan and bring to boil; reduce heat. Simmer, uncovered, for 10 to 15 minutes or until desired thickness is reached, stirring often.
2. Trim fat from ribs.
3. Preheat griddle to medium-high.
4. Place ribs, bone-side down, on griddle and cook for 1-½ to 2 hours or until tender, brushing occasionally with sauce during the last 10 minutes of cooking.
5. Serve with remaining sauce and enjoy!
Nutrition: Calories: 404, Sodium: 733mg, Dietary Fiber: 0.4g, Fat: 8.1g, Carbs: 15.2g, Protein: 60.4g.

Brined Pork Sirloin Roast

Servings: 4 to 6
Preparation Time: 20 minutes
Cooking Time: 3 to 3½ hours
Ingredients:
- 1 (3 to 3½-pound) pork sirloin roast

Directions:
1. Trim all fat and silver skin from the pork roast.
2. Place the roast and buttermilk brine in a 1-gallon sealable plastic sack or brining holder.
3. Refrigerate medium-term, turning the roast like clockwork whenever the situation allows.
4. Remove the brined pork sirloin roast from the brine and pat dry with a paper towel.
5. Supplement a meat probe into the thickest part of the roast.
6. Design the griddle for a non-direct cooking and preheat to 225°F.
7. Smoke the roast until the internal temperature arrives at 145°F, 3 to 3½ hours.
8. Rest the roast under a free foil tent for 15 minutes, at that point cut contrary to what would be expected.
Nutrition: Calories: 311 kCal Protein: 25 g Fat: 18 g

BBQ Pork Ribs

Servings: 6
Preparation Time: 12 Hours
Cooking Time: 3 Hours
Ingredients:
- 2 racks of pork spareribs
- ½ C of "Burning' Love" Rub
- 1 C Carolina Basting Sauce
- 1 C Carolina BBQ Sauce

Directions:
1. Prepare ribs by removing the membrane from the underside. Trim off any loose fat, and season ribs with rub, wrap in plastic wrap and refrigerate overnight.
2. Allow ribs to warm 1 hour. Preheat griddle to 280F.
3. If you want to sauce the ribs, do so 5 minutes before they're done, turning ever minute, and observe.
Nutrition: Calories: 290 Carbs: 5g Fat: 23g Protein: 15g

Worcestershire Pork Kabobs

Servings: 6
Preparation Time: 24 Hours
Cooking Time: 10 minutes
Ingredients:
- 2 lbs. boneless pork, 1-inch cubes
- ¾ C olive oil
- 1 Tbsp. Worcestershire sauce
- 1 tsp dried thyme
- 2 tsp black pepper
- ½ tsp cayenne
- ¾ C cider vinegar
- ¼ C sugar
- 4 Tbsp. lemon juice
- 1 Tbsp. oregano
- 2 cloves garlic, minced
- 1 tsp salt

Directions:
1. Mix together first 11 ingredients, place in sealable bag and refrigerate 24 hours: thread onto skewers.
2. Griddle on high heat, basting with reserved marinade, for 4-5 minutes; turn and griddle another 4-5 minutes.
3. Sprinkle with salt and serve.
Nutrition: Calories: 160 Carbs: 2g Fat: 5g Protein: 28g

Garlic Pork Kabobs with Parsley

Servings: 6
Preparation Time: 24 Hours
Cooking Time: 15 minutes
Ingredients:
- 3 lbs. Pork tenderloin
- 3 C margarita mix
- 3 clove garlic – minced
- 2 lg bell peppers
- 4 lbs. whole mushrooms
- ¼ C butter - softened
- 4 tsp lime juice
- 1 teaspoon sugar
- 3 Tbsp. minced parsley

Directions:
1. Cut pork into 1-inch cubes, place in a sealable plastic bag; pour marinade over to cover. Marinate overnight.
2. Blend together the butter, lime juice, Splenda, and parsley; set aside.
3. Thread pork cubes onto skewers, alternating with mushrooms and pepper, cut into eighths.
4. Griddle over high heat, basting with butter mixture, for 10-15 minutes, turning frequently.
5. If you're using bamboo skewers, soak them in water 20-30 minutes before using.
Nutrition: Calories: 160Carbs: 2g Fat: 5g Protein: 28g

Soy Pork Sliders with Lettuce

Servings: 8
Preparation Time: 24 Hours
Cooking Time: 15 minutes
Ingredients:
- 2 lbs. ground pork
- 1 C diced green onion
- 2 tsp garlic powder
- 2 Tbsp. soy sauce
- 2 tsp brown sugar
- 1 C shredded lettuce
- 1 tsp cornstarch
- Honey-mustard dressing
- 16 sesame rolls, split

Directions:
1. Mix all ingredients (except soy sauce) and form 16 equal patties. Brush each patty with soy sauce, and griddle over high heat, turning once.
2. Serve with honey mustard and cucumber spears.
3. I like to chill the seasoned meat and then spread it on an oiled cutting board, using a rolling pin for an even ¼-inch thickness.
4. Then, I just grab a biscuit cutter, and voila.perfectly round sliders!
Nutrition: Calories: 280 Carbs: 31g Fat: 9g Protein: 26g

Fabulous Luau Pork

Servings:50
Preparation Time: 12 Hours
Cooking Time: 12 Hours
Ingredients:
- 2 - boneless pork shoulders (6 lbs.)
- 2 C hot water
- 3 Qtrs. gal Hawaiian Mojo
- 2 Tbsp. seasoned salt
- ¼ C Stubbs liquid smoke
- 4 Tbsp. garlic powder
- ½ C Adobo Criollo spices

Directions:
1. Marinate pork in Hawaiian Mojo overnight. Remove from marinade, pat dry, and inject each shoulder with 6-8ozs of remaining marinade.
2. Score pork on all sides, rub with salt, then brush with liquid smoke, and sprinkle with garlic. Wrap entirely in banana leaves, tie with string.
3. Heat one side of your griddle to high, covered.
4. Once pre-heated, place the butts on the "cool" side of the griddle, roast 3 hours, and then remove banana leaves. Baste with mojo every 45 minutes throughout the rest of the cooking time. The shoulders should not be over any exposed flame.
5. Cover the griddle and vent slightly. Slow cook the shoulders for a total of 6 to 8 hours, until the meat is very tender, or you reach 195 F on the meat thermometer.
6. Chop the meat and then mix with a wash of ½ cup liquid smoke, 4 cups hot water, ¼ cup Adobo Criollo spices, and 2 Tbsp. seasoned salt.
7. Let that sit about 15 minutes, drain remaining liquid, and serve with Sweet Hawaiian Pork Sauce
Nutrition: Calories: 116 Carbs: 4g Fat: 5g Protein: 12g

Rosemary Italian Pancetta Sandwiches

Servings: 24
Preparation Time: 48 Hours
Cooking Time: 8 Hours
Ingredients:
- 2 - 8lbs. pork shoulders, butterflied
- 6 Tbsp. fennel Seeds
- 24 cloves garlic, peeled
- Salt & pepper
- 12 Tbsp. fresh rosemary
- 2 C red wine
- 32 oz sliced pancetta
- 24 crusty Italian rolls
- 4 C caramelized onions
- 6 C Italian parsley

Directions:
1. Place the fennel, garlic, rosemary, salt, pepper, wine, and pancetta in a food processor and pulse until well mixed.
2. Spread the pancetta mixture evenly over the opened pork butt. Roll the pork up firmly, and tie with kitchen twine in four places to hold the pork together.
3. The pork is done when it reaches an internal temperature of 195 degrees.
4. If you don't have an instant read thermometer (you should really get one) the meat is done when it pulls apart quickly with a fork.
5. Heat the rolls. Place ¼ cup of meat on the warm roll and spoon over a little of the pan juices onto the sandwich.
6. Top meat with caramelized onions, the ¼ cup of fresh chopped parsley.
Nutrition: Calories: 324 Carbs: 0g Fat: 28g Protein: 18g

Pork Tenderloin in Bourbon

Servings: 10
Preparation Time: 24 Hours
Cooking Time: 1 Hour
Ingredients:
- 2 C white sugar
- ½ C Jim Beam® Bourbon
- 2 C water
- 2 tsp vanilla extract
- 3 to 4 lbs. pork tenderloin
- 2 tsp black pepper
- 2 tsp garlic powder
- 2 Tbsp. salt

Directions:
1. In medium bowl, combine sugar, Jim Beam® Bourbon, water, salt and vanilla. Mix well. Place tenderloin in a large zip bag and pour ½ of marinade over the top. Refrigerate 24 hours. Season tenderloin with garlic and pepper.
2. Heat your griddle for two-zone griddling and brush the rack with vegetable oil.
3. Remove to a cutting board and slice against the grain.
Nutrition: Calories: 100 Carbs: 5g Fat: 2g Protein: 15g

Hot Pork Sandwiches

Servings: 30
Preparation Time: 24 Hours
Cooking Time: 12 Hour
Ingredients:
- 1 boneless pork butt (5-6 pounds)
- 2 Tbsp. smoked paprika
- 2 Tbsp. hickory salt
- 1 Tbsp. black pepper
- 2 cups cider vinegar
- 1 cup Southern Comfort
- 1 cup water
- 2 Tbsp. molasses
- 2 Tbsp. salt
- ¼ cup hot sauce
- 1 Tbsp. red pepper flakes
- 1 Tbsp. black pepper
- 2 teaspoons ground cayenne

Directions:
1. In a bowl, combine paprika, hickory salt, 1 Tbsp. black pepper, and cayenne. Coat pork shoulder with seasonings and cover with plastic wrap. Refrigerate 24 hours.
2. Preheat griddle to medium heat. Place pork shoulder on griddle and smoke. Place a thermometer on the grate to track temperature. Combine remaining ingredients for baste.
3. Remove from heat and allow to rest 20 minutes (still in foil) and then unwrap and rest another 10 minutes. Shred pork, tossing with reserved pan juices.
4. Serve on soft white rolls, topped with your favorite coleslaw.
Nutrition: Calories: 692Carbs: 6g Fat: 42g Protein: 70g

BBQ Sauce Pork Chops

Servings: 6
Preparation Time: 4 Hours
Cooking Time: 15 minutes
Ingredients:
- 6 boneless pork chops, thick
- 1 Tbsp. salt and sugar
- Pepper to taste
- 1 cup water
- 1 cup sweet barbecue sauce
- ¼ cup cider vinegar

Directions:
1. Place chops in a baggie with 1 cup of water and sugar (boiled and cooled), and brine 4 hours.
2. Preheat your griddle for high heat.
3. In a small saucepan, combine barbecue sauce and vinegar. Bring to a simmer and allow to cook 20-30 minutes, uncovered, stirring often. Brush grate lightly with oil before placing pork chops on the griddle. Cook over high heat for 10 to 12 minutes, turning once. Brush with sauce just before removing chops from griddle. Serve with remaining sauce.
Nutrition: Calories: 220 Carbs: 12g Fat: 9g Protein: 22g

Peach Mojo Pork Shoulder with Peaches

Servings: 12
Preparation Time: 1 Hours
Cooking Time: 6 hours
Ingredients:
- 1 - 6lbs. pork shoulder
- 1 qt Hawaiian Mojo
- ½ cup sea-salt
- 1 can peach slices, in syrup
- 2 Tbsp. garlic powder
- 2 Tbsp. red pepper flakes
- 15 oz sliced peaches in syrup
- 16 oz peach preserves
- 12oz apricot & pineapple preserves
- ½ cup Stubbs Mesquite Liquid Smoke

Directions:
1. Inject the pork with mojo and marinate overnight. Then, allow pork to come to room temp just before roasting. Smoke pork shoulder for 5-6 hours or until internal temperatures reach 185°F.
2. Slice the pork and pile in a pan, slather the top with a generous layer of peach-pineapple glaze and then place pans under a hot broiler for another 5-10 minutes to brown the glaze.
3. Serve with sweet Hawaiian rolls and white rice.

Nutrition: Calories: 210 Carbs: 18g Fat: 6g Protein: 23g

Flavorful Bacon Wrapped Dates with Gorgonzola

Servings: 16
Preparation Time: 30 minutes
Cooking Time: 30 minutes
Ingredients:
- 1 lb. thick-sliced bacon, cut in half
- 1 lb. pitted dates
- 4 ounces gorgonzola cheese
- 32 toothpicks

Directions:

1. Slice dates up one side and open them up. Pinch off a piece of cheese and place it into the center of the date. Close the halves of the dates and wrap a half-slice of bacon around the outside, secure with a toothpick. Lay a single sheet of foil over griddle grates and add the wraps in a single layer. Griddle until bacon starts to crisp, then flip each wrap over.
2. When the second side is crisped, remove to a platter lined with paper towels, allow to cool slightly before serving.

Nutrition: Calories: 248 Carbs: 33g Fat: 10g Protein: 10g

Creamy Jalapeño Pepper Bombs

Servings: 10
Preparation Time: 10 minutes
Cooking Time: 15 minutes
Ingredients:
- 10 fresh jalapenos
- 20 Cheddar Little Smokies
- 8 oz. Cream Cheese
- 2 lbs. Bacon (½ strip each)
- ⅛ Sweet Onion (diced)
- 1 Tbsp. Sugar

Directions:
1. Soften cream cheese and blend in sugar and onions.
2. Slice Jalapenos in half, lengthwise, and trim away all seeds and membranes, rinse.
3. Spoon 1 teaspoon of cream cheese mixture into each side. Place 1 smokie on each half and press it into the cream cheese.
4. Add the bombs in a single layer. Griddle until bacon starts to crisp, moving to cool side of the griddle starts flaring up, and then remove to a platter lined with paper towels.
5. Allow to cool slightly and serve.

Nutrition: Calories: 281 Carbs: 10g Fat: 24g Protein: 6g

Garlic Soy Beef with Vegetables

Servings: 6
Preparation Time: 10 minutes
Cooking Time: 15 minutes
Ingredients:
Steak:
- 2- 1 lb. sirloin steaks
- 1 tablespoon garlic powder
- 2 tablespoons soy sauce
- 1 white onion, sliced into large rounds
- 1 zucchini, sliced into ¼ inch thick flats
- 2 cups snap peas
- 3 tablespoons vegetable oil
- 3 tablespoons butter
- Salt and black pepper

Directions:
1. Season the steak with salt, pepper, and garlic powder.
2. Set your griddle to high heat on one side and medium-high heat on the other side.
3. Add some vegetable oil to the medium-hot side and add the onion rings, zucchini, and snap peas. Season with a little salt and pepper.
4. Add the steaks to the hot side and cook for 3 minutes. Flip, top with butter and add soy sauce to the steaks. Continue cooking an additional 4 minutes.
5. Remove the steak and vegetables from the griddle and slice the steak across the grain before serving.
Nutrition: Calories: 484, Sodium: 755 mg, Dietary Fiber: 4.2g, Fat: 24.7g, Carbs: 13.8g Protein: 50.9g

Herbed NY Strip Steak

Servings: 2
Preparation Time: 8 - 12 hours
Cooking Time: 15 minutes
Ingredients:
- 2 (1-pound) New York strip steaks, trimmed
- For the rub:
- 1 bunch thyme sprigs
- 1 bunch rosemary sprigs
- 1 bunch sage sprigs
- 1 ½ teaspoons black pepper, divided
- ¾ teaspoon sea salt, divided
- ½ teaspoon garlic powder
- 2 tablespoons chopped fresh flat-leaf parsley
- 2 tablespoons extra-virgin olive oil

Directions:
1. Preheat griddle to high heat.
2. Combine rub ingredients in a small mixing bowl and rub steaks with spice mixture; let rest 10 minutes.
3. Place steaks on grill and cook 1 minute per side.
4. Turn griddle down to medium heat.
5. Turn steaks and grill 3 additional minutes per side; or until thermometer registers 135°F for medium rare.
6. Remove steaks to a platter.

7. Let rest 5 minutes. Cut steaks across grain into thin slices.
Nutrition: Calories: 347, Sodium: 831 mg, Dietary Fiber: 1.9g, Fat: 20.4g, Carbs:3.7g Protein: 38.7g

Juicy NY Strip Steak Griddle

Servings 1
Preparation Time: 45 minutes
Cooking Time: 8 minutes
Ingredients:
- (8 ounce) NY strip steak
- Olive oil –
- Sea salt
- Fresh ground black pepper

Directions:
1. Remove the steak from the refrigerator and let it come to room temperature, about 30 to 45 minutes.
2. Preheat griddle to medium-high heat and brush with olive oil.
3. Season the steak on all sides with salt and pepper.
4. Cook steak about 4 to 5 minutes.
5. Flip and cook about 4 minutes more for medium rare steak; between 125°F and 130°F on a meat thermometer.
6. Transfer the steak to a plate and let it rest for 5 minutes before serving.
Nutrition: Calories:1560, Sodium: 8468 mg, Dietary Fiber: 0.g, Fat: 86g, Carbs: 0.1g Protein: 184g

Caprese Basil Flank Steak

Servings: 4
Preparation Time: 10 minutes
Cooking Time: 10 minutes
Ingredients:
- (6 ounce) flank steaks
- Sea salt, for seasoning
- Flakey sea salt, for serving
- Fresh ground pepper
- Olive oil
- 2 roma tomatoes, sliced
- ounces fresh buffalo mozzarella, cut into four slices
- 8 fresh basil leaves
- Balsamic vinegar glaze, for drizzling

Directions:
1. Lightly brush each filet, on all sides, with olive oil and season with salt and pepper.
2. Preheat griddle to high. Place steaks on griddle, reduce heat to medium, tent with foil and cook for 5 minutes. Flip, re-tent, and cook for an additional 5 minutes; during the last 2 minutes of cooking, top each with a slice of mozzarella.
3. Remove steaks from the griddle and top each with a few tomato slices, 2 basil leafs. Drizzle with balsamic glaze, and sprinkle with flakey salt and a little more black peppers.
Nutrition: Calories: 461, Sodium:485 mg, Dietary Fiber: 0.8g, Fat: 22.8g, Carbs: 5.7g Protein: 55.9g

Balsamic Porterhouse Steak with Potatoes

Servings: 4
Preparation Time: 30 minutes
Cooking Time: 35 minutes
Ingredients:
- 2 bone-in porterhouse steaks
- 1 ½ lb. small potatoes, like Yukon Gold, scrubbed but skins left on, halved
- 3 tablespoons extra-virgin olive oil, divided
- Sea salt and freshly ground pepper, to taste
- 2 teaspoons red wine, like Sangiovese or Montepulciano
- 1 teaspoon balsamic vinegar
- pinch red pepper flakes
- 2 fresh rosemary sprigs, needles removed (discard stems)

Directions:
1. Add potatoes to a large pot and cover with water, bring to a boil over high heat, then reduce the heat to medium-high and cook until the potatoes are almost tender, about 10 minutes. Drain, add to a medium mixing bowl, coat with 2 tablespoons olive oil, and set aside. Preheat griddle to medium heat. Whisk 2 tablespoons olive oil, rosemary, red wine, vinegar, and pepper flakes; add steaks to marinade and set aside until ready to cook.
2. Sprinkle potatoes with salt and pepper.
3. Add steaks to one side of the griddle and potatoes to the other.
4. Cook steak for 5 minutes, flip and 4 minutes on the other side for medium rare.
5. Add the potatoes to cook for 5 minutes.
6. Transfer steaks to a cutting board and tent with aluminum foil and let rest for 5 minutes while potatoes are cooking.
7. Divide each steak into 2 pieces and divide among 4 dinner plates. Spoon some potatoes around the steak and serve hot!
Nutrition: Calories:366, Sodium: 153 mg, Dietary Fiber: 4.5g, Fat: 23.3g, Carbs: 27.3g Protein: 13.4g

Caprese Grilled Filet Mignon with Basil

Servings: 4
Preparation Time: 10 minutes
Cooking Time: 10 minutes
Ingredients:
- (6 ounce) filets
- 2 teaspoon garlic salt
- Italian Olive oil
- 2 roma tomatoes, sliced
- 2 ounces fresh buffalo mozzarella, cut into four slices
- 8 fresh basil leaves
- Balsamic vinegar glaze, for drizzling
- Sea salt, for seasoning
- Fresh ground pepper

Directions:
1. Lightly brush each filet, on all sides, with olive oil and rub with garlic salt. Preheat griddle to high. Place steaks on griddle, reduce heat to medium, tent with foil and cook for 5 minutes.
2. Flip, re-tent, and cook for an additional 5 minutes; during the last 2 minutes of grilling top each with a slice of mozzarella.
3. Remove steaks from the griddle and top each with a few tomato slices, 2 basil leafs. Drizzle with balsamic, sprinkle with sea salt and black pepper and serve.
Nutrition: Calories: 406, Sodium: 688 mg, Dietary Fiber: 0.8g, Fat: 21.8g, Carbs: 7.2g Protein: 45.1g

Worcestershire Beef Burger Patties

Serve: 6
Preparation Time: 10 minutes
Cooking Time: 12 minutes
Ingredients:
- 2 lbs ground beef
- 2 tbsp Worcestershire sauce
- ¾ cup onion, chopped
- ½ tsp pepper
- ½ tsp salt

Directions:
1. Add all ingredients into the bowl and mix until well combined.
2. Preheat the griddle to high heat.
3. Spray griddle top with cooking spray.
4. Make patties from mixture and place on hot griddle top and cook for 5 minutes on each side.
5. Serve and enjoy.
Nutrition: Calories 292 Fat 9.4 g Carbohydrates 2.5 g Sugar 1.6 g Protein 46.1 g Cholesterol 135 mg

Mayo Roast Beef Sandwich

Serve: 1
Preparation Time: 10 minutes
Cooking Time: 5 minutes
Ingredients:
- 2 bread slices
- 2 cheese slices
- 4 deli roast beef, sliced
- 2 tsp butter
- 1 tbsp mayonnaise
- ¼ cup caramelized onions, sliced

Directions:
1. Spread butter on one side of each bread slice.
2. Take 1 bread slice and spread with mayo top with beef, onion, and cheese.
3. Cover with remaining bread slice.
4. Preheat the griddle to high heat.
5. Spray griddle top with cooking spray.
6. Place sandwich on hot griddle top and cook for 5 minutes or until golden brown from both sides.
7. Serve and enjoy.
Nutrition: Calories 859 Fat 44.6 g Carbohydrates 25.4 g Sugar 5.5 g Protein 83.4 g Cholesterol 265 mg

Buttered Rib-Eye Steak

Servings: 2 - 4
Preparation Time: 12 hours
Cooking Time: 50 minutes
Ingredients:
• 1 (24-ounce) bone-in Tomahawk rib-eye, about 2 ½ inches thick
• Olive oil -
• Sea salt
• Fresh cracked pepper
• 2 tablespoons premium French butter
• ½ teaspoon Herbes de Provence
Directions:
1. Beat butter with herbs in a small mixing bowl, cover and refrigerate until ready to grill rib-eye.
2. Rub the rib-eye liberally with olive oil, salt and pepper until entire steak is covered.
3. Wrap lightly with cling wrap and place in the refrigerator to marinate for 12 hours.
4. Preheat the griddle to high heat on one side and medium low on the other side, at least one hour prior to cooking.
5. Remove the steak from the refrigerator and leave at room temperature during the hour that the griddle is preheating.
6. Place the steak on the center of the hottest side of the griddle. Do this for both sides, about 10 minutes.
7. Move the rib-eye to the cooler side of the griddle and cook to rare, about 25 to 30 minutes.
8. Transfer rib-eye to a grill rack, add herbed butter on top, and lightly tent it with tin foil to rest for at least 15 minutes before carving.
9. Serve with your favorite sides!
Nutrition: Calories: 549, Sodium: 607 mg, Dietary Fiber: 1.5g, Fat: 40.3g, Carbs: 3.5g Protein: 40.9g

Texas-Style Rubbed Brisket

Servings: 6
Preparation Time: 10 minutes
Cooking Time: 6 hours 20 minutes
Ingredients:
• 1 (4 ½ lb) flat cut beef brisket (about 3 inches thick)
• For the rub:
• 1 tablespoon sea salt
• 1 tablespoon dark brown sugar
• 2 teaspoons smoked paprika
• 2 teaspoons chili powder
• 1 teaspoon garlic powder
• 1 teaspoon onion powder
• 1 teaspoon ground black pepper
• 1 teaspoon mesquite liquid smoke, like Colgin
Directions:
1. Combine the rub ingredients in a small mixing bowl.
2. Rinse and pat brisket dry and rub with coffee mix.
3. Preheat the griddle for two zone cooking; heat one side to high and leaving one side with low heat.
4. Sear on high heat side for 3 - 5 minutes on each side or until nicely charred.

5. Move to low heat side, tent with foil, and cook for 6 hours or until a meat thermometer registers 195°F.
6. Remove from griddle. Let stand, covered, 30 minutes.
7. Cut brisket across grain into thin slices and serve.
Nutrition: Calories:591, Sodium: 3953 mg, Dietary Fiber: 0.7g, Fat: 42.8g, Carbs: 3.2g Protein: 45.9g

Beef Zucchini Skewers

Serve: 4
Preparation Time: 10 minutes
Cooking Time: 15 minutes
Ingredients:
• 1 lb beef sirloin tips
• 1 zucchini, cut into chunks
For marinade:
• ¼ cup olive oil
• 1 jalapeno pepper
• ½ tbsp lime juice
• 1 ½ tbsp red wine vinegar
• 1 tsp dried oregano
• 2 garlic cloves
• 1 cup cilantro
Directions:
1. Add all marinade ingredients into the blender and blend until smooth.
2. Pour the blended mixture into the mixing bowl. Add beef tips and mix well and let it marinate for 30 minutes.
3. Thread marinated beef tips and zucchini chunks onto the skewers.
4. Preheat the griddle to high heat.
5. Spray griddle top with cooking spray.
6. Place skewers on a hot griddle top and cooks for 7-8 minutes or until beef tips are cooked.
7. Serve and enjoy.
Nutrition: Calories 179 Fat 14.3 g Carbohydrates 3.3 g Sugar 1.2 g Protein 11.4 g Cholesterol 0 mg

Homemade Sirloin Steaks

Serve: 4
Preparation Time: 10 minutes
Cooking Time: 15 minutes
Ingredients:
• 4 top sirloin steaks
• 1 tbsp Montreal steak seasoning
• Pepper
• Salt
Directions:
1. Season steaks with Montreal steak seasoning, pepper, and salt.
2. Preheat the griddle to medium heat.
3. Spray griddle top with cooking spray.
4. Place steaks on a hot griddle top and cook for 3-5 minutes on each side or until the internal temperature reaches 145 F.
5. Serve and enjoy.
Nutrition: Calories 163 Fat 5.3 g Carbohydrates 0 g Sugar 0 g Protein 25.8 g Cholesterol 76 mg

Garlic Tender Steak with Pine-apple Rice

Servings: 4
Preparation Time: 10 minutes
Cooking Time: 10 minutes
Ingredients:
- (4-ounce) beef fillets
- ¼ cup soy sauce
- ½ teaspoon black pepper
- ½ teaspoon garlic powder
- (8-ounce) can pineapple chunks, in juice, drained
- 2 scallions, thin sliced
- 1 (8.8-ounce) packages pre-cooked brown rice, like Uncle Ben's
- 7/8 teaspoon kosher salt
- Olive oil, for brushing

Directions:
1. Combine soy sauce, pepper, garlic powder, and beef in a large sealable plastic bag.
2. Seal and massage sauce into beef; let stand at room temperature for 7 minutes, turning bag occasionally.
3. Preheat griddle to medium-high heat and brush with olive oil.
4. Add pineapple and green onions to grill and cook 5 minutes or until well charred, turning to char evenly.
5. Remove pineapple mix and brush with additional olive oil.
6. Add steaks and cook 3 minutes on each side, for rare, or until desired temperature is reached.
7. Cook rice according to package instructions.
8. Add rice, pineapple, onions, and salt to a bowl and stir gently to combine.
9. Plate steaks with pineapple rice and serve!
Nutrition: Calories: 369, Sodium: 1408 mg, Dietary Fiber: 2.1g, Fat: 12.4g, Carbs: 37g Protein: 27.9g

Rosemary Flank Steak with Garlic

Servings: 4
Preparation Time: 10 minutes
Cooking Time: 20 minutes
Ingredients:
- 2 (8 ounce) flank steaks
- For the marinade:
- 1 tablespoon extra-virgin olive oil, plus more for brushing
- 2 tablespoons fresh rosemary, chopped
- 2 cloves garlic, minced
- 2 teaspoons sea salt
- ¼ teaspoon black pepper

Directions:
1. Add marinade ingredients to a food processor or blender and pulse until garlic and rosemary are pulverized.
2. Use a fork to pierce the steaks 10 times on each side.
3. Rub each evenly with the marinade on both sides.
4. Place in a covered dish and refrigerate for at least 1 hour or overnight.

5. Preheat griddle to high and brush with olive oil and preheat to high.
6. Cook steaks for 5 minutes, flip, tent with foil, and cook for about 3-4 minutes more.
7. Transfer meat to rest on a cutting board, cover with aluminum foil, for about 15 minutes.
8. Slice very thin against the grain and serve immediately.
Nutrition: Calories: 260, Sodium: 1001 mg, Dietary Fiber: 0.8g, Fat: 13.2g, Carbs:

Greek Flank Steak Gyros with Feta

Servings: 4
Preparation Time: 5 minutes
Cooking Time: 20 minutes
Ingredients:
- 1 pound flank steak
- 1 white onion, thinly sliced
- 1 roma tomato, thinly sliced
- 1 cucumber, peeled and thinly sliced
- ¼ cup crumbled feta cheese
- 6-inch pita pockets
- For the marinade:
- ¼ cup olive oil, plus more for brushing
- 1 teaspoon dried oregano
- 1 teaspoon balsamic vinegar
- 1 teaspoon garlic powder
- Sea salt and freshly ground pepper, to taste
- For the sauce:
- 1 cup plain yogurt
- 2 tablespoons fresh dill (can use dried), chopped
- 1 teaspoon garlic, minced
- 2 tablespoons lemon juice

Directions:
1. Cut the flank steak into thin strips against the grain. Add the marinade ingredients to a large sealable plastic bag, add the sliced meat, seal, and turn to coat.
2. Place in the refrigerator to marinate for 2 hours or overnight.
3. Preheat the griddle to medium-high heat, and an oven to 250°F.
4. Combine the sauce ingredients in small mixing bowl and set aside.
5. Spritz the pitas with a little water, wrap in foil and place in the oven to warm.
6. Brush griddle with olive oil.
7. Add meat to grill and discard marinade. Cook until brown and cooked through, about 5 minutes.
8. Remove the pitas from the oven, and cut in half.
9. Arrange the pitas on plates and stuff with cucumber, tomato, onions, and beef. Spoon some yogurt sauce over the meat and top with feta and serve.
Nutrition: Calories:901, Sodium: 1221 mg, Dietary Fiber: 5.7g, Fat: 27.2g, Carbs:107.8g Protein: 53.5g

Balsamic Marinated Skirt Steak

Servings: 4
Preparation Time: 30 minutes
Cooking Time: 45 minutes
Ingredients:
- 2 (8 ounce) skirt steaks
- For the marinade:
- 2 tablespoons balsamic vinegar
- 2 teaspoons olive oil, more for brushing
- 2 garlic cloves, minced
- Sea salt, to taste
- Black pepper, to taste

Directions:
1. Combine marinade ingredients in a sealable plastic bag, add steaks, seal bag, turn to coat; let stand at room temperature for 30 minutes.
2. Preheat griddle to medium-high heat.
3. Remove steaks and discard marinade, place on griddle and cook about 3 minutes per side. Transfer steaks to cutting board and rest for 5 Minutes. Cut across the grain into slices and serve with your favorite sides.
Nutrition: Calories: 256, Sodium: 204 mg, Dietary Fiber: 0g, Fat: 13.8g, Carbs: 0.6g Protein: 30.3g

Crusted Skirt Steak with Cinnamon

Servings: 8
Preparation Time: 10 minutes
Cooking Time: 20 minutes
Ingredients:
- ¼ cup coffee beans, finely ground
- ¼ cup dark brown sugar, firmly packed - ½ teaspoon sea salt
- ⅛ teaspoon ground cinnamon
- Pinch cayenne pepper
- ½ lb. skirt steak, cut into 4 pieces
- 1 tablespoon olive oil

Directions:
1. Heat griddle to high.
2. Combine coffee, brown sugar, salt, cinnamon, and cayenne pepper in a bowl to make rub.
3. Remove steak from refrigerator and let come to room temperature, about 15 minutes. Rub steak with oil, and sprinkle with spice rub. Massage spice rub into meat. Sear until charred and medium-rare, 2 to 4 minutes per side. Transfer to a cutting board, cover with foil and let rest 5 minutes before thinly slicing against the grain.
Nutrition: Calories:324, Sodium: 461 mg, Dietary Fiber: 0.1g, Fat: 16g, Carbs: 4.6g Protein: 37.9g

Grilled Steak with Cilantro

Servings: 4
Preparation Time: 1 - 2 hours
Cooking Time: 15 minutes
Ingredients:
- 1 lb. hanger steak or shirt steak
- ¼ cup olive oil
- 1 lime, juiced
- 1 orange, juiced
- 1 garlic clove, finely chopped
- ½ teaspoon cumin
- ¼ teaspoon salt
- ¼ teaspoon ground pepper
- handful of fresh cilantro, chopped

Directions:
1. Combine all of the ingredients in a large sealable plastic bag. Marinate in the refrigerator for 1 to 2 hours.
2. Preheat to medium/high heat, cook for 3 minutes on each side or until just cooked through.
3. Transfer to cutting board to rest for 10 minutes.
4. Slice against the grain and serve.
Nutrition: Calories: 363, Sodium: 200mg, Dietary Fiber: 1.7g, Fat: 18.4g, Carbs: 7.7g Protein: 41.6g

Lime Steak Salad

Servings: 2
Preparation Time: 10 minutes
Cooking Time: 10 minutes
Ingredients:
Steak marinade:
- 2 tablespoons olive oil
- 3 garlic cloves, minced
- 2 teaspoons chili powder
- 1 teaspoon ground cumin
- 1 teaspoon kosher salt
- 1 teaspoon freshly ground pepper
- 1 ½ pounds skirt or flap steak, cut into 4-inch lengths
- ½ cup lager beer
Salad:
- 12 ounces romaine hearts, trimmed and chopped
- 1 can black beans, drained and rinsed
- 1 pint cherry tomatoes, halved
- 1 large ripe avocado, pitted, peeled, and cut into chunks
- About ⅓ cup crumbled queso fresco
- Chopped fresh cilantro, for garnish
- Kosher salt
Dressing:
- ½ cup plain whole milk yogurt
- ⅓ cup chopped fresh cilantro
- Zest of 1 lime
- Juice of 2 limes

Directions:
1. Make marinade, then marinate steak for 4 hours to overnight.
2. Combine salad ingredients in a large bowl; add dressing and mix well. Place salad on separate plates. Preheat griddle to high. Place marinated steak on griddle, reduce heat to medium, tent with foil and cook for 5 minutes.
3. Flip, re-tent, and cook for an additional 5 minutes.
4. Remove steak from the griddle and slice into 2 inch strips.
5. Place steak strips on individual salads, and sprinkle with flakey salt and a little black pepper. Garnish with cilantro.
Nutrition: Calories:1332, Sodium: 2011 mg, Dietary Fiber: 13.3g, Fat: 65.1g, Carbs:29.4g Protein: 152.3g

Ginger Pineapple Beef Burger Patties

Serve: 4
Preparation Time: 10 minutes
Cooking Time: 8 minutes
Ingredients:
- 1 ¼ lbs ground beef
- 2 pineapple slices, chopped
- ¼ tsp pepper
- 1 garlic clove, minced
- 1 tsp ginger, grated
- ¼ cup green onions, chopped
- ¼ cup soy sauce
- Salt

Directions:
1. Add all ingredients into the bowl and mix until well combined.
2. Preheat the griddle to high heat.
3. Spray griddle top with cooking spray.
4. Make patties from mixture and place on hot griddle top and cook for 4 minutes on each side.
5. Serve and enjoy.

Nutrition: Calories 135 Fat 5.3 g Carbohydrates 13.1 g Sugar 8.6 g Protein 9.8 g Cholesterol 28 mg

Chimichurri Steak Sandwich

Serve: 2
Preparation Time: 10 minutes
Cooking Time: 10 minutes
Ingredients:
- ¼ lb steaks, cooked & sliced
- 2 tbsp chimichurri sauce
- 1 tbsp butter
- 4 bread slices
- 4 cheese slices

Directions:
1. Spread butter on one side of each bread slice.
2. Take 2 bread slices and spread with chimichurri sauce and top with steak and cheese.
3. Cover with remaining bread slices.
4. Preheat the griddle to high heat.
5. Spray griddle top with cooking spray.
6. Place sandwich on hot griddle top and cook for 5 minutes or until golden brown from both sides.
7. Serve and enjoy.

Nutrition: Calories 617 Fat 46.8 g Carbohydrates 11.8 g Sugar 1.6 g Protein 36.4 g Cholesterol 125 mg

Buttered Tomato Roast Beef Sandwich

Serve: 2
Preparation Time: 10 minutes
Cooking Time: 10 minutes
Ingredients:
- 4 bread slices
- ½ lb deli roast beef slices
- 2 tbsp mayonnaise
- 1 tbsp butter
- ½ onion, sliced
- 1 tomato, sliced
- 4 cheese slices

Directions:
1. Spread butter on one side of each bread slice.
2. Take 4 bread slices and spread with mayo and top with beef, cheese, tomatoes, and onion.
3. Cover with remaining bread slices.
4. Preheat the griddle to high heat.
5. Spray griddle top with cooking spray.
6. Place sandwich on hot griddle top and cook for 5 minutes or until golden brown from both sides.
7. Serve and enjoy.

Nutrition: Calories 617 Fat 35.9 g Carbohydrates 17.1 g Sugar 4 g Protein 53.9 g Cholesterol 177 mg

Dijon Beef Burger Patties with Parsley

Serve: 4
Preparation Time: 10 minutes
Cooking Time: 10 minutes
Ingredients:
- 1 lb ground beef
- ½ tsp pepper
- ¾ tbsp Worcestershire sauce
- 1 tbsp Dijon mustard
- ⅛ tsp cayenne
- ⅛ tsp chili flakes
- 1 tbsp parsley, chopped
- ½ tsp kosher salt

Directions:
1. Add all ingredients into the bowl and mix until well combined.
2. Preheat the griddle to high heat.
3. Spray griddle top with cooking spray.
4. Make patties from mixture and place on hot griddle top and cook for 5 minutes on each side.
5. Serve and enjoy.

Nutrition: Calories 217 Fat 7.3 g Carbohydrates 1 g Sugar 0.6 g Protein 34.6 g Cholesterol 101 mg

Basil Salmon Fillets with Broccolini

Servings: 2
Preparation Time: 10 minutes
Cooking Time: 12 minutes
Ingredients:
- 2 (6 ounce) salmon fillets, skin removed
- 2 tablespoons butter, unsalted
- 2 basil leaves, minced
- 1 garlic clove, minced
- 6 ounces broccolini
- 2 teaspoons olive oil - Sea salt, to taste

Directions:
1. Blend butter, basil, and garlic together until well-incorporated. Form into a ball and place in refrigerator until ready to serve.
2. Preheat griddle to medium-high heat.
3. Season both sides of the salmon fillets with salt and set aside.
4. Add broccolini, a pinch of salt, and olive oil to a bowl, toss to coat, and set aside.
5. Brush griddle with olive oil, and cook salmon, skin side down, for 12 minutes. Turn the salmon and cook for an additional 4 minutes. Remove from the griddle and allow to rest while the broccolini cooks.
6. Add the broccolini to the griddle, turning occasionally, until slightly charred, about 6 minutes.
7. Top each salmon fillet with a slice of basil butter and serve with a side of broccolini.
Nutrition: Calories: 398, Sodium: 303mg, Dietary Fiber: 2.2g, Fat: 26.7g, Carbs: 6.2g, Protein: 35.6g.

Tandoori Snapper with Salsa

Servings: 4
Preparation Time: 10 minutes
Cooking Time: 20 minutes
Ingredients:
- 2 red snappers, cleaned
- Sea salt
- ⅓ cup tandoori spice
- Olive oil, plus more for griddle
- Extra-virgin olive oil, for drizzling
- Lime wedges, for serving
- For the salsa:
- 1 ripe but firm mango, peeled and chopped
- 1 small red onion, thinly sliced
- 1 bunch cilantro, coarsely chopped
- 3 tablespoons fresh lime juice

Directions:
1. Toss mango, onion, cilantro, lime juice, and a big pinch of salt in a medium mixing bowl; drizzle with a bit of olive oil and toss again to coat.
2. Place snapper on a cutting board and pat dry with paper towels. Cut slashes crosswise on a diagonal along the body every 2" on both sides, with a sharp knife, cutting all the way down to the bones.
3. Season fish generously inside and out with salt. Coat fish with tandoori spice.
4. Preheat griddle medium-high heat and brush with oil.
5. Griddle fish for 10 minutes, undisturbed, until skin is puffed and charred.
6. Flip and griddle fish until the other side is lightly charred and skin is puffed, about 8 to 12 minutes.
7. Transfer to a platter. Top with mango salad and serve with lime wedges.
Nutrition: Calories: 211, Sodium: 170mg, Dietary Fiber: 2.5g, Fat: 5.4g, Carbs: 18.9g, Protein: 23.6g.

Spiced Crab Legs Griddle

Servings: 4
Preparation Time: 5 minutes
Cooking Time: 5 minutes
Ingredients:
- 4 lbs king crab legs, cooked
- 2 tablespoons chili oil

Directions:
1. Preheat griddle to high.
2. Brush both sides of crab legs with chili oil and place on griddle. Tent with foil.
3. Cook 4 to 5 minutes, turning once.
4. Transfer to plates and serve with drawn butter.
Nutrition: Calories: 518, Sodium: 4857mg, Dietary Fiber: 0g, Fat: 13.9g, Carbs: 0g, Protein: 87.1g.

Pineapple Shrimp Skewers with Cilantro

Servings: 4
Preparation Time: 1 hour 20 minutes
Cooking Time: 5 minutes
Ingredients:
- 1-½ pounds uncooked jumbo shrimp, peeled and deveined
- ½ cup light coconut milk
- 1 tablespoon cilantro, chopped
- 4 teaspoons Tabasco Original Red Sauce
- 2 teaspoons soy sauce
- ¼ cup freshly squeezed orange juice
- ¼ cup freshly squeezed lime juice (from about 2 large limes)
- ¾ pound pineapple, cut into 1 inch chunks
- Olive oil, for griddling

Directions:
1. Combine the coconut milk, cilantro, Tabasco sauce, soy sauce, orange juice, lime juice. Add the shrimp and toss to coat.
2. Cover and place in the refrigerator to marinate for 1 hour.
3. Thread shrimp and pineapple onto metal skewers, alternating each.
4. Preheat griddle to medium heat.
5. Cook 5-6 minutes, flipping once, until shrimp turn opaque pink.
6. Serve immediately.
Nutrition: Calories: 150, Sodium: 190mg, Dietary Fiber: 1.9g, Fat: 10.8g, Carbs: 14.9g, Protein: 1.5g.

Honey Tilapia and Corn Foil Pack with Lime

Servings: 4
Preparation Time: 10 minutes
Cooking Time: 10 minutes
Ingredients:
- 4 fillets tilapia
- 2 tablespoons honey
- 4 limes, thinly sliced
- 2 ears corn, shucked
- 2 tablespoons fresh cilantro leaves
- ¼ cup olive oil
- Kosher salt
- Freshly ground black pepper

Directions:
1. Preheat griddle to high.
2. Cut 4 squares of foil about 12" long.
3. Top each piece of foil with a piece of tilapia.
4. Brush tilapia with honey and top with lime, corn and cilantro.
5. Drizzle with olive oil and season with sea salt and pepper.
6. Cook until tilapia is cooked through and corn tender, about 15 minutes.

Nutrition: Calories: 319, Sodium: 92mg, Dietary Fiber: 4g, Fat: 14.7g, Carbs: 30.3g, Protein: 24g.

Halibut Fillets and Spinach Mix with Olives

Servings: 4
Preparation Time: 10 minutes
Cooking Time: 10 minutes
Ingredients:
- 4 (6 ounce) halibut fillets
- ⅓ cup olive oil
- 4 cups baby spinach
- ¼ cup lemon juice
- 2 ounces pitted black olives, halved
- 2 tablespoons flat leaf parsley, chopped
- 2 teaspoons fresh dill, chopped
- Lemon wedges, to serve

Directions:
1. Preheat griddle to medium heat.
2. Toss spinach with lemon juice in a mixing bowl and set aside.
3. Brush fish with olive oil and cook for 3-4 minutes per side, or until cooked through.
4. Remove from heat, cover with foil and let rest for 5 minutes.
5. Add remaining oil and cook spinach for 2 minutes, or until just wilted. Remove from heat.
6. Toss with olives and herbs, then transfer to serving plates with fish, and serve with lemon wedges.

Nutrition: Calories: 773, Sodium: 1112mg, Dietary Fiber: 1.4g, Fat: 36.6g, Carbs: 2.9g, Protein: 109.3g.

Lime Basil Butter Lobster Tails

Servings: 4
Preparation Time: 5 minutes
Cooking Time: 6 minutes
Ingredients:
- 4 lobster tails (cut in half lengthwise)
- 3 tablespoons olive oil
- Lime wedges (to serve) - Sea salt, to taste
- For the lime basil butter:
- 1 stick unsalted butter, softened
- ½ bunch basil, roughly chopped
- 1 lime, zested and juiced
- 2 cloves garlic, minced
- ¼ teaspoon red pepper flakes

Directions:
1. Add the butter ingredients to a mixing bowl and combine; set aside until ready to use.
2. Preheat griddle to medium-high heat.
3. Drizzle the lobster tail halves with olive oil and season with salt and pepper.
4. Place the lobster tails, flesh-side down, on the griddle.
5. Allow to cook until opaque, about 3 minutes, flip and cook another 3 minutes.
6. Add a dollop of the lime basil butter during the last minute of cooking. Serve immediately.

Nutrition: Calories: 430, Sodium: 926mg, Dietary Fiber: 0.5g, Fat: 34.7g, Carbs: 2.4g, Protein: 28g.

Spicy Lemon Shrimp with Parsley

Servings: 4
Preparation Time: 10 minutes
Cooking Time: 10 minutes
Ingredients:
- 1 ½ lbs shrimp, peeled and deveined
- 3 garlic cloves, minced
- 1 small onion, minced
- ½ cup butter
- 1 ½ tbsp fresh parsley, chopped
- 1 tbsp fresh lemon juice
- ¼ tsp red pepper flakes
- Pepper
- Salt

Directions:
1. Preheat the griddle to high heat.
2. Melt butter on the griddle top.
3. Add garlic, onion, red chili flakes, pepper, and salt and stir for 2 minutes.
4. Season shrimp with pepper and salt and thread onto skewers.
5. Brush shrimp skewers with butter mixture.
6. Place shrimp skewers on griddle top and cook until shrimp turns to pink, about 3-4 minutes.
7. Transfer shrimp to the serving plate.
8. Drizzle lemon juice over shrimp and garnish with parsley.
9. Serve and enjoy.

Nutrition: Calories 419 Fat 25 g Carbohydrates 5.2 g Sugar 0.9 g Protein 39.4 g Cholesterol 419 mg

Flavorful Crab Cakes

Servings: 4
Preparation Time: 10 minutes
Cooking Time: 15 minutes
Ingredients:
- 1 lb lump crab meat
- ½ cup panko breadcrumbs
- ⅓ cup mayonnaise
- 1 egg, beaten
- 2 tablespoons Dijon mustard
- 2 teaspoons Worcestershire sauce
- ½ teaspoon paprika
- ½ teaspoon salt
- ¼ teaspoon black pepper
- 3 tablespoons vegetable oil

Directions:
1. Preheat griddle to medium heat.
2. In a large bowl, combine the crab, breadcrumbs, mayo, egg, mustard Worcestershire sauce, paprika, salt and pepper. Mix well to combine.
3. Form the crab mixture into 4 large balls and flatten them slightly.
4. Add the oil to the griddle and cook the crab cakes for approximately 5 minutes per side or until browned and crispy. Serve immediately.

Nutrition: Calories: 282, Sodium: 1205mg, Dietary Fiber: 0.6g, Fat: 27.4g, Carbs: 9.5g, Protein: 18.8g.

Spiced Grilled Jumbo Shrimp

Servings: 6
Preparation Time: 15 minutes
Cooking Time: 8 minutes
Ingredients:
- 1-½ pounds uncooked jumbo shrimp, peeled and deveined
- For the marinade:
- 2 tablespoons fresh parsley
- 1 bay leaf, dried
- 1 teaspoon chili powder
- 1 teaspoon garlic powder
- ¼ teaspoon cayenne pepper
- ¼ cup olive oil
- ¼ teaspoon salt
- ⅛ teaspoon pepper

Directions:
1. Add marinade ingredients to a food processor and process until smooth.
2. Transfer marinade to a large mixing bowl.
3. Fold in shrimp and toss to coat; refrigerate, covered, 30 minutes.
4. Thread shrimp onto metal skewers.
5. Preheat griddle to medium heat.
6. Cook 5-6 minutes, flipping once, until shrimp turn opaque pink.
7. Serve immediately.

Nutrition: Calories: 131, Sodium: 980mg, Dietary Fiber: 0.4g, Fat: 8.5g, Carbs: 1g, Protein: 13.7g.

Mouthwatering Gremolata Swordfish Skewers

Servings: 4
Preparation Time: 20 minutes
Cooking Time: 10 minutes
Ingredients:
- 1-½ lb. skinless swordfish fillet
- 2 teaspoons lemon zest
- 3 tablespoons lemon juice
- ½ cup finely chopped parsley
- 2 teaspoons garlic, minced
- ¾ teaspoon sea salt
- ¼ teaspoon black pepper
- 2 tablespoons extra-virgin olive oil, plus extra for serving
- ½ teaspoon red pepper flakes
- 3 lemons, cut into slices

Directions:
1. Preheat griddle to medium-high.
2. Combine lemon zest, parsley, garlic, ¼ teaspoon of the salt, and pepper in a small bowl with a fork to make gremolata and set aside.
3. Mix swordfish pieces with reserved lemon juice, olive oil, red pepper flakes, and remaining salt.
4. Thread swordfish and lemon slices, alternating each, onto the metal skewers.
5. Griddle skewers 8 to 10 minutes, flipping halfway through, or until fish is cooked through.
6. Place skewers on a serving platter and sprinkle with gremolata.
7. Drizzle with olive oil and serve.

Nutrition: Calories: 333, Sodium: 554mg, Dietary Fiber: 0.5g, Fat: 16g, Carbs: 1.6g, Protein: 43.7g.

Enticing Bacon-Wrapped Scallops

Servings: 4
Preparation Time: 15 minutes
Cooking Time: 4 minutes
Ingredients:
- 12 large sea scallops, side muscle removed
- 8 slices of bacon
- 1 tablespoon vegetable oil
- 12 toothpicks

Directions:
1. Heat your griddle to medium heat and cook the bacon until fat has rendered but bacon is still flexible. Remove bacon from the griddle and place on paper towels.
2. Raise griddle heat to medium-high.
3. Wrap each scallop with a half slice of bacon and skewer with a toothpick to keep the bacon in place.
4. Place the scallops on the griddle and cook for 90 seconds per side. They should be lightly browned on both sides.
5. Remove from the griddle and serve immediately.

Nutrition: Calories: 315, Sodium: 1023mg, Dietary Fiber: 0g, Fat: 20g, Carbs: 2.7g, Protein: 29.2g.

Lemon Clams with Horseradish-Tabasco Sauce

Servings: 4
Preparation Time: 5 minutes
Cooking Time: 10 minutes
Ingredients:
- 2 dozen littleneck clams, scrubbed
- 4 tablespoons unsalted butter, softened
- 2 tablespoons horseradish, drained
- 1 tablespoon hot sauce, like Tabasco
- ¼ teaspoon lemon zest, finely grated
- 1 tablespoon fresh lemon juice
- ¼ teaspoon smoked paprika
- Sea salt

Directions:
1. Preheat the griddle to high.
2. Blend the butter with the horseradish, hot sauce, lemon zest, lemon juice, paprika, and pinch of salt.
3. Arrange the clams over high heat and griddle until they pop open, about 25 seconds.
4. Carefully turn the clams over using tongs, so the meat side is down.
5. Griddle for about 20 seconds longer, until the clam juices start to simmer.
6. Transfer the clams to a serving bowl.
7. Top each with about ½ teaspoon of the sauce and serve.
Nutrition: Calories: 191, Sodium: 382mg, Dietary Fiber: 0.3g, Fat: 12.7g, Carbs: 4g, Protein: 14.8g.

Sesame Marinated Griddle Squid

Servings: 4
Preparation Time: 5 minutes
Cooking Time: 5 minutes
Ingredients:
- 1-½ lbs. Squid, red - Olive oil
- For the marinade:
- 2 cloves garlic cloves, minced
- ½ teaspoon ginger, minced
- 3 tablespoons gochujang
- 3 tablespoons corn syrup
- 1 teaspoon yellow mustard
- 1 teaspoon soy sauce
- 2 teaspoons sesame oil
- 1 teaspoon sesame seeds
- 2 green onions, chopped

Directions:
1. Preheat griddle to medium high heat and brush with olive oil. Add the squid and tentacles to the griddle and cook for 1 minute until the bottom looks firm and opaque. Turn them over and cook for another minute; straighten out the body with tongs if it curls. Baste with sauce on top of the squid and cook 2 additional minutes.
2. Flip and baste the other side, cook 1 minute until the sauce evaporates and the squid turns red and shiny.
Nutrition: Calories: 292, Sodium: 466mg, Dietary Fiber: 2.7g, Fat: 8.6g, Carbs: 25.1g, Protein: 27.8g.

Mexican Shrimp Tacos with Salsa

Servings: 4
Preparation Time: 10 minutes
Cooking Time: 10 minutes
Ingredients:
- 2 lbs. medium shrimp, peeled and deveined
- 8 flour tortillas, warmed
- 1 bag cabbage slaw
- 1 cup salsa
- 1 cup Mexican crema
- For marinade:
- 2 tablespoons olive oil
- 1 tablespoon chili powder
- 1 tablespoon cumin
- 1 tablespoon garlic powder
- 1 tablespoon fresh lime juice
- ¼ teaspoon sea salt
- ⅛ teaspoon fresh ground pepper

Directions:
1. Preheat a griddle to medium-high.
2. Combine oil marinade in a large sealable plastic bag. Add shrimp and toss coat; let marinate in the refrigerator for 30 minutes.
3. Cook shrimp for 3 minutes, on each side, until cooked through.
4. Transfer to a plate.
5. Lay two tortillas on each plate. Evenly divide the shrimp, cabbage slaw, salsa in the middle of each tortilla.
6. Drizzle with Mexican crema and serve.
Nutrition: Calories: 400, Sodium: 92mg, Dietary Fiber: 4g, Fat: 14.7g, Carbs: 30.3g, Protein: 24g.

Buttered Oysters

Servings: 6
Preparation Time: 5 minutes
Cooking Time: 25 minutes
Ingredients:
- 3 dozen medium oysters, scrubbed and shucked
- Flakey sea salt, for serving
- For the butter:
- ¼ teaspoon crushed red pepper
- 7 tablespoons unsalted butter
- ¼ teaspoon chili oil
- 1 teaspoon dried oregano
- 2 tablespoons freshly squeezed lemon juice
- 2 tablespoons Tequila Blanco, like Espolon

Directions:
1. Combine butter ingredients in a small mixing bowl until well-incorporated and set aside.
2. Preheat griddle to high.
3. Griddle the oysters about 1 to 2 minutes.
4. Sprinkle the oysters with salt flakes.
5. Warm the butter in a microwave for 30 seconds, and spoon the warm Tequila butter over the oysters and serve.
Nutrition: Calories: 184, Sodium: 300mg, Dietary Fiber: 0.2g, Fat: 15g, Carbs: 3.8g, Protein: 0.2g.

Lemon Garlic Shrimp with Parsley

Servings: 4
Preparation Time: 10 minutes
Cooking Time: 15 minutes
Ingredients:
- 1 ½ lbs shrimp, peeled and deveined
- 1 tbsp garlic, minced
- ¼ cup butter
- ¼ cup fresh parsley, chopped
- ¼ cup fresh lemon juice
- Pepper
- Salt

Directions:
1. Preheat the griddle to high heat.
2. Melt butter on the griddle top.
3. Add garlic and sauté for 30 seconds.
4. Add shrimp and season with pepper and salt and cook for 4-5 minutes or until it turns to pink.
5. Add lemon juice and parsley and stir well and cook for 2 minutes.
6. Serve and enjoy.
Nutrition: Calories 312 Fat 14.6 g Carbohydrates 3.9 g Sugar 0.4 g Protein 39.2 g Cholesterol 389 mg

Enticing Mexican Shrimp

Servings: 4
Preparation Time: 10 minutes
Cooking Time: 12 minutes
Ingredients:
- 1 lb shrimp, cleaned
- 3 tbsp fresh parsley, chopped
- 1 tbsp garlic, minced
- ¼ onion, sliced
- ¼ tsp paprika
- ¼ tsp ground cumin
- 2 fresh lime juice
- 2 tbsp olive oil
- ¼ cup butter
- Pepper
- Salt

Directions:
1. Season shrimp with paprika, cumin, pepper, and salt.
2. Preheat the griddle to high heat.
3. Add oil and butter to the griddle top.
4. Add onion and garlic and sauté for 5 minutes.
5. Add shrimp and cook for 5-8 minutes or until cooked.
6. Add parsley and lime juice.
7. Stir well and serve.
Nutrition: Calories 311 Fat 20.5 g Carbohydrates 5 g Sugar 0.7 g Protein 26.4 g Cholesterol 269 mg

Lime Shrimp with Shrimp Butter

Servings: 4
Preparation Time: 15 minutes
Cooking Time: 15 minutes

Ingredients:
- 6 tbsp unsalted butter
- ½ cup finely chopped red onion
- 1 ½ tsp crushed red pepper
- 1 tsp Malaysian shrimp paste
- 1 ½ tsp lime juice
- salt
- grounded black pepper
- 24 shelled and deveined large shrimp
- 6 wooden skewers (better if soaked in water for 30 minutes)
- Torn mint leaves and assorted sprouts
Intolerances:
- Gluten-Free - Egg-Free

Directions:
1. In a little griddle, liquefy 3 tbsps. of butter. Add the onion then cook over moderate heat for about 3 minutes.
2. Add in the squashed red pepper and shrimp paste and cook until fragrant, about 2 minutes.
3. Add in the lime juice and the remaining 3 tbsps. of butter and season with salt. Keep the shrimp sauce warm.
4. Set up the griddle. Season the shrimp with salt and pepper and string onto the skewers, not too tightly.
5. Griddle over high heat, turning once until gently singed and cooked through, around 4 minutes.
6. Move onto a platter and spoon with shrimp sauce. Spread on the mint leaves and sprouts and serve.
Nutrition: Calories: 224 Fat: 10g Cholesterol: 260mg Carbs: 1g Protein: 30g

Stir-Fried Shrimp and Veggie Mix

Servings: 2
Preparation Time: 10 minutes
Cooking Time: 10 minutes
Ingredients:
- ½ lb shrimp, peeled and deveined
- 1 tbsp garlic, minced
- ⅓ cup olives
- 1 cup mushrooms, sliced
- 2 tbsp olive oil
- 1 cup tomatoes, diced
- 1 small onion, chopped
- Pepper
- Salt

Directions:
1. Preheat the griddle to high heat. Add oil.
2. Add onion, mushrooms, and garlic and sauté until onion soften.
3. Add shrimp and tomatoes and stir until shrimp is cooked through.
4. Add olives and stir well.
5. Remove pan from heat and set aside for 5 minutes. Season with pepper and salt.
6. Serve and enjoy.
Nutrition: Calories 325 Fat 18.7 g Carbohydrates 12.5 g Sugar 4.5 g Protein 28.6 g Cholesterol 239 mg

Tasty Pesto Shrimp

Servings: 4
Preparation Time: 10 minutes
Cooking Time: 5 minutes
Ingredients:
- 1 lb shrimp, remove shells and tails
- ½ cup basil pesto
- Pepper
- Salt

Directions:
1. Add shrimp, pesto, pepper, and salt into the large bowl and toss well. Set aside for 15 minutes.
2. Heat griddle over medium-high heat.
3. Thread marinated shrimp onto the skewers and place onto the hot griddle top and cook for 1-2 minutes on each side.
4. Serve and enjoy.
Nutrition: Calories 270 Fat 15 g Carbohydrates 3.7 g Sugar 2 g Protein 28.8 g Cholesterol 246 mg

Hearty Mayo Salmon Patties

Servings: 2
Preparation Time: 10 minutes
Cooking Time: 10 minutes
Ingredients:
- 6 oz can salmon, drained, remove bones, and pat dry
- 2 tbsp mayonnaise
- ½ cup almond flour
- ¼ tsp thyme
- 1 egg, lightly beaten
- 2 tbsp olive oil
- Pepper
- Salt

Directions:
1. Add salmon, thyme, egg, mayonnaise, almond flour, pepper, and salt into the mixing bowl and mix until well combined.
2. Preheat the griddle to high heat.
3. Add oil to the griddle top.
4. Make small patties from salmon mixture and place onto the hot griddle top and cook for 5-6 minutes.
5. Turn patties and cook for 3-4 minutes more. Serve and enjoy.
Nutrition: Calories 530 Fat 41 g Carbohydrates 9.8 g Sugar 1.1 g Protein 30.6 g Cholesterol 146 mg

Buttery Blackened Salmon

Servings: 5
Preparation Time: 10 minutes
Cooking Time: 10 minutes
Ingredients:
- 1 ¼ lbs salmon fillets
- 2 tbsp blackened seasoning
- 2 tbsp butter

Directions:
1. Season salmon fillets with blackened seasoning.
2. Preheat the griddle to high heat.
3. Melt butter on the griddle top.
4. Place salmon fillets onto the hot griddle top and cook for 4-5 minutes.

5. Turn salmon and cook for 4-5 minutes more. Serve and enjoy.
Nutrition: Calories 190 Fat 11 g Carbohydrates 0 g Sugar 0 g Protein 21.1 g Cholesterol 62 mg

Blackened Tilapia with Cumin

Servings: 4
Preparation Time: 10 minutes
Cooking Time: 6 minutes
Ingredients:
- 4 tilapia fillets
- 2 tbsp butter
- 1 tbsp olive oil
- For seasoning:
- 1 ½ tsp paprika
- 1 lemon, sliced
- ½ tsp ground cumin
- 1 tsp oregano
- ½ tsp garlic powder
- Pepper
- Salt

Directions:
1. In a small bowl, mix together all seasoning ingredients and rub over fish fillets.
2. Preheat the griddle to high heat.
3. Add butter and oil on the hot griddle top.
4. Place fish fillets onto the griddle top and cook for 3 minutes.
5. Turn fish fillets and cook for 3 minutes more or until cooked through. Serve and enjoy.
Nutrition: Calories 181 Fat 10.5 g Carbohydrates 1.2 g Sugar 0.2 g Protein 21.4 g Cholesterol 70 mg

Lime Salmon Zucchini Patties

Servings: 6
Preparation Time:10 minutes
Cooking Time: 10 minutes
Ingredients:
- 2 eggs
- 1 ½ lbs salmon, cooked
- 2 cups zucchini, shredded
- 2 tbsp onion, minced
- ¼ cup fresh cilantro, chopped
- ¼ cup olive oil
- ¾ cup almond flour
- 3 tbsp fresh lime juice
- 2 tbsp jalapeno, minced
- 2 tsp salt

Directions:
1. Add salmon, lime juice, cilantro, zucchini, jalapenos, onion, eggs, and salt into the food processor and process until the mixture is combined.
2. Add almond flour to a shallow dish. Preheat the griddle to high heat. Add oil to griddle.
3. Take ¼ cup salmon mixture and form patties, coat patties with almond flour then place onto the hot griddle top and cook for 5 minutes per side.
4. Serve and enjoy.
Nutrition: Calories 330 Fat 24 g Carbohydrates 5 g Sugar 1.5 g Protein 27.4 g Cholesterol 105 mg

Italian Shrimp with Paprika

Servings: 4
Preparation Time: 10 minutes
Cooking Time: 5 minutes
Ingredients:
* 1 lb shrimp, deveined
* 1 tsp Italian seasoning
* 1 tsp paprika
* 1 ½ tsp garlic, minced
* 1 stick butter
* 1 fresh lemon juice
* ¼ tsp pepper
* ½ tsp salt

Directions:
1. Preheat the griddle to high heat.
2. Melt butter on the hot griddle top.
3. Add garlic and cook for 30 seconds.
4. Toss shrimp with paprika, Italian seasoning, pepper, and salt.
5. Add shrimp into the pan and cook for 2-3 minutes per side.
6. Drizzle lemon juice over shrimp.
7. Stir and serve.
Nutrition: Calories 346 Fat 25 g Carbohydrates 2.6 g Sugar 0.2 g Protein 26.2 g Cholesterol 300 mg

Mouthwatering Lemon Scallops with Garlic

Servings: 2
Preparation Time: 10 minutes
Cooking Time: 5 minutes
Ingredients:
* 1 lb frozen bay scallops, thawed, rinsed & pat dry
* 1 tsp garlic, minced
* 2 tbsp olive oil
* 1 tsp parsley, chopped
* 1 tsp lemon juice
* Pepper
* Salt

Directions:
1. Preheat the griddle to high heat.
2. Add oil to the griddle top.
3. Add garlic and sauté for 30 seconds.
4. Add scallops, lemon juice, pepper, and salt, and sauté until scallops turn opaque.
5. Garnish with parsley and serve.
Nutrition: Calories 123 Fat 14 g Carbohydrates 0.6 g Sugar 0.1 g Protein 0.1 g Cholesterol 0 mg

Oregano Shrimp Skewers

Servings: 6
Preparation Time: 10 minutes
Cooking Time: 7 minutes
Ingredients:
* 1 ½ lbs shrimp, peeled and deveined
* 1 tbsp dried oregano
* 2 tsp garlic paste
* 2 lemon juice
* ¼ cup olive oil
* 1 tsp paprika
* Pepper
* Salt

Directions:
1. Add all ingredients into the mixing bowl and mix well and place in the refrigerator for 1 hour.
2. Remove marinated shrimp from refrigerator and thread onto the skewers.
3. Preheat the griddle to high heat.
4. Place skewers onto the griddle top and cook for 5-7 minutes.
5. Serve and enjoy.
Nutrition: Calories 212 Fat 10.5 g Carbohydrates 2.7 g Sugar 0.1 g Protein 26 g Cholesterol 239 mg

Flavorful Balsamic Salmon

Servings: 6
Preparation Time: 10 minutes
Cooking Time: 10 minutes
Ingredients:
* 6 salmon fillets
* 5 tbsp balsamic vinaigrette
* 2 tbsp olive oil
* 1 ½ tsp garlic powder
* Pepper
* Salt

Directions:
1. In a mixing bowl, add salmon, garlic powder, balsamic vinaigrette, pepper, and salt and mix well. Set aside.
2. Preheat the griddle to high heat.
3. Add oil to the hot griddle top.
4. Place salmon onto the griddle top and cook for 3-5 minutes on each side or until cooked through.
5. Serve and enjoy.
Nutrition: Calories 328 Fat 20.7 g Carbohydrates 1.4 g Sugar 1 g Protein 34.7 g Cholesterol 78 mg

Buttered Garlic Shrimp

Servings: 4
Preparation Time: 10 minutes
Cooking Time: 5 minutes
Ingredients:
* 1 lb shrimp, peeled and cleaned
* 5 garlic cloves, chopped
* 2 tbsp olive oil
* 1 tbsp fresh parsley, chopped
* 1 tsp paprika
* 2 tbsp butter
* ½ tsp sea salt

Directions:
1. Add shrimp, 1 tbsp oil, garlic, and salt in a large bowl and toss well and place in the refrigerator for 1 hour.
2. Preheat the griddle to high heat.
3. Add remaining oil and butter on the hot griddle top.
4. Once butter is melted then add marinated shrimp and paprika and stir constantly for 2-3 minutes or until shrimp is cooked.
5. Garnish with parsley and serve.
Nutrition: Calories 253 Fat 15 g Carbohydrates 3.3 g Sugar 0.1 g Protein 26.2 g Cholesterol 254 mg

Garlic Salmon

Servings: 2
Preparation Time: 10 minutes
Cooking Time: 6 minutes
Ingredients:
- 12 oz salmon, cut into two pieces
- 1 tsp Greek seasoning
- 1 tbsp olive oil
- ½ tsp lemon zest
- 1 garlic clove, minced
- Pepper
- Salt

Directions:
1. In a large bowl, mix olive oil, lemon zest, garlic, pepper, salt, and Greek seasoning.
2. Add salmon in a bowl and coat well with marinade and set aside for 15 minutes.
3. Preheat the griddle to high heat.
4. Place marinated salmon on hot griddle top and cook for 2-3 minutes. Turn salmon to the other side and cook for 2-3 minutes more.
5. Serve and enjoy.
Nutrition: Calories 290 - Fat 17.6 g Carbohydrates 1.4 g Sugar 0.1 g - Protein 33.2 g Cholesterol 75 mg

Lemon Garlic Butter Tilapia

Servings: 6
Preparation Time: 10 minutes
Cooking Time: 8 minutes
Ingredients:
- 2 lbs tilapia fillets
- 1 tsp garlic powder
- ½ fresh lemon juice
- 1 tbsp butter, melted
- Pepper - Salt

Directions:
1. In a small bowl, combine together lemon juice, garlic powder, and butter and microwave for 10 seconds.
2. Brush both the side of the fish fillet with lemon mixture. Season fillet with pepper and salt.
3. Preheat the griddle to high heat.
4. Spray griddle top with cooking spray.
5. Place fillets on hot griddle top and cook for 4 minutes on each side.
6. Serve and enjoy.
Nutrition: Calories 143 Fat 3 g Carbohydrates 0.4 g Sugar 0.1 g Protein 28.2 g Cholesterol 79 mg

Caper Basil Halibut with Garlic

Servings: 4
Preparation Time: 10 minutes
Cooking Time: 8 minutes
Ingredients:
- 24 oz halibut fillets
- 2 garlic cloves, crushed
- 2 tbsp olive oil
- 2 tsp capers, drained
- 3 tbsp fresh basil, sliced
- 2 ½ tbsp fresh lemon juice

Directions:
1. In a small bowl, whisk together garlic, olive oil, and lemon juice. Stir in 2 tbsp basil.

2. Season garlic mixture with pepper and salt.
3. Season fish fillets with pepper and salt and brush with garlic mixture.
4. Preheat the griddle to high heat.
5. Place fish fillets on hot griddle and cook for 4 minutes on each side.
6. Transfer fish fillets on serving plate and top with remaining garlic mixture and basil.
7. Serve and enjoy.
Nutrition: Calories 250 Fat 10.5 g Carbohydrates 0.8 g Sugar 0.2 g Protein 39.1 g Cholesterol 59 mg

Greek-Style Lemon Salmon Fillets

Servings: 2
Preparation Time: 10 minutes
Cooking Time: 6 minutes
Ingredients:
- 2 salmon fillets
- 1 tbsp fresh basil, minced
- 1 tbsp butter, melted
- 1 tbsp fresh lemon juice
- ⅛ tsp salt

Directions:
1. Preheat the griddle to high heat.
2. In a small bowl, mix together lemon juice, basil, butter, and salt.
3. Brush salmon fillets with lemon mixture and place them on the hot griddle top.
4. Cook salmon for 2-3 minutes. Flip salmon and cook for 2-3 minutes more. Serve and enjoy.
Nutrition: Calories 290 Fat 16.8 g Carbohydrates 0.3 g Sugar 0.2 g Protein 34.7 g Cholesterol 46 mg

Sesame Soy Salmon Skewers

Servings: 4
Preparation Time: 10 minutes
Cooking Time: 10 minutes
Ingredients:
- 1 lb salmon fillets, cut into 1-inch cubes
- 2 tbsp soy sauce
- 1 tbsp toasted sesame seeds
- 1 lime zest
- 2 tsp olive oil
- 1 ½ tbsp maple syrup
- 1 tsp ginger, crushed
- 1 lime juice

Directions:
1. In a bowl, mix together olive oil, soy sauce, lime zest, lime juice, maple syrup, and ginger.
2. Add salmon and stir to coat. Set aside for 10 minutes.
3. Preheat the griddle to high heat.
4. Slide marinated salmon pieces onto the skewers and cook on a hot griddle top for 8-10 minutes or until cooked through.
5. Sprinkle salmon skewers with sesame seeds and serve.
Nutrition: Calories 209 Fat 10 g Carbohydrates 6.5 g Sugar 4.6 g Protein 22.9 g Cholesterol 50 mg

Parmesan Shrimp with Nuts

Servings: 4
Preparation Time: 10 minutes
Cooking Time: 6 minutes
Ingredients:
- 1 lb shrimp, peeled and deveined
- 2 tbsp parmesan cheese, grated
- 1 tbsp fresh lemon juice
- 1 tbsp pine nuts, toasted
- 1 garlic clove
- ½ cup basil
- 1 tbsp olive oil
- Pepper
- Salt

Directions:
1. Add basil, lemon juice, cheese, pine nuts, garlic, pepper, and salt in a blender and blend until smooth.
2. Add shrimp and basil paste in a bowl and mix well.
3. Place shrimp bowl in the fridge for 20 minutes.
4. Preheat the griddle to high heat.
5. Spray griddle top with cooking spray.
6. Thread marinated shrimp onto skewers and place skewers on the hot griddle top.
7. Cook shrimp for 3 minutes on each side or until cooked.
8. Serve and enjoy.
Nutrition: Calories 225 Fat 11.2 g Carbohydrates 2.2 g Sugar 0.2 g Protein 27.2 g Cholesterol 241 mg

Roasted Yellowtail Fillet with Salsa Verde

Servings: 4
Preparation Time: 10 minutes
Cooking Time: 30 minutes
Ingredients:
- 4 Yellowtail Filets (6 oz.)
- 1 lb. new Potatoes
- 2 tbsp. Olive oil
- 1 lb. Mushrooms, oyster
- 1 tsp. ground Black pepper
- 4 tbsp. of olive oil
Salsa Verde:
- 1 tbsp. Cilantro, chopped
- 2 tbsp. Mint, chopped
- ½ cup Parsley, chopped
- 2 cloves of garlic, minced
- 1 tbsp. Oregano, chopped
- 1 Lemon, the juice
- 1 cup of Olive oil
- ⅛ tsp. Pepper Flake
- Salt

Directions:
1. Preheat the griddle to high with closed lid.
2. Place an iron pan directly on the griddle. Let it heat for 10 minutes.
3. Rub the fish with oil. Season with black pepper and salt.
4. In a 2 different bowls place the mushrooms and potatoes, drizzle with oil and season with black pepper and salt. Toss. Place the potatoes in the pan. Cook 10 minutes. Add the mushrooms.

5. Place the fillets on the grate with the skin down. Cook for 6 minutes and flip. Cook for 4 minutes more.
6. While the potatoes, mushrooms, and fish are cooking make the Salsa Verde. In a bowl combine all the ingredients and stir to combine.
7. Place the mushrooms and potatoes on a plate, top with a fillet and drizzle with the Salsa Verde. Serve and Enjoy!
Nutrition: Calories: 398 Protein: 52g Carbs: 20g Fat: 18gg

Baked Lemon Steelhead with Shallot

Servings: 4 - 6
Preparation Time: 15 minutes
Cooking Time: 20 minutes
Ingredients:
- 1 Lemon
- 2 Garlic cloves, minced
- ½ Shallot, minced
- 3 tbsp. Butter, unsalted
- Saskatchewan seasoning, blackened
- Italian Dressing
- 1 Steelhead, (a fillet)

Directions:
1. Preheat the griddle to 350 degrees F with closed lid.
2. In an iron pan place the butter. Place the pan in the griddle while preheating so that the butter melts. Coat the fillet with Italian dressing. Rub with Saskatchewan rub. Make sure the layer is thin.
3. Mince the garlic and shallot. Remove the pan from the griddle and add the garlic and shallots.
4. Spread the mixture on the fillet. Slice the lemon into slices. Place the slice on the butter mix.
5. Place the fish on the grate. Cook 20 - 30 minutes.
6. Remove from the griddle and serve. Enjoy!
Nutrition: Calories: 230 Protein: 28g Carbs 2g: Fat: 14g

Easy Mahi-Mahi

Servings: 4
Preparation Time: 10 minutes
Cooking Time: 10 minutes
Ingredients:
- 4 (6-ounce) mahi-mahi fillets
- 2 tablespoons olive oil
- Salt and ground black pepper, as required
Directions:
1. Preheat the griddle to 350 degrees F.
2. Coat fish fillets with olive oil and season with salt and black pepper evenly.
3. Place the fish fillets onto the griddle and cook for about 5 minutes per side.
4. Remove the fish fillets from griddle and serve hot.
Nutrition: Calories 195 Total Fat 7 g Saturated Fat 1 g Cholesterol 60 mg Sodium 182 mg Total Carbs 0 g Fiber 0 g Sugar 0 g Protein 31.6g

Wine-Brined Soy Salmon

Servings: 4
Preparation Time: 15 minutes
Cooking Time: 5 hours
Ingredients:
- 2 cups low-sodium soy sauce
- 1 cup dry white wine
- 1 cup water
- ½ teaspoon Tabasco sauce
- ⅓ cup sugar
- ¼ cup salt
- ½ teaspoon garlic powder
- ½ teaspoon onion powder
- Ground black pepper, as required
- 4 (6-ounce) salmon fillets

Directions:
1. In a large bowl, add all ingredients except salmon and stir until sugar is dissolved.
2. Add salmon fillets and coat with brine well.
3. Refrigerate, covered overnight.
4. Remove salmon from bowl and rinse under cold running water.
5. With paper towels, pat dry the salmon fillets.
6. Arrange a wire rack in a sheet pan.
7. Place the salmon fillets onto wire rack, skin side down and set aside to cool for about 1 hour.
8. Preheat the Griddle to 165 degrees F.
9. Arrange the salmon fillets onto the griddle, skin side down and cook for about 3-5 hours or until desired doneness.
10. Remove the salmon fillets from griddle and serve hot.
Nutrition: Calories 379 Total Fat 10.5 g Saturated Fat 1.5 g Cholesterol 75 mg Sodium 14000 mg Total Carbs 26.8 g Fiber 0.1 g Sugar 25.3 g Protein 41.1 g

Tasty Lime Salmon

Servings: 6
Preparation Time: 15 minutes
Cooking Time: 30 minutes
Ingredients:
- 2 (1-pound) salmon fillets
- Salt and ground black pepper, as required
- 1 tablespoon seafood seasoning
- 2 lemons, sliced
- 2 limes, sliced

Directions:
1. Preheat the griddle to 225 degrees F.
2. Season the salmon fillets with salt, black pepper and seafood seasoning evenly.
3. Place the salmon fillets onto the griddle and top each with lemon and lime slices evenly.
4. Cook for about 30 minutes.
5. Remove the salmon fillets from griddle and serve hot.
Nutrition: Calories 327 Total Fat 19.8 g Saturated Fat 3.6 g Cholesterol 81 mg Sodium 237 mg Total Carbs 1 g Fiber 0.3 g Sugar 0.2 g Protein 36.1 g

Enticing Rosemary Trout

Servings: 8

Preparation Time: 10 minutes
Cooking Time: 5 hours
Ingredients:
- 1(7-pound) whole lake trout, butterflied
- ½ cup kosher salt
- ½ cup fresh rosemary, chopped
- 2 teaspoons lemon zest, grated finely

Directions:
1. Rub the trout with salt generously and then, sprinkle with rosemary and lemon zest.
2. Arrange the trout in a large baking dish and refrigerate for about 7-8 hours.
3. Remove the trout from baking dish and rinse under cold running water to remove the salt.
4. With paper towels, pat dry the trout completely.
5. Arrange a wire rack in a sheet pan.
6. Place the trout onto the wire rack, skin side down and refrigerate for about 24 hours.
7. Preheat the griddle to 180 degrees F, using charcoal.
8. Place the trout onto the griddle and cook for about 2-4 hours or until desired doneness.
9. Remove the trout from griddle and place onto a cutting board for about 5 minutes before serving.
Nutrition: Calories 633 Total Fat 31.8 g Saturated Fat 7.9 g Cholesterol 153 mg Sodium 5000 mg Total Carbs 2.4 g Fiber 1.6 g Sugar 0 g Protein 85.2 g

Herbed Lemon Salmon Kebabs

Servings: 4
Preparation Time: 20 minutes
Cooking Time: 25 minutes
Ingredients:
- 2 tbsp of chopped fresh oregano
- 2 tsp of sesame seeds
- 1 tsp ground cumin
- 1 tsp Kosher salt
- ¼ tsp crushed red pepper flakes
- 1 ½ pounds of skinless salmon fillets, cut into 1" pieces
- 2 lemons, thinly sliced into rounds
- 2 tbsp of olive oil
- 16 bamboo skewers, soaked in water for one hour

Intolerances:
- Gluten-Free
- Egg-Free
- Lactose-Free

Directions:
1. Set up the griddle for medium heat. Mix the oregano, sesame seeds, cumin, salt, and red pepper flakes in a little bowl. Put the spice blend aside.
2. String the salmon and the lemon slices onto 8 sets of parallel skewers in order to make 8 kebabs.
3. Spoon with oil and season with the spice blend.
4. Griddle and turn at times until the fish is cooked.
Nutrition: Calories: 230 Fat: 10g Carbs: 1g Protein: 30g

Sesame Flounder Fillet

Servings: 4
Preparation Time: 15 minutes
Cooking Time: 2½ hours
Ingredients:
- ½ cup sesame seeds, toasted
- ½ teaspoon kosher salt flakes
- 1 tablespoon canola oil
- 1 teaspoon sesame oil
- 4 (6-ounce) flounder fillets
Directions:
1. Preheat the griddle to 225 degrees F.
2. With a mortar and pestle, crush sesame seeds with kosher salt slightly.
3. In a small bowl, mix together both oils.
4. Coat fish fillets with oil mixture generously and then, rub with sesame seeds mixture.
5. Place fish fillets onto the lower rack of griddle and cook for about 2-2½ hours.
6. Remove the fish fillets from griddle and serve hot.
Nutrition: Calories 343 Total Fat 16.2 g Saturated Fat 2.3 g Cholesterol 116 mg Sodium 476 mg Total Carbs 4.2 g Fiber 2.1 g Sugar 0.1 g Protein 44.3 g

Garlic Parsley Prawn Skewers

Servings: 5
Preparation Time: 15 minutes
Cooking Time: 8 minutes
Ingredients:
- ¼ cup fresh parsley leaves, minced
- 1 tablespoon garlic, crushed
- 2½ tablespoons olive oil
- 2 tablespoons Thai chili sauce
- 1 tablespoon fresh lime juice
- 1½ pounds prawns, peeled and deveined
Directions:
1. In a large bowl, add all ingredients except for prawns and mix well.
2. In a resealable plastic bag, add marinade and prawns.
3. Seal the bag and shake to coat well
4. Refrigerate for about 20-30 minutes.
5. Preheat the griddle to 450 degrees F.
6. Remove the prawns from marinade and thread onto metal skewers.
7. Arrange the skewers onto the griddle and cook for about 4 minutes per side.
8. Remove the skewers from griddle and serve hot.
Nutrition: Calories 234 Total Fat 9.3 g Saturated Fat 1.7 g Cholesterol 287 mg Sodium 562 mg Total Carbs 4.9 g Fiber 0.1 g Sugar 1.7 g Protein 31.2 g

BBQ Buttered Jumbo Shrimp

Servings: 6
Preparation Time: 15 minutes
Cooking Time: 30 minutes
Ingredients:
- 8 ounces salted butter, melted
- ¼ cup Worcestershire sauce
- ¼ cup fresh parsley, chopped
- 1 lemon, quartered
- 2 pounds jumbo shrimp, peeled and deveined
- 3 tablespoons BBQ rub
Directions:
1. In a metal baking pan, add all ingredients except for shrimp and BBQ rub and mix well.
2. Season the shrimp with BBQ rub evenly.
3. Add shrimp in the pan with butter mixture and coat well.
4. Set aside for about 20-30 minutes.
5. Preheat the griddle to 250 degrees F.
6. Place the pan onto the griddle and cook for about 25-30 minutes.
7. Remove the pan from griddle and serve hot.
Nutrition: Calories 462 Total Fat 33.3 g Saturated Fat 20.2 g Cholesterol 400 mg Sodium 485 mg Total Carbs 4.7 g Fiber 0.2 g Sugar 2.1 g Protein 34.9 g

Garlic Lime Clams Bread

Servings: 4
Preparation Time: 10 minutes
Cooking Time: 25 minutes
Ingredients:
- 6 tbsp unsalted pieces of butter
- 2 large shallots, chopped
- 4 thinly sliced garlic cloves
- 1 tbsp of tomato paste
- 1 cup of beer
- 1 cup cherry tomatoes
- 1 ½ ounce can-chickpeas, rinsed
- 2 tbsp sambal oelek
- 24 scrubbed littleneck clams
- 1 tbsp fresh lime juice
- 4 thick slices of country-style bread
- 2 tbsp olive oil
- Kosher salt
- ½ cup cilantro leaves
- lime wedges
Intolerances:
- Gluten-Free
- Egg-Free
Directions:
1. Set up the griddle for medium, indirect heat. Put a large griddle on the griddle over direct heat and melt 4 tbsp of butter in it.
2. Add the shallots and garlic and keep cooking, often stirring, until they soften, about 4 minutes.
3. Add the tomato paste and keep cooking, continually stirring, until paste darkens to a rich brick red color. Add the beer and tomatoes.
4. Cook until the beer is reduced nearly by half, about 4 minutes. Add in the chickpeas and sambal oelek, then the clams.
5. Cover and keep cooking until clams have opened, maybe from 5 to 10 minutes depending on the size of clams and the heat. Discard any clams that don't open. Pour in the lime juice and the remaining 2 tbsp of butter.
6. While griddling the clams, you can sprinkle the bread with oil and season with salt. Griddle until it becomes golden brown and crisp.
7. Put the toasts onto plates and spoon with clam mixture, then top with cilantro. Serve with lime wedges.
Nutrition: Calories: 400 Fat: 21g Carbs: 33g Protein: 17g

Savory Prosciutto-Wrapped Scallops

Servings: 4
Preparation Time: 15 minutes
Cooking Time: 40 minutes
Ingredients:
- 8 large scallops, shelled and cleaned
- 8 extra-thin prosciutto slices

Directions:
1. Preheat the griddle to 225-250 degrees F.
2. Arrange the prosciutto slices onto a smooth surface.
3. Place 1 scallop on the edge of 1 prosciutto slice and roll it up tucking in the sides of the prosciutto to cover completely.
4. Repeat with remaining scallops and prosciutto slices
5. Arrange the wrapped scallops onto a small wire rack.
6. Place the wire rack onto the griddle and cook for about 40 minutes.
7. Remove the scallops from griddle and serve hot.
Nutrition: Calories 160 Total Fat 6.7 g Saturated Fat 2.3 g Cholesterol 64 mg Sodium 1000 mg Total Carbs 1.4 g Fiber 0 g Sugar 0 g Protein 23.5 g

Garlic Buttered Clams with Parsley

Servings: 6
Preparation Time: 15 minutes
Cooking Time: 8 minutes
Ingredients:
- 24 littleneck clams
- ½ cup cold butter, chopped
- 2 tablespoons fresh parsley, minced
- 3 garlic cloves, minced
- 1 teaspoon fresh lemon juice

Directions:
1. Preheat the griddle to 450 degrees F.
2. Scrub the clams under cold running water.
3. In a large casserole dish, mix together remaining ingredients.
4. Place the casserole dish onto the griddle.
5. Now, arrange the clams directly onto the griddle and cook for about 5-8 minutes or until they are opened. (Discard any that fail to open).
6. With tongs, carefully transfer the opened clams into the casserole dish and remove from the griddle.
7. Serve immediately.
Nutrition: Calories 306 Total Fat 17.6 g Saturated Fat 9.9 g Cholesterol 118 mg Sodium 237 mg Total Carbs 6.4 g Fiber 0.1 g Sugar 0.1 g Protein 29.3 g

Lemony Lobster Tails with Garlic

Servings: 4
Preparation Time: 15 minutes

Cooking Time: 25 hours
Ingredients:
- ½ cup butter, melted
- 2 garlic cloves, minced
- 2 teaspoons fresh lemon juice
- Salt and ground black pepper, as required
- 4 (8-ounce) lobster tails

Directions:
1. Preheat the griddle to 450 degrees F.
2. In a metal pan, add all ingredients except for lobster tails and mix well.
3. Place the pan onto the griddle and cook for about 10 minutes.
4. Meanwhile, cut down the top of the shell and expose lobster meat.
5. Remove pan of butter mixture rom griddle.
6. Coat the lobster meat with butter mixture.
7. Place the lobster tails onto the griddle and cook for about 15 minutes, coating with butter mixture once halfway through.
8. Remove from the griddle and serve hot.
Nutrition: Calories 409 Total Fat 24.9 g Saturated Fat 15.1 g Cholesterol 392 mg Sodium 1305 mg Total Carbs 0.6 g Fiber 0 g Sugar 0.1 g Protein 43.5 g

Buttered Lobster with Parsley

Servings: 4
Preparation Time: 15 minutes
Cooking Time: 40 minutes
Ingredients:
- 1 lobster (or more)
- ½ cup fresh butter
- 2 lemons juice (freshly squeezed)
- 2 tbsp parsley
- Salt and freshly ground pepper to taste
Intolerances:
- Gluten-Free
- Egg-Free

Directions:
1. Use a pot large enough large to hold the lobsters and fill water and salt. Bring to boil and put in lobster. Boil for 4 - 5 minutes.
2. Remove lobster to the working surface.
3. Pull the body to the base of the head and divide the head.
4. Firmly hold the body, with the abdomen upward, and with a sharp knife cut it along in the middle.
5. Start your griddle with the lid open until the fire is established (4 to 5 minutes). Set the temperature to 350ºF and preheat, lid closed for 10 to 15 minutes.
6. Melt the butter and beat it with a lemon juice, parsley, salt, and pepper. Spread butter mixture over lobster and put directly on a griddle grate.
7. Griddle lobsters cut side down about 7 - 8 minutes until the shells are bright in color (also, depends on its size).
8. Turn the lobster over and brush with butter mixture. Griddle for another 4 - 5 minutes.
9. Serve hot sprinkled with lemon butter and parsley finely chopped.
Nutrition: Calories: 385 Fat: 24g Cholesterol: 346mg Carbs: 2g Protein: 37g

Mayo Orange Fish with Salsa Verde

Servings: 4
Preparation Time: 15 minutes
Cooking Time: 30 minutes
Ingredients:
- 2 garlic cloves
- 3 tbsp fresh orange juice
- 1 tsp dried oregano
- 2 cups of chopped white onion
- ¾ cup chopped cilantro
- ¼ cup extra virgin olive oil and more for the griddle
- 5 tbsp fresh lime juice
- 1 lb. of tilapia, striped bass or sturgeon fillets
- Kosher salt and grounded pepper
- 1 cup of mayonnaise
- 1 tbsp of milk
- 4 corn tortillas
- 2 avocados, peeled and sliced
- ½ small head of cabbage, cored and thinly sliced
- Salsa Verde -
- Lime wedges
Intolerances:
- Gluten-Free
- Egg-Free
Directions:
1. Mix the garlic, orange juice, oregano, one cup onion, ¼ cup cilantro, ¼ cup oil, and 3 tbsp of lime juice in a medium bowl.
2. Season the fish with salt and grounded pepper. Spoon the ½ onion mixture on a glass baking dish then put the fish on it.
3. Spoon the remaining onion mixture over the fish and chill for half hour. Turn the fish, cover and chill for another half hour.
4. Mix the mayo, milk, and the remaining two tbsps. of lime juice in a little bowl.
5. Set up the griddle for medium-high heat and brush the grate with oil.
6. Griddle the fish, with some marinade on, till opaque in the center, about 3–5 minutes for each side.
7. Griddle the tortilla still slightly burned, about ten seconds per side. Coarsely chop the fish and put it onto a platter.
8. Serve with lime mayonnaise, tortillas, avocados, cabbage, Salsa Verde, lime wedges and the remaining cup of sliced onion and ½ cup cilantro.
Nutrition: Calories: 270 Fat: 22g Cholesterol: 11mg Carbs: 2g Protein: 20g

Honey Garlic Salmon Steaks

Servings: 4
Preparation Time: 10 minutes
Cooking Time: 20 minutes
Ingredients:
- Vegetable oil (for the griddle)
- 2 serrano chilis
- 2 garlic cloves
- 1 cup cilantro leaves
- ½ cup plain whole-milk Greek yogurt
- 1 tbsp of extra virgin olive oil
- 1 tsp honey
- Kosher salt
- 2 12oz bone-in salmon steaks
Intolerances:
- Gluten-Free
- Egg-Free
Directions:
1. Set up the griddle for medium-high heat, then oil the grate.
2. Expel and dispose of seeds from one chili. Mix the two chilis, garlic, cilantro, the yogurt, oil, the nectar, and ¼ cup water in a blender until it becomes smooth, then season well with salt.
3. Move half of the sauce to a little bowl and put it aside. Season the salmon steaks with salt.
4. Griddle it, turning more than once, until it's beginning to turn dark, about 4 minutes.
5. Keep on griddling, turning frequently, and seasoning with residual sauce for at least 4 minutes longer.
Nutrition: Calories: 290 Fat: 14g Cholesterol: 80g Carbs: 1g Protein: 38g

Marinated Trout with Parsley

Servings: 4
Preparation Time: 20 minutes
Cooking Time: 45 minutes
Ingredients:
- ¼ cup olive oil
- 1 lemon juice
- ½ cup of white wine
- 2 cloves garlic minced
- 2 tbsp fresh parsley, finely chopped
- 1 tsp fresh basil, finely chopped
- Salt and freshly ground black pepper to taste
- 4 trout fish, cleaned
- Lemon slices for garnish
Intolerances:
- Gluten-Free
- Egg-Free
- Lactose-Free
Directions:
1. In a large container, stir olive oil, lemon juice, wine, garlic, parsley, basil and salt and freshly ground black pepper to taste.
2. Submerge fish in sauce and toss to combine well.
3. Cover and marinate in refrigerate overnight.
4. When ready to cook, start the griddle on Smoke with the lid open for 4 to 5 minutes. Set the temperature to 400ºF and preheat, lid closed, for 10 to 15 minutes.
5. Remove the fish from marinade and pat dry on paper towel; reserve marinade.
6. Griddle trout for 5 minutes from both sides (be careful not to overcook the fish).
7. Pour fish with marinade and serve hot with lemon slices.
Nutrition: Calories: 267 Fat: 18g Carbs: 3g Protein: 16g

Savory Scallops with Lemony Salsa Verde

Servings: 2
Preparation Time: 15 minutes
Cooking Time: 15 minutes
Ingredients:
• 2 tbsp of vegetable oil and more for the griddle
• 12 large sea scallops, side muscle removed
• Kosher salt and grounded black pepper
• Lemony Salsa Verde
Intolerances:
• Gluten-Free - Egg-Free - Lactose-Free
Directions:
1. Set up the griddle for medium-high heat, then oil the grate. Toss the scallops with 2 tbsp of oil on a rimmed baking sheet and season with salt and pepper.
2. Utilizing a fish spatula or your hands, place the scallops on the griddle.
3. Griddle them, occasionally turning, until gently singed and cooked through, around 2 minutes for each side.
4. Serve the scallops with Lemony Salsa Verde.
Nutrition: Calories: 30 Fat: 1g Cholesterol: 17mg Carbs: 1g Protein: 6g

Basil Sea Scallops and Corn Salad

Servings: 6
Preparation Time: 25 minutes
Cooking Time: 30 minutes
Ingredients:
• 6 shucked ears of corn
• 1-pint grape tomatoes, halved
• 3 sliced scallions, white and light green parts only
• ⅓ cup basil leaves, finely shredded
• Salt and grounded pepper
• 1 small shallot, minced
• 2 tbsp balsamic vinegar
• 2 tbsp hot water
• 1 tsp Dijon mustard ¼ cup
• 3 tbsp sunflower oil
• 1 ½ pounds sea scallops
Intolerances:
• Gluten-Free
• Egg-Free
• Lactose-Free
Directions:
1. In a pot of boiling salted water, cook the corn for about 5 minutes. Drain and cool.
2. Place the corn into a big bowl and cut off the kernels. Add the tomatoes, the scallions and basil then season with salt and grounded pepper.
3. In a blender, mix the minced shallot with the vinegar, heated water, and mustard. With the blender on, gradually add 6 tbsps. of the sunflower oil.
4. Season the vinaigrette with salt and pepper; at that point, add it to the corn salad.

5. In a huge bowl, toss the remaining 1 tbsp. of oil with the scallops, then season with salt and grounded pepper.
6. Heat a griddle pan. Put on half of the scallops and griddle over high heat, turning once, until singed, around 4 minutes.
7. Repeat with the other half of the scallops. Place the corn salad on plates, then top with the scallops and serve.
Nutrition: Calories: 230 Fat: 5g Cholesterol: 60mg Carbs: 13g Protein: 33g

Herbed Oysters with Tequila Butter

Servings: 6
Preparation Time: 20 minutes
Cooking Time: 25 minutes
Ingredients:
• ½ tsp fennel seeds
• ¼ tsp crushed red pepper
• 7 tbsp of unsalted butter
• ¼ cup of sage leaves, plus 36 small leaves for the garnish
• 1 tsp of dried oregano
• 2 tbsp lemon juice
• 2 tbsp of tequila
• Kosher salt
• rock salt, for the serving
• 3 dozen scrubbed medium oysters
Intolerances:
• Gluten-Free
• Egg-Free
• Lactose-Free
Directions:
1. Using a griddle, toast the fennel seeds and squashed red pepper over moderate heat until fragrant for 1 minute.
2. Move onto a mortar and let it cool. With a pestle, pound the spices to a coarse powder, then move into a bowl.
3. Using the same griddle, cook 3 ½ tbsp. of the butter over moderate heat until it becomes dark-colored, about two minutes. Add ¼ cup of sage and keep cooking, occasionally turning, for about 2 minutes. Move the sage onto a plate. Transfer the butter into the bowl with the spices. Repeat with the remaining butter and sage leaves. Put some aside for decoration.
4. Put the fried sage leaves onto the mortar and squash them with the pestle. Add the squashed sage to the butter along with the oregano, lemon juice, and tequila and season with salt. Keep warm.
5. Set up the griddle. Line a platter with rock salt. Griddle the oysters over high heat until they open, about 1 to 2 minutes.
6. Dispose of the top shell and spot the oysters on the rock salt, being careful not to spill their juice. Spoon the warm tequila sauce over the oysters, decorate with a fresh sage leaf, and serve.
Nutrition: Calories: 68 Fat: 3g Carbs: 4g Protein: 10g

Oregano Cuttlefish and Spinach Salad

Servings: 6
Preparation Time: 15 minutes
Cooking Time: 30 minutes
Ingredients:
- ½ cup of olive oil
- 1 tbsp of lemon juice
- 1 tsp oregano
- Pinch of salt
- 8 large cuttlefish, cleaned
- Spinach, pine nuts, olive oil and vinegar for serving

Intolerances:
- Gluten-Free
- Egg-Free
- Lactose-Free

Directions:
1. Prepare marinade with olive oil, lemon juice, oregano and a pinch of salt pepper (be careful, cuttlefish do not need too much salt).
2. Place the cuttlefish in the marinade, tossing to cover evenly. Cover and marinate for about 1 hour.
3. Remove the cuttlefish from marinade and pat dry them on paper towel.
4. Start the griddle, and set the temperature to high and preheat, lid closed, for 10 to 15 minutes.
5. Griddle the cuttlefish just 3 - 4 minutes on each side.
6. Serve hot with spinach, pine nuts, olive oil, and vinegar.
Nutrition: Calories: 299 Fat: 19g Cholesterol: 186mg Carbs: 3g Protein: 28g

Dijon Rosemary Catfish Fillets

Servings: 6
Preparation Time: 15 minutes
Cooking Time: 25 minutes
Ingredients:
- ½ cup olive oil
- Juice of 4 lemons
- 2 tbsp Dijon mustard
- ½ tsp salt
- 1 tsp paprika
- Fresh rosemary chopped
- 4 (6- to 8-oz.) catfish fillets, ½-inch thick

Intolerances:
- Gluten-Free
- Egg-Free
- Lactose-Free

Directions:
1. Set the temperature to Medium and preheat, lid closed, for 10 to 15 minutes.
2. Whisk the olive oil, lemon juice, mustard, salt, paprika and chopped rosemary in a bowl.
3. Brush one side of each fish fillet with half of the olive oil-lemon mixture; season with salt and pepper to taste.
4. Griddle fillets, covered, 4 to 5 minutes. Turn fillets and brush with remaining olive oil-lemon mixture.
5. Griddle 4 to 5 minutes more (do not cover).
6. Remove fish fillets to a serving platter, sprinkle with rosemary and serve.

Nutrition: Calories: 295 Fat: 24g Cholesterol: 58mg Carbs: 3g Protein: 16g

Mirin Soy Squid

Servings: 4
Preparation Time: 15 minutes
Cooking Time: 45 minutes
Ingredients:
- 1 cup mirin
- 1 cup of soy sauce
- ⅓ cup yuzu juice or fresh lemon juice
- 2 cups of water
- 2 pounds squid tentacles left whole; bodies cut crosswise 1 inch thick

Intolerances:
- Gluten-Free
- Egg-Free
- Lactose-Free

Directions:
1. In a bowl, mix the mirin, soy sauce, the yuzu juice, and water.
2. Put a bit of the marinade in a container and refrigerate it for later use.
3. Add the squid to the bowl with the rest of the marinade and let it sit for about 30 minutes or refrigerate for 4 hours.
4. Set up the griddle. Drain the squid.
5. Griddle over medium-high heat, turning once until white all through for 3 minutes.
6. Serve hot.
Nutrition: Calories: 110 Fat: 6g Carbs: 6g Protein: 8g

Buttered Codwith Onion

Servings: 4
Preparation Time: 10 minutes
Cooking Time: 15 minutes
Ingredients:
- ¼ cup butter
- 1 finely chopped small onion
- ¼ cup white wine
- 4 (6ounce) cod fillets
- 1 tbsp of extra virgin olive oil
- ½ tsp salt (or to taste)
- ½ tsp black pepper
- Lemon wedges

Intolerances:
- Gluten-Free
- Egg-Free

Directions:
1. Set up the griddle for medium-high heat.
2. In a little griddle liquefy the butter. Add the onion and cook for 1or2 minutes.
3. Add the white wine and let stew for an extra 3 minutes. Take away and let it cool for 5 minutes.
4. Spoon the fillets with extra virgin olive oil and sprinkle with salt and pepper. Put the fish on a well-oiled rack and cook for 8 minutes.
5. Season it with sauce and cautiously flip it over. Cook for 6 to 7 minutes more, turning more times or until the fish arrives at an inside temperature of 145ºF.
6. Take away from the griddle, top with lemon wedges, and serve.
Nutrition: Calories: 140 Fat: 5g Cholesterol: 46mg Carbs: 4g Protein: 20g

Oregano Lemon Calamari with Mustard

Servings: 6
Preparation Time: 10 minutes
Cooking Time: 35 minutes
Ingredients:
- 8 Calamari, cleaned
- 2 cups of milk
- Sauce
- 4 tsp of sweet mustard
- Juice from 2 lemons
- ½ cup of olive oil
- 2 tbsp fresh oregano, finely chopped
- Pepper, ground
- ½ bunch of parsley, finely chopped

Intolerances:
- Gluten-Free
- Egg-Free
- Lactose-Free

Directions:
1. Clean calamari well and cut into slices.
2. Place calamari in a large metal bow, cover and marinate with milk overnight.
3. Remove calamari from the milk and drain well on paper towel. Grease the fish lightly with olive oil.
4. In a bowl, combine mustard and the juice from the two lemons.
5. Beat lightly and pour the olive oil very slowly; stir until all the ingredients are combined well.
6. Add the oregano and pepper and stir well.
7. Start the griddle and set the temperature to moderate; preheat, lid closed, for 10 to 15 minutes.
8. Place the calamari on the griddle and cook for 2-3 minutes per side or until it has a bit of char and remove from the griddle.
9. Transfer calamari to serving platter and pour them over with mustard sauce and chopped parsley.

Nutrition: Calories: 212 Fat: 19g Cholesterol: 651mg Carbs: 7g Protein: 3g

Rosemary Chili Halibut Fillets

Servings: 6
Preparation Time: 15 minutes
Cooking Time: 55 minutes
Ingredients:
- 1 cup of virgin olive oil
- 2 large red chili peppers, chopped
- 2 cloves garlic, cut into quarters
- 1 bay leaf
- 1 twig of rosemary
- 2 lemons
- 4 tbsp of white vinegar
- 4 halibut fillets

Intolerances:
- Gluten-Free
- Egg-Free
- Lactose-Free

Directions:
1. In a large container, mix olive oil, chopped red chili, garlic, bay leaf, rosemary, lemon juice and white vinegar. Submerge halibut fillets and toss to combine well.
2. Cover and marinate in the refrigerator for several hours or overnight. Remove anchovies from marinade and pat dry on paper towels for 30 minutes.
3. Start the griddle, set the temperature to medium and preheat, lid closed for 10 to 15 minutes. Griddle the anchovies, skin side down for about 10 minutes, or until the flesh of the fish becomes white (thinner cuts and fillets can cook in as little time as 6 minutes).
4. Turn once during cooking to avoid having the halibut fall apart. Transfer to a large serving platter, pour a little lemon juice over the fish, sprinkle with rosemary and serve.
Nutrition: Calories: 259 Fat: 4g Cholesterol: 133mg Carbs: 5g Protein: 51g

Montreal Seasoned Cornish Hen

Servings: 2
Preparation Time: 10 minutes
Cooking Time: 60 minutes
Ingredients:
* 1 cornish hen
* 1 tbsp olive oil
* 1 tbsp Montreal chicken seasoning

Directions:
1. Cut the backbone of hens and flatten the breastplate.
2. Brush hen with oil and rub with Montreal chicken seasoning.
3. Wrap hens in plastic wrap and place in the refrigerator for 4 hours.
4. Preheat the griddle to high heat.
5. Spray griddle top with cooking spray.
6. Place marinated hen on hot griddle top and cook for 60 minutes or until internal temperature reaches 180 F.
7. Serve and enjoy.
Nutrition: Calories 228 Fat 18 g Carbohydrates 0 g Sugar 0 g Protein 14 g Cholesterol 85 mg

Glazed Orange Cornish Hen

Servings: 2
Preparation Time: 10 minutes
Cooking Time: 60 minutes
Ingredients:
* 1 cornish hen
* ¼ onion, cut into chunks
* ¼ orange cut into wedges
* 2 garlic cloves
* 4 fresh sage leaves
* 1 ½ fresh rosemary sprigs
* For glaze:
* 2-star anise
* 1 tbsp honey
* 1 cup orange juice
* ¼ fresh orange, sliced
* ½ orange zest
* 1.5 oz Grand Marnier
* ½ cinnamon stick

Directions:
1. Stuff hen with orange wedges, garlic, onions, and herbs. Season with pepper and salt.
2. Preheat the griddle to high heat.
3. Spray griddle top with cooking spray.
4. Place hen on hot griddle top and cook for 60 minutes or until the internal temperature of hens reaches 165 F.
5. Meanwhile, in a saucepan heat, all glaze ingredients until reduce by half over medium-high heat.
6. Brush hen with glaze.
7. Slice and serve.
Nutrition: Calories 351 Fat 12.1 g Carbohydrates 29.2 g Sugar 40.9 g Protein 16 g Cholesterol 85 mg

Marinated Cornish Hen with Cinnamon

Servings: 2
Preparation Time: 10 minutes
Cooking Time: 60 minutes
Ingredients:
* 1 cornish hen
* 1 cup cold water
* 16 oz apple juice
* ⅛ cup brown sugar
* 1 cinnamon stick
* 1 cup hot water
* ¼ cup kosher salt

Directions:
1. Add cinnamon, hot water, cold water, apple juice, brown sugar, and salt into the large pot and stir until sugar is dissolved.
2. Add hen in the brine and place in the refrigerator for 4 hours.
3. Preheat the griddle to high heat.
4. Spray griddle top with cooking spray.
5. Remove hens from brine and place on hot griddle top and cook for 60 minutes or until internal temperature reaches 160 F.
6. Slice and serve.
Nutrition: Calories 938 Fat 9.5 g Carbohydrates 232 g Sugar 200 g Protein 10 g Cholesterol 51 mg

Scrumptious Garlic Honey Cornish Hen

Servings: 2
Preparation Time: 10 minutes
Cooking Time: 60 minutes
Ingredients:
* 1 cornish hen
* 2 garlic cloves, minced
* ⅛ cup honey
* ¼ cup soy sauce
* ¾ cup warm water
* 1 tbsp cornstarch
* ¼ cup brown sugar

Directions:
1. Mix together soy sauce, warm water, brown sugar, garlic, cornstarch, and honey.
2. Place Cornish hen in baking dish and season with pepper and salt.
3. Pour marinade over hen and place in the refrigerator for 10 hours.
4. Preheat the griddle to high heat.
5. Spray griddle top with cooking spray. Place marinated hen on hot griddle top and cook for 60 minutes or until internal temperature reaches 165 F.
6. Serve and enjoy.
Nutrition: Calories 338 Fat 11.8 g Carbohydrates 42.3 g Sugar 35.6 g Protein 16.6 g Cholesterol 85 mg

Buttered Rosemary Hen

Servings: 2
Preparation Time: 10 minutes
Cooking Time: 60 minutes
Ingredients:
- 1 cornish game hen
- 1 tbsp butter, melted
- ½ tbsp rosemary, minced
- 1 tsp chicken rub

Directions:
1. Brush hens with melted butter.
2. Mix together rosemary and chicken rub.
3. Rub hen with rosemary and chicken rub mixture.
4. Preheat the griddle to high heat.
5. Spray griddle top with cooking spray.
6. Place hen on hot griddle top and cook for 60 minutes or until internal temperature reaches 165 F.
7. Serve and enjoy.
Nutrition: Calories 221 Fat 17 g Carbohydrates 0.5 g Sugar 0 g Protein 14.5 g Cholesterol 100 mg

BBQ Griddle Hen

Servings: 8
Preparation Time: 10 minutes
Cooking Time: 1 hour 30 minutes
Ingredients:
- 1 cornish hen
- 2 tbsp BBQ rub

Directions:
1. Preheat the griddle to high heat.
2. Spray griddle top with cooking spray.
3. Coat hens with BBQ rub and place on hot griddle top and cook for 1 ½ hours or until the internal temperature of hens reach 165 F.
4. Slice and serve.
Nutrition: Calories 168 Fat 11 g Carbohydrates 0 g Sugar 0 g Protein 14 g Cholesterol 85 mg

Herbed Cornish Hen with Paprika

Servings: 2
Preparation Time: 10 minutes
Cooking Time: 60 minutes
Ingredients:
- 1 cornish hen
- ½ tbsp paprika
- ¼ tsp pepper
- ¼ tsp sage
- ½ tsp thyme
- ½ tbsp onion powder

Directions:
1. In a small bowl, mix together paprika, onion powder, thyme, sage, and pepper.
2. Rub hen with paprika mixture.
3. Preheat the griddle to high heat.
4. Spray griddle top with cooking spray.
5. Place hen on hot griddle top and cook for 60 minutes or until internal temperature reaches 185 F.
6. Serve and enjoy.
Nutrition: Calories 180 Fat 12 g Carbohydrates 2.7 g Sugar 0.8 g Protein 14.9 g Cholesterol 85 mg

Asian Spiced Cornish Hen

Servings: 2
Preparation Time: 10 minutes
Cooking Time: 60 minutes
Ingredients:
- 1 cornish hen
- 1 ½ tsp Chinese five-spice powder
- 1 ½ tsp rice wine
- ½ tsp pepper
- 2 cups of water
- 3 tbsp soy sauce
- 2 tbsp sugar
- Salt

Directions:
1. In a large bowl, mix together water, soy sauce, sugar, rice wine, five-spice, pepper, and salt.
2. Place Cornish hen in the bowl and place in the refrigerator for overnight.
3. Preheat the griddle to high heat.
4. Spray griddle top with cooking spray.
5. Remove Cornish hen from marinade and place on hot griddle top and cook for 60 minutes or until internal temperature reaches 185 F.
6. Slice and serve.
Nutrition: Calories 233 Fat 11.8 g Carbohydrates 15.9 g Sugar 13.4 g Protein 15.9 g Cholesterol 85 mg

Rosemary Butter Griddle Cornish Hen

Servings: 2
Preparation Time: 10 minutes
Cooking Time: 60 minutes
Ingredients:
- 1 cornish hen, rinse and pat dry with paper towels
- 1 tbsp butter, melted
- 1 rosemary sprigs
- 1 tsp poultry seasoning

Directions:
1. Stuff rosemary sprigs into the hen cavity.
2. Brush hen with melted butter and season with poultry seasoning.
3. Preheat the griddle to high heat.
4. Spray griddle top with cooking spray.
5. Place hen on hot griddle top and cook for 60 minutes or until the internal temperature of hens reaches 165 F.
6. Slice and serve.
Nutrition: Calories 127 Fat 8 g Carbohydrates 0.5 g Sugar 0 g Protein 13 g Cholesterol 74 mg

Tasty Cornish Game Hen

Servings: 2
Preparation Time: 10 minutes
Cooking Time: 60 minutes

Ingredients:
- 1 cornish game hen
- ½ tbsp olive oil
- ¼ tbsp poultry seasoning

Directions:
1. Brush hen with oil and rub with poultry seasoning.
2. Preheat the griddle to high heat.
3. Spray griddle top with cooking spray.
4. Place hen on hot griddle top and cook from all the sides until brown.
5. Cover hen with lid or pan and cook for 60 minutes or until the internal temperature of hen reaches 180 F.
6. Slice and serve.

Nutrition: Calories 366 Fat 26.9 g Carbohydrates 0.3 g Sugar 0 g Protein 28 g Cholesterol 168 mg

Cheese Stuffed Jalapeno Peppers

Servings: 10
Preparation Time: 30 minutes
Cooking Time: 1 hour and 30 minutes
Ingredients:
• 8 ounces regular cream cheese (room temp)
• 10 jalapeno peppers (medium)
• ¾ cup cheddar cheese blend and shredded Monterey Jack (not necessary)
• 1 teaspoon smoked paprika
• 1 teaspoon garlic powder
• ½ teaspoon red pepper flakes (not necessary)
• Little Smokies sausages (20)
• 10 bacon strips, thinly sliced and halved
Intolerances:
• Egg-Free
Directions:
1. Wash the jalapenos, then slice them up along the length. Get a spoon, or a paring knife if you prefer, and use that to take out the seeds and the veins.
2. Place the scooped-out jalapenos on a veggie griddleing tray and put it all aside.
3. Get a small bowl and mix the shredded cheese, cream cheese, paprika, cayenne pepper, garlic powder, and red pepper flakes. Mix them thoroughly.
4. Get your jalapenos which you've hollowed out, and then stuff them with the cream cheese mix.
5. Get your little Smokies sausage, and then put it right onto each of the cheese stuffed jalapenos.
6. Grab some of the thinly sliced and halved bacon strips and wrap them around each of the stuffed jalapenos and their sausage.
7. Grab some toothpicks. Use them to keep the bacon nicely secured to the sausage.
8. Set up your griddle so it's ready for indirect cooking. Get it preheated to 250ºF.
9. Put your jalapeno peppers in and smoke them at 250ºF for anywhere from 90 minutes to 120 minutes. You want to keep it going until the bacon is nice and crispy.
10. Take out the atomic buffalo turds, and then let them rest for about 5 minutes. Serve!
Nutrition: Calories: 198 Fat: 17g Cholesterol: 48mg Carbs: 3g Protein: 8g

Brisket and Beans

Servings: 10
Preparation Time: 20 minutes
Cooking Time: 1 hour and 30 minutes
Ingredients:
• 1 green bell pepper (medium, diced)
• 1 red bell pepper (medium, diced)
• 1 yellow onion (large, diced)
• 2 - 6 jalapeno peppers (diced)
• 2 tablespoons olive oil (extra-virgin)
• 3 cups brisket flat (chopped)
• 1 can baked beans (28 ounces)
• 1 can red kidney beans (1 4ounces, rinsed, drained)
• 1 cup barbecue sauce
• ½ cup brown sugar (packed)
• 2 teaspoons mustard (ground)
• 3 cloves of garlic (chopped)
• 1 ½ teaspoon black pepper
• 1 ½ teaspoon kosher salt
Intolerances:
• Gluten-Free Egg-Free
• Lactose-Free
Directions:
1. Put a griddle on the fire, on medium heat. Warm up your olive oil. Toss in the diced jalapenos, peppers, and onions. Stir every now and then for 8 minutes.
2. Grab a 4-quart casserole dish. Now, in your dish, mix in the pork and beans, kidney beans, baked beans, chopped brisket, cooked peppers and onions, brown sugar, barbecue sauce, garlic, mustard, salt, and black pepper.
3. Set up your griddle so it's ready for indirect cooking.
4. Preheat your griddle to 325ºF.
5. Cook your brisket beans on the griddle, for 90 minutes to 120 minutes. Keep it uncovered as you cook. When it's ready, you'll know, because the beans will get thicker and will have bubbles as well.
6. Rest the food for 15 minutes, before you finally move on to step number 5.
7. Serve!
Nutrition: Calories: 200 Fat: 2g Cholesterol: 10mg Carbs: 35g Protein: 9g

Taco Chicken Drumsticks

Servings: 8
Preparation Time: 10 minutes
Cooking Time: 30 minutes
Ingredients:
• 2 lbs. Chicken legs
• 2 tbsps. Taco seasoning
• 2 tbsps. Olive oil
Intolerances:
• Gluten-Free
• Egg-Free
• Lactose-Free
Directions:
1. Preheat the griddle to a medium-high heat and oil grates.
2. Brush chicken legs with oil and rub with taco seasoning.
3. Place chicken legs on the hot griddle and cook for 30 minutes.
4. Turn chicken legs after every 10 minutes.
5. Serve.
Nutrition: Calories: 165 Fat: 12g Carbs: 1g Protein: 10g

Twice-Baked Spaghetti Squash with Cheeses

Servings: 2
Preparation Time: 15 minutes
Cooking Time: 1 hour
Ingredients:
- 1 spaghetti squash (medium)
- 1 tablespoon olive oil (extra virgin)
- 1 teaspoon salt
- ½ teaspoon pepper
- ½ cup Parmesan cheese (grated, divided)
- ½ cup mozzarella cheese (shredded, divided)

Intolerances:
- Egg-Free

Directions:
1. Cut the squash along the length in half. Make sure you're using a knife that's large enough, and sharp enough. Once you're done, take out the pulp and the seeds from each half with a spoon.
2. Rub the insides of each half of the squash with some olive oil. When you're done with that, sprinkle the salt and pepper.
3. Set up your griddle for indirect cooking.
4. Preheat your griddle to 375ºF.
5. Put each half of the squash on the griddle. Make sure they're both facing upwards on the griddle grates, which should be nice and hot.
6. Bake for 45 minutes, keeping it on the griddle until the internal temperature of the squash hits 170ºF. You'll know you're done when you find it easy to pierce the squash with a fork.
7. Move the squash to your cutting board. Let it sit there for 10 minutes so that it can cool a bit.
8. Turn up the temp on your griddle to 425ºF.
9. Use a fork to remove the flesh from the squash in strands by raking it back and forth. Do be careful, because you want the shells to remain intact. The strands you rake off should look like spaghetti, if you're doing it right.
10. Put the spaghetti squash strands in a large bowl, and then add in half of your mozzarella and half of your Parmesan cheeses. Combine them by stirring.
11. Take the mix, and stuff it into the squash shells. When you're done, sprinkle them with the rest of the Parmesan and mozzarella cheeses. Optional: You can top these with some bacon bits, if you like.
12. Allow the stuffed spaghetti squash shells you've now stuffed to bake at 435ºF for 15 minutes, or however long it takes the cheese to go brown.
13. Serve and enjoy.
Nutrition: Calories: 214 Fat: 3g Cholesterol: 17mg Carbs: 27g Protein: 16g

Healthy Bacon-Wrapped Asparagus

Servings: 6
Preparation Time: 15 minutes
Cooking Time: 25 - 30 minutes
Ingredients:
- 15 - 20 spears of fresh asparagus (1 pound)
- Olive oil (extra virgin)
- 5 slices bacon (thinly sliced)
- 1 teaspoon salt and pepper (or your preferred rub)

Intolerances:
- Gluten-Free
- Egg-Free
- Lactose-Free

Directions:
1. Break off the ends of the asparagus, then trim it all so they're down to the same length.
2. Separate the asparagus into bundles—3 spears per bundle. Then spritz them with some olive oil.
3. Use a piece of bacon to wrap up each bundle. When you're done, lightly dust the wrapped bundle with some salt and pepper to taste, or your preferred rub.
4. Set up your griddle so that it's ready for indirect cooking.
5. Put some fiberglass mats on your grates. Make sure they're the fiberglass kind. This will keep your asparagus from getting stuck on your griddle gates.
6. Preheat your griddle to 400ºF.
7. Griddle the wraps for 25 minutes to 30 minutes, tops. The goal is to get your asparagus looking nice and tender, and the bacon deliciously crispy.
Nutrition: Calories: 71 Fat: 3g Carbs: 1g Protein: 6g

Mayo Potato Skewers

Servings: 8
Preparation Time: 15 minutes
Cooking Time: 25 minutes
Ingredients:
- 2 lbs. quartered Potatoes
- 1 tsp. Garlic powder
- 2 tsps. Crushed dried rosemary
- 4 tbsps. Dry white wine
- ½ cup Mayonnaise
- ½ cup Water

Intolerances:
- Gluten-Free
- Egg-Free
- Lactose-Free

Directions:
1. Add potatoes and water in a microwave-safe bowl and cook in the microwave for 15 minutes or until potatoes are tender.
2. Drain potatoes well and let them cool. In a large mixing bowl, stir together mayonnaise, garlic powder, rosemary, and wine.
3. Add potatoes and toss to coat. Cover bowl and place in the refrigerator for 1 hour.
4. Preheat the griddle to a high heat and oil grates. Remove potatoes from the marinade and thread onto the skewers.
5. Place potato skewers on a hot griddle, cover, and cook for 6-8 minutes. Turn skewers halfway through.
6. Serve.
Nutrition: Calories: 135 Fat: 5g Carbs: 20g Protein: 2g

Garlic Parmesan Potato Wedges

Servings: 3
Preparation Time: 15 minutes
Cooking Time: 35 minutes
Ingredients:
- 3 russet potatoes (large)
- 2 teaspoons of garlic powder
- ¾ teaspoon black pepper
- 1 ½ teaspoons of salt
- ¾ cup Parmesan cheese (grated)
- 3 tablespoons fresh cilantro (chopped, optional. You can replace this with flat-leaf parsley)
- ½ cup blue cheese (per serving, as optional dip. Can be replaced with ranch dressing)

Intolerances:
- Gluten-Free
- Egg-Free

Directions:
1. Use some cold water to scrub your potatoes as gently as you can with a veggie brush. When done, let them dry.
2. Slice your potatoes along the length in half. Cut each half into a third.
3. Get all the extra moisture off your potato by wiping it all away with a paper towel. If you don't do this, then you're not going to have crispy wedges!
4. In a large bowl, throw in your potato wedges, some olive oil, garlic powder, salt, garlic, and pepper, and then toss them with your hands, lightly. You want to make sure the spices and oil get on every wedge.
5. Place your wedges on a nonstick tray, or pan, or basked. The single layer kind. Make sure it's at least 15 x 12 inches.
6. Set up your griddle so it's ready for indirect cooking.
7. Preheat your griddle to 425ºF.
8. Set the tray upon your preheated griddle. Roast the wedges for 15 minutes before you flip them. Once you turn them, roast them for another 15 minutes, or 20 tops. The outside should be a nice, crispy, golden brown.
9. Sprinkle your wedges generously with the Parmesan cheese. When you're done, garnish it with some parsley, or cilantro, if you like. Serve these bad boys up with some ranch dressing, or some blue cheese, or just eat them that way!
Nutrition: Calories: 194 Fat: 5g Cholesterol: 5mg Carbs: 32g Protein: 5g

Mayo Bacon Cheddar Beef Slider

Servings: 2
Preparation Time: 30 minutes
Cooking Time: 15 minutes
Ingredients:
- 1 pound ground beef (80% lean)
- ½ teaspoon of garlic salt
- ½ teaspoon salt
- ½ teaspoon of garlic
- ½ teaspoon onion
- ½ teaspoon black pepper
- 6 bacon slices, cut in half
- ½ Cup mayonnaise
- 2 teaspoons of creamy wasabi (optional)
- 6 (1 oz) sliced sharp cheddar cheese, cut in half (optional)
- Sliced red onion
- ½ Cup sliced kosher dill pickles
- 12 mini breads sliced horizontally
- Ketchup

Intolerances:
- Egg-Free

Directions:
1. Place ground beef, garlic salt, seasoned salt, garlic powder, onion powder and black hupe pepper in a medium bowl.
2. Divide the meat mixture into 12 equal parts, shape into small thin round patties (about 2 ounces each) and save.
3. Cook the bacon on medium heat over medium heat for 5-8 minutes until crunchy. Set aside.
4. To make the sauce, mix the mayonnaise and horseradish in a small bowl, if used.
5. Preheat griddle to 350°F. Griddle surface should be approximately 400°F.
6. Spray a cooking spray on the griddle cooking surface for best non-stick results.
7. Griddle the putty for 3-4 minutes each until the internal temperature reaches 160°F.
8. If necessary, place a sharp cheddar cheese slice on each patty while the patty is on the griddle or after the patty is removed from the griddle.
9. Place a small amount of mayonnaise mixture, a slice of red onion, and a hamburger pate in the lower half of each roll.
10. Pickled slices, bacon and ketchup.
Nutrition: Calories: 160 Fat: 11g Carbs: 20g Protein: 10g

Sweet Potato Sticks

Servings: 4
Preparation Time: 10 minutes
Cooking Time: 12 minutes
Ingredients:
- 2 lbs. peeled and cut into ½-inch wedges Sweet potatoes
- 2 tbsps. Olive oil
- Pepper and salt to taste

Intolerances:
- Gluten-Free Egg-Free
- Lactose-Free

Directions:
1. Preheat the griddle to medium-high heat.
2. Toss sweet potatoes with oil, pepper, and salt.
3. Place sweet potato wedges on a hot griddle and cook over a medium heat for 6 minutes.
4. Flip and cook for 6-8 minutes more. Serve.
Nutrition: Calories: 230 Fat: 6g Carbs: 40g Protein: 4g

Mashed Potato and Bacon Casserole

Servings: 8
Preparation Time: 30 minutes
Cooking Time: 45 - 60 minutes
Ingredients:
* 1 small red onion, thinly sliced
* 1 small green bell pepper, thinly sliced
* 1 small red bell pepper, thinly sliced
* 1 small yellow bell pepper, thinly sliced
* 3 cups mashed potatoes
* 8 - 10 bacon slices
* ¼ cup bacon grease or salted butter (½ stick)
* ¾ cup sour cream
* 1 ½ teaspoons barbecue rub
* 3 cups shredded sharp cheddar cheese (divided)
* 4 cups hash brown potatoes (frozen)
Intolerances:
* Gluten-Free Egg-Free
Directions:
1. Get that bacon cooking over medium heat in a large griddle. Cook till nice and crisp. Aim for 5 minutes on both sides. Then set aside your bacon.
2. Pour the bacon grease into a glass container and set aside.
3. Using the same griddle, warm up the butter or bacon grease over medium heat. When warm enough, sauté bell peppers and red onions. You're aiming for al dente. When done, set it all aside.
4. Grab a casserole dish, preferably one that is 9 by 11 inches. Spray with some nonstick cooking spray, then spread the mashed potatoes out, covering the entire bottom of the dish. Add the sour cream to the next layer over the potatoes. When you're done, season it with some of the barbecue rub. Create a new layer with the sautéed veggies over the potatoes, leaving the butter or grease in the pan.
5. Sprinkle your sharp cheddar cheese—just 1½ of the cups. Then add the frozen hash brown potatoes. Scoop out the rest of the bacon grease or butter from the sautéed veggies, all over the hash browns, and then top it all off with some delicious crumbled bacon bits.
6. Add the rest of the sharp cheddar cheese (1½ cups) over the whole thing, and then use some aluminum foil to cover the casserole dish.
7. Set up your griddle for indirect cooking. Preheat to 350ºF. Let the whole thing bake for 45 - 60 minutes. Ideally, you want the cheese to bubble. Take it out and let it sit for about 10 minutes. Serve!
Nutrition: Calories: 232 Fat: 2g Carbs: 48g Protein: 9g

BBQ Smoked Parmesan Moink Ball Skewers

Servings: 6
Preparation Time: 30 minutes

Cooking Time: 1 hour and 15 minutes
Ingredients:
* ½ pound pork sausage (ground)
* ½ pound ground beef (80% lean)
* 1 egg (large)
* ½ cup red onions (minced)
* ½ cup Parmesan cheese (grated)
* ½ cup Italian breadcrumbs
* ¼ cup parsley (finely chopped)
* ¼ cup milk (whole)
* 2 garlic cloves (minced) or 1 teaspoon garlic (crushed)
* 1 teaspoon oregano
* ½ teaspoon kosher salt
* ½ teaspoon black pepper
* ¼ cup barbecue sauce
* ½ pound bacon slices (thinly sliced, halved)
Intolerances:
* Egg-Free
Directions:
1. Mix up the ground pork sausage, ground beef, breadcrumbs, onion, egg, parsley, Parmesan cheese, garlic, milk, oregano, salt, and pepper in a large bowl. Whatever you do, don't overwork your meat.
2. Make meatballs of 1½ ounces each. They should be about 1½ in width. Put them on your Teflon-coated fiberglass mat.
3. Wrap up each meatball in half a slice of your thinly sliced bacon.
4. Spear your moink balls, three to a skewer.
5. Set up your griddle so that it's nice and ready for indirect cooking.
6. Preheat your griddle to 225ºF.
7. Smoke the skewered moink balls for half an hour.
8. Turn up the temperature to 350ºF, and keep it that way until the internal temperature of your skewered moink balls hits 175ºF, which should take about 40 to 45 minutes, max.
9. When the bacon gets nice and crispy, brush your moink balls with whatever barbecue sauce you like. Ideally, you should do this in the last five minutes of your cook time.
10. Serve the moink ball skewers while they're hot.
Nutrition: Calories: 314 Fat: 28g Protein: 15g

Stuffed Portobello Mushrooms

Servings: 6
Preparation Time: 20 minutes
Cooking Time: 30 – 45 minutes
Ingredients:
- 6 medium-sized portobello mushrooms
- Extra virgin olive oil
- ⅓ Grated parmesan cheese cup
- Club Beat Staffing:
- 8 oz fresh crab meat or canned or imitation crab meat
- 2 tablespoons extra virgin olive oil
- ⅓ Chopped celery
- Chopped red peppers
- ½ cup chopped green onion
- ½ cup Italian breadcrumbs
- ½ Cup mayonnaise
- 8 oz cream cheese at room temperature
- ½ teaspoon of garlic
- 1 tablespoon dried parsley
- Grated parmesan cheese cup
- 1 1 teaspoon of Old Bay seasoning
- ¼ teaspoon of kosher salt
- ¼ teaspoon black pepper

Intolerances:
- Egg-Free

Directions:
1. Clean the mushroom cap with a damp paper towel. Cut off the stem and save it.
2. Remove the brown gills from the bottom of the mushroom cap with a spoon and discard.
3. Prepare crab meat stuffing. If you are using canned crab meat, drain, rinse, and remove shellfish.
4. Heat the olive oil in a frying pan over medium high heat. Add celery, peppers and green onions and fry for 5 minutes. Set aside for cooling.
5. Gently pour the chilled sautéed vegetables and the remaining ingredients into a large bowl.
6. Cover and refrigerate crab meat stuffing until ready to use.
7. Put the crab mixture in each mushroom cap and make a mound in the center.
8. Sprinkle extra virgin olive oil and sprinkle parmesan cheese on each stuffed mushroom cap. Put the mushrooms in a 10 x 15-inch baking dish.
9. Use the griddle to indirect heating and preheat to 375°F.
10. Bake for 30-45 minutes until the filling becomes hot (165°F as measured by an instant-read digital thermometer) and the mushrooms begin to release juice.
Nutrition: Calories: 60 Fat: 4g Cholesterol: 20mg Carbs: 2g Protein: 2g

Rosemary Garlic Parmesan Tomatoes

Servings: 6
Preparation Time: 110 minutes
Cooking Time: 20 minutes
Ingredients:
- 9 halved Tomatoes
- 1 cup grated Parmesan cheese
- ½ tsp. Ground black pepper
- ¼ tsp. Onion powder
- 1 tbsp. Dried rosemary
- 2 tbsps. Olive oil
- 5 minced Garlic cloves
- 1 tsp. Kosher salt

Intolerances:
- Gluten-Free
- Egg-Free

Directions:
1. Heat a griddle to medium-low heat and oil grates.
2. Place tomatoes halves cut side down, onto the griddle and cook for 5-7 minutes.
3. Heat olive oil in a pan over a medium heat. Add garlic, rosemary, black pepper, onion powder, and salt and cook for 3-5 minutes.
4. Remove from heat and set aside. Flip each tomato half and brush with olive oil garlic mixture and top with grated parmesan cheese.
5. Close griddle and cook for 7-10 minutes more until cheese is melted.
6. Remove tomatoes from the griddle and serve immediately.
Nutrition: Calories: 130 Fat: 8g Carbs: 9g Protein: 6g

Feta Peppered Spinach Turkey Burgers

Servings: 4
Preparation Time: 10 minutes
Cooking Time: 10 minutes
Ingredients:
- 1 lb. Ground turkey
- 1 tbsp. Breadcrumbs
- ¼ tsp. Crushed red pepper
- 1 tsp. Parsley
- 1 tsp. Oregano
- 1 tsp. Garlic powder
- ⅓ cup. Sun-dried tomatoes
- ½ cup, crumbled Feta cheese
- ½ cup, chopped Baby spinach
- ½ tsp. Pepper
- ½ tsp. Sea salt

Intolerances:
- Egg-Free

Directions:
1. Add all ingredients into the mixing bowl and mix until just combined.
2. Make four equal shaped patties from the mixture.
3. Preheat the griddle to high heat.
4. Place patties on a hot griddle and cook for 3-5 minutes on each side or until internal temperature reaches to 165°F. Serve
Nutrition: Calories: 215 Fat: 6g Carbs: 9g Protein: 30g

Curried Lemon Cauliflower Skewers

Servings: 6
Preparation Time: 15 minutes
Cooking Time: 15 minutes
Ingredients:
- 1 cut into florets large cauliflower head
- 1 cut into wedges onion
- 1 cut into squares yellow bell pepper
- 1 fresh lemon juice
- ¼ cup olive oil
- ½ tsp. garlic powder
- ½ tsp. ground ginger
- 3 tsps. curry powder
- ½ tsp. salt

Intolerances:
- Gluten-Free
- Egg-Free
- Lactose-Free

Directions:
1. In a large mixing bowl, whisk together oil, lemon juice, garlic, ginger, curry powder, and salt. Add cauliflower florets and toss until well coated.
2. Heat the griddle to medium heat.
3. Thread cauliflower florets, onion, and bell pepper onto the skewers.
4. Place skewers onto the hot griddle and cook for 6-7 minutes on each side.
5. Serve.

Nutrition: Calories: 100 Fat: 8g Carbs: 6g Protein: 1g

Thyme Soy Mushroom Skewers

Servings: 4
Preparation Time: 10 minutes
Cooking Time: 10 minutes
Ingredients:
- 2 lbs. sliced ¼-inch thick Mushrooms
- ½ tsp. chopped Thyme
- 3 chopped Garlic cloves
- 1 tbsp. Soy sauce
- 2 tbsps. Balsamic vinegar
- Pepper and salt to taste

Intolerances:
- Gluten-Free
- Egg-Free
- Lactose-Free

Directions:
1. Add mushrooms and remaining ingredients into the mixing bowl, cover, and place in the refrigerator for 30 minutes.
2. Thread marinated mushrooms onto the skewers.
3. Heat the griddle to medium-high heat. Place mushroom skewers onto the hot griddle and cook for 2-3 minutes per side.
4. Serve.

Nutrition: Calories: 60 Fat: 1g Carbs: 8g Protein: 6g

Spicy Cheddar Sausage Balls

Servings: 4
Preparation Time: 20 minutes
Cooking Time: 40 minutes
Ingredients:
- 1 lb Hot Breakfast Sausage
- 2 cups Bisquick Baking Mix
- 8 ounces Cream Cheese
- 8 ounces Extra Sharp Cheddar Cheese
- ¼ cup Fresno Peppers
- 1 tablespoon Dried Parsley
- 1 teaspoon Killer Hogs AP Rub
- ½ teaspoon Onion Powder

Directions:
1. Get ready griddle or flame broil for roundabout cooking at 400 degrees F.
2. Blend Sausage, Baking Mix, destroyed cheddar, cream cheddar, and remaining fixings in a huge bowl until all-around fused.
3. Utilize a little scoop to parcel blend into chomp to estimate balls and roll tenderly fit as a fiddle.
4. Spot wiener and cheddar balls on a cast-iron container and cook for 15mins.
5. Present with your most loved plunging sauces.
Nutrition: Calories: 95 Carbs: 4g Fat: 7g Protein: 5g

Bourbon White Chocolate Bread Pudding

Servings: 12
Preparation Time: 20 minutes
Cooking Time: 1hr 15 minutes
Ingredients:
- 1 loaf French bread
- 4 cups Heavy Cream
- 3 Large Eggs
- 2 cups White Sugar
- 1 package White Chocolate morsels
- ¼ cup Melted Butter
- 2 teaspoons Vanilla
- 1 teaspoon Ground Nutmeg
- 1 teaspoon Salt
- Bourbon White Chocolate Sauce
- 1 package White Chocolate morsels
- 1 cup Heavy Cream
- 2 tablespoons Melted Butter
- 2 tablespoons Bourbon
- ½ teaspoon Salt

Directions:
1. Preheat the griddle at 350 degrees F.
2. Tear French bread into little portions and spot in a massive bowl. Pour four cups of Heavy Cream over Bread and douse for 30mins.
3. Join eggs, sugar, softened spread, and vanilla in a medium to estimate bowl. Include a package of white chocolate pieces and a delicate blend. Season with Nutmeg and Salt.
4. Pour egg combo over the splashed French bread and blend to sign up for.

5. Pour the combination right into a properly to buttered nine X 13 to dish inchmeal and spot it at the griddle.
6. Cook for 60Secs or until bread pudding has set and the top is darker.
7. For the sauce: Melt margarine in a saucepot over medium warm temperature. Add whiskey and hold on cooking for three to 4mins until liquor vanished and margarine begins to darkish-colored.
8. Include vast cream and heat till a mild stew. Take from the warmth and consist of white chocolate pieces a bit at a time continuously blending until the complete percent has softened. Season with a hint of salt and serve over bread pudding.
Nutrition: Calories: 372 Carbs: 31g Fat: 25g Protein: 5g

Mayo Jalapeño Griddle Dip

Servings: 8
Preparation Time: 10 minutes
Cooking Time: 15 minutes
Ingredients:
- 8 ounces cream cheese
- 16 ounces shredded cheese
- ⅓ cup mayonnaise
- 4 ounces diced green chilies
- 3 fresh jalapeños
- 2 teaspoons Killer Hogs AP Rub
- 2 teaspoons Mexican Style Seasoning
For the topping:
- ¼ cup Mexican Blend Shredded Cheese
- Sliced jalapeños
- Mexican Style Seasoning
- 3 tablespoons Killer Hogs AP Rub
- 2 tablespoons Chili Powder
- 2 tablespoons Paprika
- 2 teaspoons Cumin
- ½ teaspoon Granulated Onion
- ¼ teaspoon Cayenne Pepper
- ¼ teaspoon Chipotle Chili Pepper ground
- ¼ teaspoon Oregano

Directions:
1. Preheat griddle or flame broil for roundabout cooking at 350 degree
2. Join fixings in a big bowl and spot in a cast to press griddle
3. Top with Mexican Blend destroyed cheddar and cuts of jalapeno's
4. Spot iron griddle on flame broil mesh and cook until cheddar hot and bubbly and the top has seared
5. Marginally about 25mins.
6. Serve warm with enormous corn chips (scoops), tortilla chips, or your preferred vegetables for plunging.
Nutrition: Calories: 150 Carbs: 22g Fat: 6g Protein: 3g

Buttery Blackberry Pie

Servings: 8
Preparation Time: 15 minutes
Cooking Time: 40 minutes
Ingredients:
- Butter, for greasing
- ½ cup all-purpose flour
- ½ cup milk
- 2 pints blackberries
- 2 cup sugar, divided
- 1 box refrigerated piecrusts
- 1 stick melted butter
- 1 stick of butter
- Vanilla ice cream

Directions:
1. Preheat your griddle, with your lid closed, until it reaches 375.
2. Butter a cast iron griddle.
3. Unroll a piecrust and lay it in the bottom and up the sides of the griddle. Use a fork to poke holes in the crust.
4. Lay the griddle on the griddle and smoke for five mins, or until the crust is browned. Set off the griddle.
5. Mix together 1 ½ c. of sugar, the flour, and the melted butter together. Add in the blackberries and toss everything together.
6. The berry mixture should be added to the griddle. The milk should be added on the top afterward. Sprinkle on half of the diced butter.
7. Unroll the second pie crust and lay it over the griddle. You can also slice it into strips and weave it on top to make it look like a lattice. Place the rest of the diced butter over the top.
8. Sprinkle the rest of the sugar over the crust and place it griddle back on the griddle. Lower the lid and smoke for 15 to 20 minutes or until it is browned and bubbly. You may want to cover with some foil to keep it from burning during the last few minutes of cooking. Serve the hot pie with some vanilla ice cream.
Nutrition: Calories: 393 Protein: 4.25g Carbs: 53.67g Fat: 18.75g

Cajun Turkey Club Sandwich

Servings: 3
Preparation Time: 5 Minutes
Cooking Time: 10 Minutes
Ingredients:
- 1 3lbs Turkey Breast
- 1 stick Butter (melted)
- 8 ounces Chicken Broth
- 1 tablespoon Killer Hogs Hot Sauce
- ¼ cup Malcolm's King Craw Seasoning
- 8 Pieces to Thick Sliced Bacon
- 1 cup Brown Sugar
- 1 head Green Leaf Lettuce
- 1 Tomato (sliced)
- 6 slices Toasted Bread
- ½ cup Cajun Mayo
- 1 cup Mayo
- 1 tablespoon Dijon Mustard
- 1 tablespoon Killer Hogs Sweet Fire Pickles (chopped)
- 1 tablespoon Horseradish
- ½ teaspoon Malcolm's King Craw Seasoning

- 1 teaspoon Killer Hogs Hot Sauce
- Pinch of Salt & Black Pepper to taste

Directions:
1. Preheat the griddle 325 degrees F
2. Join dissolved margarine, chicken stock, hot sauce, and 1 tbsp of Cajun Seasoning in a blending bowl. Infuse the blend into the turkey bosom scattering the infusion destinations for even inclusion.
3. Shower the outside of the turkey bosom with a Vegetable cooking splash and season with Malcolm's King Craw Seasoning.
4. Spot the turkey bosom on the griddle and cook until the inside temperature arrives at 165 degrees F. Utilize a moment read thermometer to screen temp during the cooking procedure.
5. Consolidate darker sugar and 1 teaspoon of King Craw in a little bowl. Spread the bacon with the sugar blend and spot on a cooling rack.
6. Cook the bacon for 12 to 15mins or until darker. Make certain to turn the bacon part of the way through for cooking.
7. Toast the bread, cut the tomatoes dainty, and wash/dry the lettuce leaves.
8. At the point when the turkey bosom arrives at 165 take it from the flame broil and rest for 15mins. Take the netting out from around the bosom and cut into slender cuts.
9. To cause the sandwich: To slather Cajun Mayo* on the toast, stack on a few cuts of turkey bosom, lettuce, tomato, and bacon. Include another bit of toast and rehash a similar procedure. Include the top bit of toast slathered with more Cajun mayo, cut the sandwich into equal parts and appreciate.
Nutrition: Calories: 130 Carbs: 1g Fat: 4g Protein: 21g

Berries Layered Cake

Servings: 6
Preparation Time: 10 minutes
Cooking Time: 20 minutes
Ingredients:
- 2 pounds cake
- 3 cups of whipped cream
- ¼ cup melted butter
- 1 cup of blueberries
- 1 cup of raspberries
- 1 cup sliced strawberries

Directions:
1. Preheat the griddle to high with closed lid.
2. Slice the cake loaf (¾ inch), about 10 per loaf. Brush both sides with butter.
3. Griddle for 7 minutes on each side. Set aside.
4. Once cooled completely start layering your cake. Place cake, berries then cream.
5. Sprinkle with berries and serve.
Nutrition: Calories: 160 Protein: 2.3g Carbs: 22g Fat: 6g

Creamy Bread Pudding

Servings: 4
Preparation Time: 15 minutes
Cooking Time: 45 minutes
Ingredients:
- 8 stale donuts
- 3 eggs
- 1 cup milk
- 1 cup heavy cream
- ½ cup brown sugar
- 1 teaspoon vanilla
- 1 pinch salt
- Blueberry Compote
- 1 pint blueberries
- ⅔ cup granulated sugar
- ¼ cup water
- 1 lemon
- Oat Topping
- 1 cup quick oats
- ½ cup brown sugar
- 1 teaspoon flour
- 2 to 3 tablespoons room temperature butter

Directions:
1. Warmth your Griddlea Griddle to 350 degrees F.
2. Cut your doughnuts into 6 pieces for every doughnut and put it in a safe spot. Blend your eggs, milk, cream, darker sugar, vanilla, and salt in a bowl until it's everything fused. Spot your doughnuts in a lubed 9 by 13 container at that point pour your custard blend over the doughnuts. Press down on the doughnuts to guarantee they get covered well and absorb the juices.
3. In another bowl, consolidate your oats, dark colored sugar, flour and gradually join the spread with your hand until the blend begins to cluster up like sand. When that is Prepared, sprinkle it over the highest point of the bread pudding and toss it on the barbecue around 40 to 45mins until it gets decent and brilliant dark-colored.
4. While the bread pudding is Preparing, place your blueberries into a griddle over medium-high warmth and begin to cook them down so the juices begin to stream. When that occurs, include your sugar and water and blend well. Diminish the warmth to drug low and let it cool down until it begins to thicken up. Right when the blend begins to thicken, pizzazz your lemon and add the get-up-and-go to the blueberry compote and afterward cut your lemon down the middle and squeeze it into the blend. What you're left with is a tasty, splendid compote that is ideal for the sweetness of the bread pudding.
5. Watch out for your bread pudding around the 40 to 50mins mark. The blend will, in any case, shake a piece in the middle however will solidify as it stands once you pull it off. You can pull it early on the off chance that you like your bread pudding more sodden however to me, the ideal bread pudding will be dimmer with some caramelization yet will at present have dampness too!

6. Presently this is the point at which I'd snatch an attractive bowl, toss a pleasant aiding of bread pudding in there then top it off with the compote and a stacking scoop of vanilla bean frozen yogurt at that point watch faces light up.
7. In addition to the fact that this is an amazingly beautiful dish, the flavor will take you out. Destined to be an enormous hit in your family unit. Give it a shot and express gratitude toward me.
8. What's more, as usual, ensure you snap a photo of your manifestations and label us in your dishes! We'd love to include your work.
Nutrition: Calories: 290 Carbs: 62g Fat: 4g Protein: 5g

Bacon Sweet Potato Pie with Pecans

Servings: 8
Preparation Time: 15 minutes
Cooking Time: 50 minutes
Ingredients:
- 1 pound 3 ounces sweet potatoes -
- 1 ¼ cups plain yogurt
- ¾ cup packed, dark brown sugar
- ½ teaspoon of cinnamon
- ¼ teaspoon of nutmeg
- 5 egg yolks –
- ¼ teaspoon of salt
- 1 (up to 9 inch) deep dish, frozen pie shell
- 1 cup chopped pecans, toasted
- 4 strips of bacon, cooked and diced
- 1 tablespoon maple syrup
- Optional: Whipped topping

Directions:
1. In the first region, 3D shapes the potatoes right into a steamer crate and sees into a good-sized pot of stew water.
2. Ensure the water is not any nearer than creeps from the base of the bushel. When steamed for 20mins, pound with a potato masher and installed a safe spot.
3. While your flame broil is preheating, location the sweet potatoes within the bowl of a stand blender and beat with the oar connection.
4. Include yogurt, dark colored sugar, cinnamon, nutmeg, yolks, and salt, to flavor, and beat until very a whole lot joined. Take this hitter into the pie shell and see onto a sheet dish. Sprinkle walnuts and bacon on pinnacle and bathe with maple syrup.
5. Heat for 45 to 60mins or until the custard arrives at 165 to 180 degree. Take out from fish fry and funky. Keep refrigerated within the wake of cooling.
Nutrition: Calories: 270 Carbs: 39g Fat: 12g Protein: 4g

Vanilla Smoked Chocolate Bacon Pie with Pecan

Servings: 8
Preparation Time: 1hr 45 minutes
Cooking Time: 45 minutes
Ingredients:
- 4 eggs
- 1 cup chopped pecans
- 1 tablespoon of vanilla
- ½ cup semi to sweet chocolate chips
- ½ cup dark corn syrup
- ½ cup light corn syrup
- ¾ cup bacon (crumbled)
- ¼ cup bourbon
- 4 tablespoons or ¼ cup of butter - ½ cup brown sugar
- ½ cup white sugar
- 1 tablespoon cornstarch
- 1 package refrigerated pie dough
- 16 ounces heavy cream
- ¾ cup white sugar
- ¼ cup bacon
- 1 tablespoon vanilla

Directions:
1. Pie:
2. Carry Griddle to 350 degrees F.
3. Blend 4 tablespoons spread, ½ cup darker sugar, and ½ cup white sugar in blending bowl.
4. In a different bowl, blend 4 eggs and 1 tablespoon cornstarch together and add to blender.
5. Include ½ cup dull corn syrup, ½ cup light corn syrup, ¼ cup whiskey, 1 cup slashed walnuts, 1 cup bacon, and 1 tablespoon vanilla to blend.
6. Spot pie batter in 9-inch pie griddle. Daintily flour mixture.
7. Uniformly place ½ cup chocolate contributes pie dish.
8. Take blend into the pie dish.
9. Smoke at 350 degrees F for 40mins or until the focus is firm.
10. Cool and top with bacon whipped cream.
11. Bacon whipped Cream:
12. Consolidate fixings (16 ounces substantial cream, ¾ cup white sugar, ¼ cup bacon to finely cleaved, and 1 tablespoon vanilla) and mix at rapid until blend thickens. This formula can be separated into 6mins pie container or custard dishes or filled in as one entire pie.
Nutrition: Calories: 200 Carbs: 18g Fat: 0g Protein: 3g

Worcestershire Juicy Cheeseburger

Servings: 6
Preparation Time: 10 minutes
Cooking Time: 10 minutes
Ingredients:
- 2 lbs. ground beef
- 1 egg beaten
- 1 Cup dry bread crumbs
- 3 tablespoons evaporated milk
- 2 tablespoons Worcestershire sauce
- 1 tablespoons Griddlea Griddles All Purpose Rub
- 4 slices of cheddar cheese
- 4 buns

Directions:
1. Start by consolidating the hamburger, egg, dissipated milk, Worcestershire and focus on a bowl. Utilize your hands to blend well. Partition this blend into 4 equivalent parts. At that point take every one of the 4 sections and partition them into equal parts. Take every one of these little parts and smooth them. The objective is to have 8 equivalent level patties that you will at that point join into 4 burgers.
2. When you have your patties smoothed, place your cheddar in the center and afterward place the other patty over this and firmly squeeze the sides to seal. You may even need to push the meat back towards the inside a piece to shape a marginally thicker patty. The patties ought to be marginally bigger than a standard burger bun as they will recoil a bit of during cooking.
3. Preheat your Kong to 300 degrees F.
4. Keep in mind during flame broiling that you fundamentally have two meager patties, one on each side, so the cooking time ought not to have a place. You will cook these for 5 to 8mins per side—closer to 5mins on the off chance that you favor an uncommon burger or more towards 8mins in the event that you like a well to done burger.
5. At the point when you flip the burgers, take a toothpick and penetrate the focal point of the burger to permit steam to getaway. This will shield you from having a hit to out or having a visitor who gets a jaw consume from liquid cheddar as they take their first nibble.
6. Toss these on a pleasant roll and top with fixings that supplement whatever your burgers are loaded down with.
Nutrition: Calories: 300 Carbs: 33g Fat: 12g Protein: 15g

Honey Fruit on the Griddle

Servings: 4
Preparation Time: 5 minutes
Cooking Time: 10 minutes
Ingredients:
- 2 plums, peaches apricots, etc. (choose seasonally)
- 3 tablespoons Sugar, turbinate
- ¼ cup of Honey
- Gelato, as desired

Directions:
1. Preheat the griddle to 450 degrees F with closed lid.
2. Slice each fruit in halves and remove pits. Brush with honey. Sprinkle with some sugar.
3. Griddle on the grate until you see that there are griddle marks. Set aside.
4. Serve each with a scoop of gelato. Enjoy.
Nutrition: Calories: 120 Protein: 1g Carbs: 15g Fat: 3g

Honey Grilled Fruit with Cream

Servings: 6
Preparation Time: 15 minutes
Cooking Time: 10 minutes
Ingredients:
- 2 halved Apricot
- 1 halved Nectarine
- 2 halved peaches
- ¼ cup of Blueberries
- ½ cup of Raspberries
- 2 tablespoons of Honey
- 1 orange, the peel
- 2 cups of Cream
- ½ cup of Balsamic Vinegar

Directions:
1. Preheat the griddle to 400 degrees F with closed lid.
2. Griddle the peaches, nectarines and apricots for 4 minutes on each side.
3. Place a pan over the stove and turn on medium heat. Add 2 tablespoons of honey, vinegar, and orange peel. Simmer until medium thick.
4. In the meantime, add honey and cream in a bowl. Whip until it reaches a soft form.
5. Place the fruits on a serving plate. Sprinkle with berries. Drizzle with balsamic reduction. Serve with cream and enjoy!
Nutrition: Calories: 230 Protein: 3g Carbs: 35g Fat: 3g

Yummy Apple Pie on the Griddle with Cinnamon

Servings: 6
Preparation Time: 15 minutes
Cooking Time: 30 minutes
Ingredients:
- ¼ cup of Sugar
- 4 Apples, sliced
- 1 tablespoon of Cornstarch
- 1 teaspoon Cinnamon, ground
- 1 Pie Crust, refrigerated, soften in according to the directions on the box
- ½ cup of Peach preserves

Directions:
1. Preheat the griddle to 375F with closed lid.
2. In a bowl combine the cinnamon, cornstarch, sugar, and apples. Set aside.
3. Place the piecrust in a pie pan. Spread the preserves and then place the apples. Fold the crust slightly.
4. Place a pan on the griddle (upside - down) so that you don't brill/bake the pie directly on the heat.
5. Cook 30 - 40 minutes. Once done, set aside to rest. Serve and enjoy
Nutrition: Calories: 160 Protein 0.5g Carbs: 35g Fat: 1g

Simple Coconut Chocolate Brownies

Servings: 6
Preparation Time: 15 minutes
Cooking Time: 25 minutes
Ingredients:
- 4 eggs
- 1 cup Cane Sugar
- ¾ cup of Coconut oil
- 4 ounces chocolate, chopped
- ½ teaspoon of Sea salt
- ¼ cup cocoa powder, unsweetened
- ½ cup flour
- 4 ounces Chocolate chips
- 1 teaspoon of Vanilla

Directions:
1. Preheat the griddle to 350F with closed lid.
2. Take a baking pan (9x9), grease it and line a parchment paper.
3. In a bowl combine the salt, cocoa powder and flour. Stir and set aside.
4. In the microwave or double boiler melt the coconut oil and chopped chocolate. Let it cool a bit.
5. Add the vanilla, eggs, and sugar. Whisk to combine.
6. Add into the flour, and add chocolate chips. Pour the mixture into a pan.
7. Place the pan on the grate. Bake for 20 minutes. If you want dryer brownies to bake for 5 - 10 minutes more. Let them cool before cutting. Cut the brownies into squares and serve.
Nutrition: Calories: 135 Protein: 2g Carbs: 16g Fat: 3g

Vanilla Bacon Chocolate Chip Cookies

Servings: 6
Preparation Time: 30 minutes
Cooking Time: 30 minutes
Ingredients:
- 8 slices cooked and crumbled bacon
- 2 ½ teaspoons apple cider vinegar
- 1 teaspoon vanilla
- 2 cups semisweet chocolate chips
- 2 room temp eggs
- 1 ½ teaspoon baking soda
- 1 cup granulated sugar
- ½ teaspoon salt
- 2 ¾ cup all-purpose flour
- 1 cup light brown sugar
- 1 ½ stick softened butter

Directions:
1. Mix salt, baking soda and flour.
2. Cream the sugar and the butter together. Lower the speed. Add in the eggs, vinegar, and vanilla.
3. Put it on low fire, slowly add in the flour mixture, bacon pieces, and chocolate chips.
4. Preheat your griddle, with your lid closed, until it reaches 375 degrees F.
5. Put a parchment paper on a baking sheet you are using and drop a teaspoonful of cookie batter on the baking sheet. Let them cook on the griddle, covered, for approximately 12 minutes or until they are browned.
Nutrition: Calories: 167 Carbs: 21g Fat: 9g Protein: 2g

Walnut Chocolate Chip Cookies

Servings: 8
Preparation Time: 30 minutes
Cooking Time: 30 minutes
Ingredients:
- 1 ½ cup chopped walnuts
- 1 teaspoon vanilla
- 2 cup chocolate chips
- 1 teaspoon baking soda
- 2 ½ cup plain flour
- ½ teaspoon salt
- 1 ½ stick softened butter
- 2 eggs
- 1 cup brown sugar
- ½ cup sugar

Directions:
1. Preheat your griddle, with your lid closed, until it reaches 350.
2. Mix the baking soda, salt, and flour.
3. Cream the brown sugar, sugar, and butter. Mix in the vanilla and eggs until it comes together.
4. Slowly add in the flour while continuing to beat. Once all flour has been incorporated, add in the chocolate chips and walnuts. Using a spoon, fold into batter.
5. Place an aluminum foil onto griddle. In an aluminum foil, drop spoonful of dough and bake for 17 minutes.
Nutrition: Calories: 150 Carbs: 18g Fat: 5g Protein: 10g

Cinnamon Apple Cobbler

Servings: 8
Preparation Time: 30 minutes
Cooking Time: 1 hour 50 minutes
Ingredients:
- 8 Granny Smith apples
- 1 cup sugar
- 1 stick melted butter
- 1 teaspoon cinnamon
- Pinch salt
- ½ cup brown sugar
- 2 eggs
- 2 teaspoons baking powder
- 2 cup plain flour
- 1 ½ cup sugar

Directions:
1. Peel and quarter apples, place into a bowl. Add in the cinnamon and one c. sugar. Stir well to coat and let it set for one hour.
2. Preheat your griddle, with your lid closed, until it reaches 350.
3. In a large bowl add the salt, baking powder, eggs, brown sugar, sugar, and flour. Mix until it forms crumbles.
4. Place apples into rack Add the crumble mixture on top and drizzle with melted butter.
5. Place on the griddle and cook for 50 minutes.
Nutrition: Calories: 152 Carbs: 26g Fat: 5g Protein: 1g

Bananas in Caramel Sauce

Servings: 4
Preparation Time: 15 minutes.
Cooking Time: 15 minutes.
Ingredients:
- ⅓ cup chopped pecans
- ½ cup sweetened condensed milk
- 4 slightly green bananas
- ½ cup brown sugar
- 2 tablespoons corn syrup
- ½ cup butter

Directions:
1. Preheat your griddle, with the lid closed, until it reaches 350.
2. Place the milk, corn syrup, butter, and brown sugar into a heavy saucepan and bring to boil. For five minutes simmer the mixture in low heat. Stir frequently.
3. Place the bananas with their peels on, on the griddle and let them griddle for five minutes. Flip and cook for five minutes more. Peels will be dark and might split.
4. Place on serving platter. Cut the ends off the bananas and split peel down the middle. Take the peel off the bananas and spoon caramel on top. Sprinkle with pecans.
Nutrition: Calories: 152 Carbs: 36g Fat: 1g Protein: 1g

Ice Cream Bread with Chocolate Chips

Servings: 6
Preparation Time: 10 minutes
Cooking Time: 1 hour
Ingredients:
- 1 ½ quart full-fat butter pecan ice cream, softened
- 1 teaspoon salt
- 2 cups semisweet chocolate chips
- 1 cup sugar
- 1 stick melted butter
- Butter, for greasing
- 4 cups self-rising flour

Directions:
1. Preheat your griddle, with your lid closed, until it reaches 350 degrees F.
2. Mix together the salt, sugar, flour, and ice cream with an electric mixer set to medium for two minutes.
3. As the mixer is still running, add in the chocolate chips, beating until everything is blended.
4. Spray a Bundt pan or tube pan with cooking spray. If you choose to use a pan that is solid, the center will take too long to cook. That's why a tube or Bundt pan works best.
5. Add the batter to your Prepared pan.
6. Set the cake on the griddle, cover, and smoke for 50 minutes to an hour. A toothpick should come out clean.
7. Take the pan off of the griddle. For 10 minutes cool the bread. Remove carefully the bread from the pan and then drizzle it with some melted butter.
Nutrition: Calories: 148.7 Protein: 3.5g Carbs: 27g Fat: 3g

Gooey S'mores Dip

Servings: 8
Preparation Time: 10 minutes
Cooking Time: 25 minutes
Ingredients:
- 12 ounces semisweet chocolate chips
- ¼ cup milk
- 2 tablespoons melted salted butter
- 16 ounces marshmallows
- Apple wedges
- Graham crackers

Directions:
1. Preheat your griddle, with your lid closed, until it reaches 450.
2. Put a cast iron griddle on your griddle and add in the milk and melted butter. Stir together for a minute.
3. Once it has heated up, top with the chocolate chips, making sure it makes a single layer. Place the marshmallows on top, standing them on their end and covering the chocolate.
4. Cover, and let it smoke for five to seven minutes. The marshmallows should be toasted lightly.
5. Take the griddle off the heat and serve with apple wedges and graham crackers.

Nutrition: Calories: 216.7 Protein: 2.7g Carbs: 41g Fat: 4.7g

Sugar Pumpkin Seeds with Cinnamon

Servings: 8
Preparation Time: 15 minutes
Cooking Time: 30 minutes
Ingredients:
- 2 tablespoons sugar
- Seeds from a pumpkin
- 1 teaspoon cinnamon
- 2 tablespoons melted butter

Directions:
1. Preheat your griddle, with your lid closed, until it reaches 350.
2. Clean the seeds and toss them in the melted butter. Add them to the sugar and cinnamon. Spread them out on a baking sheet, place on the griddle, and smoke for 25 minutes. Serve.

Nutrition: Calories: 127 Protein: 5g Carbs: 15g Fat: 21g

Conclusion

The Outdoor Gas Griddle is a good tool that is both helpful and healthy. Understanding the mechanism and how this tool is used is crucial in using it effectively. The Outdoor Gas Griddle will help you get a better cooking result. It will also help you to cook with less stress. I made several mistakes when I newly bought mine. Nevertheless, I gained more experience and understood how to use it more productively over time.

After reading this book, you should know the recipes you can cook with the Outdoor Gas Griddle. A challenge many people who buy the griddle face is that they do not have enough knowledge of the myriad of recipes they can cook with the grill. But with this cookbook, you can relax and take your time to use your griddle to the fullest of its capacity. If you are ever lost or don't know the next recipe to cook, open to this book and begin the journey of an interesting meal Preparation.

Appendix 1 Measurement Conversion Chart

WEIGHT EQUIVALENTS

US STANDARD	METRIC (APPROXINATE)
1 ounce	28 g
2 ounces	57 g
5 ounces	142 g
10 ounces	284 g
15 ounces	425 g
16 ounces (1 pound)	455 g
1.5 pounds	680 g
2 pounds	907 g

TEMPERATURES EQUIVALENTS

FAHRENHEIT(F)	CELSIUS©
225 °F	107 °C
250 °F	120 °C
275 °F	135 °C
300 °F	150 °C
325 °F	160 °C
350 °F	180 °C
375 °F	190 °C
400 °F	205 °C
425 °F	220 °C
450 °F	235 °C
475 °F	245 °C
500 °F	260 °C

VOLUME EQUIVALENTS (DRY)

US STANDARD	METRIC (APPROXIMATE)
⅛ teaspoon	0.5 mL
¼ teaspoon	1 mL
½ teaspoon	2 mL
¾ teaspoon	4 mL
1 teaspoon	5 mL
1 teaspoon	15 mL
¼ cup	59 mL
½ cup	118 mL
¾ cup	177 mL
1 cup	235 mL
2 cups	475 mL
3 cups	700 mL
4 cups	1 L

VOLUME EQUIVALENTS (LIQUID)

US STANDARD	US STANDARD (OUNCES)	METRIC
2 tablespoons	1 fl.oz	30 mL
¼ cup	2 fl.oz	60 mL
½ cup	4 fl.oz	120 mL
1 cup	8 fl.oz	240 mL
1½ cup	12 fl.oz	355 mL
2 cups or 1 pint	16 fl.oz	475 mL
4 cups or 1 quart	32 fl.oz	1 L
1 gallon	128 fl.oz	4 L

Appendix 2 Recipes Index

Made in the USA
Monee, IL
29 November 2024